☆ A BROOKLANDS ☆
'ROAD TEST' LIMITED EDITION

NSU
Ro80

Compiled by
R.M.Clarke

ISBN 1 85520 4088

BROOKLANDS BOOKS LTD.
P.O. BOX 146, COBHAM,
SURREY, KT11 1LG. UK

Brooklands Books

MOTORING

BROOKLANDS ROAD TEST SERIES

Abarth Gold Portfolio 1950-1971
AC Ace & Aceca 1953-1983
Alfa Romeo Giulietta Gold Portfolio 1954-1965
Alfa Romeo Giulia Coupés 1963-1976
Alfa Romeo Giulia Coupés Gold Port. 1963-1976
Alfa Romeo Spider 1966-1990
Alfa Romeo Spider Gold Portfolio 1966-1991
Alfa Romeo Alfasud 1972-1984
Alfa Romeo Alfetta Gold Portfolio 1972-1987
Alfa Romeo Alfetta GTV6 1980-1986
Allard Gold Portfolio 1937-1959
Alvis Gold Portfolio 1919-1967
AMX & Javelin Muscle Portfolio 1968-1974
Armstrong Siddeley Gold Portfolio 1945-1960
Aston Martin Gold Portfolio 1948-1971
Aston Martin Gold Portfolio 1972-1985
Aston Martin Gold Portfolio 1985-1995
Audi Quattro Gold Portfolio 1980-1991
Austin A30 & A35 1951-1962
Austin-Healey 100 & 100/6 Gold Port. 1952-1959
Austin-Healey 3000 Ultimate Portfolio 1959-1967
Austin-Healey Sprite Gold Portfolio 1958-1971
BMW 6 & 8 Cyl. Cars Limited Edition 1935-1960
BMW 1600 Collection No. 1 1966-1981
BMW 2002 Gold Portfolio 1968-1976
BMW 6 Cylinder Coupés & Saloons Gold P. 1969-1976
BMW 316, 318, 320 (4 cyl.) Gold Port. 1975-1990
BMW 320, 323, 325 (6 cyl.) Gold Port. 1977-1990
BMW 3 Series Gold Portfolio 1991-1997
BMW 5 Series Gold Portfolio 1981-1987
BMW 5 Series Gold Portfolio 1988-1995
BMW 6 Series Gold Portfolio 1976-1989
BMW 7 Series Performance Portfolio 1977-1986
BMW Alpina Performance Portfolio 1967-1987
BMW Alpina Performance Portfolio 1988-1998
BMW M Series Gold Portfolio 1976-1997
BMW Z3 & Z3M Limited Edition
Borgward Isabella Limited Edition
Bricklin Gold Portfolio 1974-1975
Bristol Cars Gold Portfolio 1946-1992
Buick Automobiles 1947-1960
Buick Muscle Cars 1965-1970
Cadillac Allanté 1986-1993
Cadillac Automobiles 1949-1959
Cadillac Automobiles 1960-1969
Checker Limited Edition
Chevrolet 1955-1957
Impala & SS Muscle Portfolio 1958-1972
Corvair Performance Portfolio 1959-1969
El Camino & SS Muscle Portfolio 1959-1987
Chevy II & Nova SS Muscle Portfolio 1962-1974
Chevelle & SS Muscle Portfolio 1964-1972
Caprice Limited Edition 1965-1976
Chevrolet Muscle Cars 1966-1971
Chevy Blazer 1969-1981
Camaro Muscle Portfolio 1967-1973
Chevrolet Camaro & Z-28 1973-1981
High Performance Camaros 1982-1988
Chevrolet Corvette Gold Portfolio 1953-1962
Chevrolet Corvette Sting Ray Gold Port. 1963-1967
Chevrolet Corvette Gold Portfolio 1968-1977
High Performance Corvettes 1983-1989
Chrysler 300 Gold Portfolio 1955-1970
Imperial Limited Edition 1955-1970
Valiant 1960-1962
Citroen Traction Avant Gold Portfolio 1934-1957
Citroen 2CV Gold Portfolio 1948-1989
Citroen DS & ID 1955-1975
Citroen DS & ID Gold Portfolio 1955-1975
Citroen SM 1970-1975
Cobras & Replicas 1962-1983
Shelby Cobra Gold Portfolio 1962-1969
Cobras & Cobra Replicas Gold Portfolio 1962-1989
Crosley & Crosley Specials Limited Edition
Cunningham Automobiles 1951-1955
Daimler SP250 Sports & V-8 250 Saloon
Ultimate Portfolio 1959-1969
Datsun Roadsters 1962-1971
Datsun 240Z & 260Z Gold Portfolio 1970-1978
Datsun 280Z & ZX 1975-1983
DeLorean Gold Portfolio 1977-1995
De Soto Limited Edition 1952-1960
Charger Muscle Portfolio 1966-1974
Dodge Viper Performance Portfolio 1990-1998
ERA Gold Portfolio 1934-1994
Excalibur Collection No.1 1952-1981
Facel Vega 1954-1964
Ferrari Limited Edition 1947-1957
Ferrari Limited Edition 1958-1963
Ferrari Dino 1965-1974
Ferrari Dino 308 & Mondial Gold Portfolio 1974-1985
Ferrari 328 348 Mondial Gold Portfolio 1986-1994
Fiat 500 Gold Portfolio 1936-1972
Fiat 600 & 850 Gold Portfolio 1955-1972
Fiat Pininfarina 124 & 2000 Spider 1968-1985
Fiat X1/9 Gold Portfolio 1973-1989
Fiat Abarth Performance Portfolio 1972-1987
Ford Consul, Zephyr, Zodiac Mk. I & II 1950-1962
Ford Zephyr, Zodiac, Executive Mk. III & IV 1962-1971
Ford Cortina 1600E & GT 1967-1970
High Performance Capris Gold Portfolio 1969-1987
Capri Muscle Portfolio 1974-1987
High Performance Fiestas 1979-1991
Ford Escort RS & Mexico Limited Edition 1970-1979
High Performance Escorts Mk. I 1968-1974
High Performance Escorts Mk. II 1975-1980
High Performance Escorts 1980-1985
High Performance Escorts 1985-1990
High Perf. Sierras & Merkurs Gold Port. 1983-1990
Ford Automobiles 1949-1959
Ford Fairlane Performance Portfolio 1955-1970
Ford Ranchero Muscle Portfolio 1957-1979
Edsel Limited Edition 1957-1960
Falcon Performance Portfolio 1960-1970
Ford Galaxie & LTD Limited Edition 1960-1973
Ford Thunderbird 1955-1957
Ford Thunderbird 1958-1963
Ford GT40 Gold Portfolio 1964-1987
Ford Torino Limited Edition 1968-1974
Ford Bronco 4x4 Performance Portfolio 1966-1977
Ford Bronco 1978-1988
Goggomobil Limited Edition
Holden 1948-1962
Honda S500 • S600 • S800 Limited Edition 1962-1970
Honda CRX 1983-1987
Hudson Limited Edition 1946-1957
International Scout Gold Portfolio 1961-1980
Isetta Gold Portfolio 1953-1964
ISO & Bizzarrini Gold Portfolio 1962-1974
Jaguar and SS Gold Portfolio 1931-1951
Jaguar C-Type & D-Type Gold Portfolio 1951-1960
Jaguar XK120, 140, 150 Gold Portfolio 1948-1960
Jaguar Mk. VII, VIII, IX, X, 420 Gold Port. 1950-1970
Jaguar Mk. 1 & Mk. 2 Gold Portfolio 1959-1969
Jaguar E-Type Gold Portfolio 1961-1971
Jaguar E-Type V-12 1971-1975
Jaguar S-Type & 420 Limited Edition
Jaguar XJ12, XJ5.3, V12 Gold Portfolio 1972-1990
Jaguar XJ6 Series I & II Gold Portfolio 1968-1979
Jaguar XJ6 Series III Perf. Portfolio 1979-1986
Jaguar XJ6 Gold Portfolio 1986-1994
Jaguar XJS Gold Portfolio 1975-1988
Jaguar XJS Gold Portfolio 1988-1995
Jaguar XK8 Limited Edition
Jeep CJ5 & CJ6 1960-1976
Jensen Interceptor Gold Portfolio 1966-1986
Jensen-Healey Limited Edition 1972-1976
Kaiser-Frazer Limited Edition 1946-1955
Lagonda Gold Portfolio 1919-1964
Lancia Aurelia & Flaminia Gold Portfolio 1950-1970
Lancia Fulvia Gold Portfolio 1963-1976
Lancia Beta Gold Portfolio 1972-1984
Lancia Delta Gold Portfolio 1979-1994
Lancia Stratos 1972-1985
Land Rover Series I 1948-1958
Land Rover Series II & IIa 1958-1971
Land Rover Series III 4x4 Perf. Portfolio 1971-1985
Land Rover 90 110 Defender Gold Portfolio 1983-1994
Land Rover Discovery 1989-1994
Land Rover Story Part One 1948-1971
Fifty Years of Selling Land Rover
Lincoln Gold Portfolio 1949-1960
Lincoln Continental 1961-1969
Lincoln Continental 1969-1976
Lotus Sports Racers Gold Portfolio 1953-1965
Lotus Seven Gold Portfolio 1957-1973
Lotus Caterham Seven Gold Portfolio 1974-1995
Lotus Elan Gold Portfolio 1962-1974
Lotus Elan & SE 1989-1992
Lotus Europa Gold Portfolio 1966-1975
Lotus Elite & Eclat 1974-1982
Marcos Coupés & Spyders Gold Portfolio 1960-1997
Matra Limited Edition 1965-1983
Mazda Miata MX-5 Performance Portfolio 1989-1997
Mazda RX-7 Gold Portfolio 1978-1991
McLaren F1 Sportscar Limited Edition
Mercedes 190 & 300 SL 1954-1963
Mercedes G-Wagen 1981-1994
Mercedes S & 600 1965-1972
Mercedes S Class 1972-1979
Mercedes 230 • 250 • 280SL Gold Portfolio 1963-1971
Mercedes SLs & SLCs Gold Portfolio 1971-1989
Mercedes SLs Performance Portfolio 1989-1994
Mercury Limited Edition 1947-1959
Mercury Comet & Cyclone Limited Edition 1960-1970
Mercury Muscle Cars 1966-1971
Cougar Limited Edition 1967-1973
Messerschmitt Gold Portfolio 1954-1964
MG Gold Portfolio 1929-1939
MG TA & TC Gold Portfolio 1936-1949
MG TD & TF Gold Portfolio 1949-1955
MGA & Twin Cam Gold Portfolio 1955-1962
MG Midget Gold Portfolio 1961-1979
MGB Roadsters 1962-1980
MGB MGC & V8 Gold Portfolio 1962-1980
MGB GT 1965-1980
MGC & MGB GT V8 Limited Edition
MG Y-Type & Magnette ZA/ZB Limited Edition
MGF Limited Edition
Mini Gold Portfolio 1959-1969
Mini Gold Portfolio 1969-1980
Mini Gold Portfolio 1981-1997
High Performance Minis Gold Portfolio 1960-1973
Mini Cooper Gold Portfolio 1961-1971
Mini Moke Gold Portfolio 1964-1994
Morgan Three-Wheeler Gold Portfolio 1910-1952
Morgan Plus 4 & Four 4 Gold Portfolio 1936-1967
Morris Minor Collection No. 1 1948-1980
Shelby Mustang Muscle Portfolio 1965-1970
High Performance Mustang IIs 1974-1978
Mustang 5.0L Muscle Portfolio 1982-1993
Nash & Nash-Healey Limited Edition 1949-1957
Nash-Austin Metropolitan Gold Portfolio 1954-1962
NSU Ro80 Limited Edition
Oldsmobile Automobiles 1955-1963
Oldsmobile Muscle Portfolio 1964-1971
Cutlass & 4-4-2 Muscle Portfolio 1964-1974
Oldsmobile Toronado 1966-1978
Opel GT Gold Portfolio 1968-1973
Opel Manta Limited Edition 1970-1975
Packard Gold Portfolio 1946-1958
Pantera Gold Portfolio 1970-1989
Panther Gold Portfolio 1972-1990
Barracuda Muscle Portfolio 1964-1974
Pontiac Limited Edition 1949-1960
Pontiac Tempest & GTO 1961-1965
GTO Muscle Portfolio 1964-1974
Firebird & Trans-Am Muscle Portfolio 1967-1972
Firebird & Trans-Am Muscle Portfolio 1973-1981
High Performance Firebirds 1982-1988
Pontiac Fiero 1984-1988
Porsche 356 Gold Portfolio 1953-1965
Porsche 912 Limited Edition
Porsche 911 1965-1969
Porsche 911 1970-1972
Porsche 911 1973-1977
Porsche 911 SC & Turbo Gold Portfolio 1978-1983
Porsche 911 Carrera & Turbo Gold Port. 1984-1989
Porsche 911 Gold Portfolio 1990-1997
Porsche 924 Gold Portfolio 1975-1988
Porsche 928 Performance Portfolio 1977-1994
Porsche 944 Gold Portfolio 1981-1991
Porsche 968 Limited Edition
Porsche Boxster Limited Edition
Railton & Brough Superior Gold Portfolio 1933-1950
Range Rover Gold Portfolio 1970-1985
Range Rover Gold Portfolio 1986-1995
Reliant Scimitar 1964-1986
Renault Alpine Gold Portfolio 1958-1994
Riley Gold Portfolio 1924-1939
R. R. Silver Cloud & Bentley 'S' Series Gold P. 1955-65
Rolls Royce Silver Shadow Ultimate Portfolio 1965-80
Rolls Royce & Bentley Gold Portfolio 1980-1989
Rolls Royce & Bentley Limited Edition 1990-1997
Rover P4 1949-1959
Rover 3 & 3.5 Litre Gold Portfolio 1958-1973
Rover 2000 & 2200 1963-1977
Rover 3500 & Vitesse 1976-1986
Saab Sonett Collection No.1 1966-1974
Saab Turbo 1976-1983
Studebaker Gold Portfolio 1947-1966
Studebaker Hawks & Larks 1956-1963
Avanti 1962-1990
Suzuki SJ Gold Portfolio 1971-1997
Vitara, Sidekick & Geo Tracker Perf. Port. 1988-1997
Sunbeam Tiger & Alpine Gold Portfolio 1959-1967
Toyota Land Cruiser Gold Portfolio 1956-1987
Toyota Land Cruiser 1988-1997
Toyota MR2 Gold Portfolio 1984-1997
Triumph TR2 & TR3 Gold Portfolio 1952-1961
Triumph TR4, TR5, TR250 1961-1968
Triumph TR6 Gold Portfolio 1969-1976
Triumph TR7 & TR8 Gold Portfolio 1975-1982
Triumph Herald 1959-1971
Triumph Vitesse 1962-1971
Triumph Spitfire Gold Portfolio 1962-1980
Triumph 2000, 2.5, 2500 1963-1977
Triumph GT6 Gold Portfolio 1966-1974
Triumph Stag Gold Portfolio 1970-1977
Triumph Dolomite Sprint Limited Edition
TVR Gold Portfolio 1959-1986
TVR Performance Portfolio 1986-1994
VW Beetle Gold Portfolio 1935-1967
VW Beetle Gold Portfolio 1968-1991
VW Beetle Collection No.1 1970-1982
VW Karmann Ghia 1955-1982
VW Bus, Camper, Van 1954-1967
VW Bus, Camper, Van 1968-1979
VW Bus, Camper, Van 1979-1989
VW Scirocco 1974-1981
VW Golf GTI 1976-1986
Volvo PV444 & PV544 1945-1965
Volvo Amazon-120 Ultimate Portfolio 1956-1970
Volvo 1800 Gold Portfolio 1960-1973
Volvo 140 & 160 Series Gold Portfolio 1966-1975
Forty Years of Selling Volvo
Westfield Limited Edition

BROOKLANDS *ROAD & TRACK* SERIES

Road & Track on Alfa Romeo 1964-1970
Road & Track on Alfa Romeo 1971-1976
Road & Track on Aston Martin 1962-1990
R & T on Auburn Cord and Duesenburg 1952-84
Road & Track on Audi & Auto Union 1952-1980
Road & Track on Audi & Auto Union 1980-1986
Road & Track on Austin Healey 1953-1970
Road & Track on BMW Cars 1966-1974
Road & Track on BMW Cars 1975-1978
Road & Track on BMW Cars 1979-1983
R & T on Cobra, Shelby & Ford GT40 1962-1992
Road & Track on Corvette 1953-1967
Road & Track on Corvette 1968-1982
Road & Track on Corvette 1982-1986
Road & Track on Corvette 1986-1990
Road & Track on Ferrari 1975-1981
Road & Track on Ferrari 1981-1984
Road & Track on Ferrari 1984-1988
Road & Track on Fiat Sports Cars 1968-1987
Road & Track on Jaguar 1950-1960
Road & Track on Jaguar 1961-1968
Road & Track on Jaguar 1968-1974
Road & Track on Jaguar 1974-1982
Road & Track on Jaguar 1983-1989
Road & Track on Lamborghini 1964-1985
Road & Track on Lotus 1972-1983
R & T on Mazda RX-7 & MX-5 Miata 1986-1991
Road & Track on Mercedes 1952-1962
Road & Track on Mercedes 1963-1970
Road & Track on Mercedes 1971-1979
Road & Track on Mercedes 1980-1987
Road & Track on MG Sports Cars 1949-1961
Road & Track on MG Sports Cars 1962-1980
R & T on Nissan 300-ZX & Turbo 1984-1989
Road & Track on Pontiac 1960-1983
Road & Track on Porsche 1951-1967
Road & Track on Porsche 1968-1971
Road & Track on Porsche 1972-1975
Road & Track on Porsche 1975-1978
Road & Track on Porsche 1979-1982
Road & Track on Porsche 1985-1988
R & T on Rolls Royce & Bentley 1950-1965
R & T on Rolls Royce & Bentley 1966-1984
Road & Track on Saab 1972-1992
R & T on Toyota Sports & GT Cars 1966-1984
R & T on Triumph Sports Cars 1953-1967
R & T on Triumph Sports Cars 1967-1974
R & T on Triumph Sports Cars 1974-1982
Road & Track on Volkswagen 1951-1968
Road & Track on Volkswagen 1968-1978
Road & Track on Volkswagen 1978-1985
Road & Track on Volvo 1957-1974
Road & Track on Volvo 1977-1994
Road & Track - Henry Manney at Large & Abroad
Road & Track - Peter Egan's "Side Glances"
Road & Track - Peter Egan "At Large"
Road & Track - Best of PS

BROOKLANDS *CAR AND DRIVER* SERIES

Car and Driver on BMW 1955-1977
Car and Driver on Corvette 1978-1982
Car and Driver on Corvette 1983-1988
C and D on Datsun Z 1600 & 2000 1966-1984
Car and Driver on Ferrari 1955-1962
Car and Driver on Ferrari 1963-1975
Car and Driver on Ferrari 1976-1983
Car and Driver on Mopar 1956-1967
Car and Driver on Mustang 1964-1972
Car and Driver on Pontiac 1961-1975
Car and Driver on Porsche 1955-1962
Car and Driver on Porsche 1963-1970
Car and Driver on Porsche 1970-1976
Car and Driver on Porsche 1977-1981
Car and Driver on Porsche 1982-1986
Car and Driver on Volvo 1955-1986

RACING

Le Mans - The Bentley & Alfa Years - 1923-1939
Le Mans - The Jaguar Years - 1949-1957
Le Mans - The Ferrari Years - 1958-1965
Le Mans - The Ford & Matra Years - 1966-1974
Le Mans - The Porsche Years - 1975-1982
Le Mans - The Porsche & Jaguar Years - 1983-91
Mille Miglia - The Alfa & Ferrari Years - 1927-1951
Mille Miglia - The Ferrari & Mercedes Years - 1952-57
Targa Florio - The Ferrari & Lancia Years - 1948-1954
Targa Florio - The Porsche & Ferrari Years - 1955-1964
Targa Florio - The Porsche Years - 1965-1973

A COMPREHENSIVE GUIDE

BMW 2002

BROOKLANDS *PRACTICAL CLASSICS* SERIES

PC on Austin A40 Restoration
PC on Land Rover Restoration
PC on Metalworking in Restoration
PC on Midget/Sprite Restoration
PC on MGB Restoration
PC on Sunbeam Rapier Restoration
PC on Triumph Herald/Vitesse

BROOKLANDS *HOT ROD* 'MUSCLECAR & HI-PO ENGINES' SERIES

Chevy 265 & 283
Chevy 302 & 327
Chevy 348 & 409
Chevy 350 & 400
Chevy 396 & 427
Chevy 454 thru 512
Chrysler Hemi
Chrysler 273, 318, 340 & 360
Chrysler 361, 383, 400, 413, 426 & 440
Ford 289, 302, Boss 302 & 351W
Ford 351C & Boss 351
Ford Big Block

BROOKLANDS RESTORATION SERIES

Auto Restoration Tips & Techniques
Basic Bodywork Tips & Techniques
BMW '02 Restoration Guide
Classic Camaro Restoration
Chevrolet High Performance Tips & Techniques
Chevy Engine Swapping Tips & Techniques
Chevy-GMC Pickup Repair
Chrysler Engine Swapping Tips & Techniques
Engine Swapping Tips & Techniques
Land Rover Restoration Tips & Techniques
MG 'T' Series Restoration Guide
MGA Restoration Guide
Mustang Restoration Tips & Techniques

MOTORCYCLING

BROOKLANDS ROAD TEST SERIES

AJS & Matchless Gold Portfolio 1945-1966
BMW Motorcycles Gold Portfolio 1950-1971
BMW Motorcycles Gold Portfolio 1971-1976
BSA Singles Gold Portfolio 1945-1963
BSA Singles Gold Portfolio 1964-1974
BSA Twins A7 & A10 Gold Portfolio 1946-1962
BSA Twins A50 & A65 Gold Portfolio 1962-1973
BSA & Triumph Triples Gold Portfolio 1968-1976
Ducati Gold Portfolio 1960-1973
Ducati Gold Portfolio 1974-1978
Ducati Gold Portfolio 1978-1982
Harley-Davidson Sportsters Perf. Port. 1965-1976
Harley-Davidson Super Glide Perf. Port. 1971-1981
Harley-Davidson FXR Series Perf. Port. 1982-1992
Honda CB750 Gold Portfolio 1969-1978
Honda CB500 & 550 Fours Perf. Port. 1971-1977
Honda Gold Wing Gold Portfolio 1975-1995
Honda CBX 1000 Gold Portfolio 1978-1982
Laverda Gold Portfolio 1967-1977
Moto Guzzi Gold Portfolio 1949-1973
Norton Commando Gold Portfolio 1968-1977
Suzuki GT750 Performance Portfolio 1971-1977
Triumph Bonneville Gold Portfolio 1959-1983
Vincent Gold Portfolio 1945-1980

BROOKLANDS *CYCLE WORLD* SERIES

Cycle World on BMW 1974-1980
Cycle World on BMW 1981-1986
Cycle World on Ducati 1982-1991
Cycle World on Harley-Davidson 1962-1968
Cycle World on Harley-Davidson 1978-1983
Cycle World on Harley-Davidson 1983-1987
Cycle World on Harley-Davidson 1987-1990
Cycle World on Harley-Davidson 1990-1992
Cycle World on Honda 1962-1967
Cycle World on Honda 1968-1971
Cycle World on Honda 1971-1974
Cycle World on Husqvarna 1966-1976
Cycle World on Husqvarna 1977-1984
Cycle World on Kawasaki 1966-1971
Cycle World on Kawasaki Off-Road Bikes 1972-1979
Cycle World on Kawasaki Street Bikes 1972-1976
Cycle World on Norton 1962-1971
Cycle World on Suzuki 1962-1970
Cycle World on Suzuki Off-Road Bikes 1971-1976
Cycle World on Suzuki Street Bikes 1971-1976
Cycle World on Triumph 1967-1972
Cycle World on Yamaha 1962-1969
Cycle World on Yamaha Off-Road Bikes 1970-1974
Cycle World on Yamaha Street Bikes 1970-1974

MILITARY

BROOKLANDS MILITARY VEHICLES SERIES

Allied Military Vehicles No. 2 1941-1946
Complete WW2 Military Jeep Manual
Dodge Military Vehicles No. 1 1940-1945
Hail To The Jeep
Military & Civilian Amphibians 1940-1990
Off Road Jeeps: Civilian & Military 1944-1971
US Military Vehicles 1941-1945
US Army Military Vehicles WW2-TM9-2800
VW Kubelwagen Military Portfolio 1940-1990
WW2 Jeep Military Portfolio 1941-1945

15019

Brooklands
Books

CONTENTS

ACKNOWLEDGEMENTS

For more than 35 years, Brooklands Books have been publishing compilations of road tests and other articles from the English speaking world's leading motoring magazines. We have already published more than 600 titles, and in these we have made available to motoring enthusiasts some 20,000 stories which would otherwise have become hard to find. For the most part, our books focus on a single model, and as such they have become an invaluable source of information. As Bill Boddy of *Motor Sport* was kind enough to write when reviewing one of our Gold Portfolio volumes, the Brooklands catalogue "must now constitute the most complete historical source of reference available, at least of the more recent makes and models."

Even so, we are constantly being asked to publish new titles on cars which have a narrower appeal than those we have already covered in our main series. The economics of book production make it impossible to cover these subjects in our main series, but Limited Edition volumes like this one give us a way to tackle these less popular but no less worthy subjects. This additional range of books is matched by a Limited Edition - Extra series, which contains volumes with further material to supplement existing titles in our Road Test and Gold Portfolio ranges.

Both the Limited Edition and Limited Edition - Extra series maintain the same high standards of presentation and reproduction set by our established ranges. However, each volume is printed in smaller quantities - which is perhaps the best reason we can think of why you should buy this book now. We would also like to remind readers that we are always open to suggestions for new titles; perhaps your club or interest group would like us to consider a book on your particular subject?

Finally, we are more than pleased to acknowledge that Brooklands Books rely on the help and co-operation of those who publish the magazines where the articles in our books originally appeared. For this present volume, we gratefully acknowledge the continued support of the publishers of *Autocar, Autosport, Car, Classic and Sportscar, Classic Cars, Modern Motor, Motor, Motor Racing, Motor Trend, NSU (Great Britain) Ltd., Road Test, Sports Car Graphic* and *What Car?* for allowing us to include their valuable and informative copyright stories.

R.M. Clarke.

1968 CARS

Serious contender

The NSU Ro80 puts the Wankel on the major market

by Charles Bulmer

BSc., A.F.R. Ae.S.

The very low front and smooth lines are assisted by the use of rectangular lights including two angled fog lights.

IT is over ten years now since NSU completed their first experimental Wankel engine. In this time they have built more than 3,000 small rotary outboard motors and, since 1963, about 2,500 single-rotor Spiders. This sports two-seater was a recognition of the need for consumer testing and NSU made it clear that they would replace any defective or troublesome engines. It gave them an enormous amount of experience but it did nothing to dam the commercial and financial pressures building up in the background and demanding some return on a vast research investment.

Six weeks ago we published a description of the Mazda Cosmo twin-rotor GT car, so the NSU Ro80 is the third Wankel-engined car to go into production. But it is the first serious commercial project of its kind. Full production should start about the end of September and it is planned to build 40 to 50 cars a day by the end of this year. If the car gains acceptance this rate will increase during 1968 to 100 cars a day, which is the limit of the factory facilities.

At the time of writing the home market price has not been announced but it is known that it will be in the region of 14,000 DM (£1,200). In Germany this puts it in the same price class as the Mercedes 230 automatic, the BMW 2000 automatic and the Citroen DS21, cars which are comparable in size, accommodation and performance although mostly rather heavier. The question of weight is of particular importance in view of the German taxation system.

It will be remembered that the Wankel engine aroused a great deal of controversy when an attempt was made to incorporate it in the capacity tax system. Taking the case of the single-rotor Spider engine with a swept volume of 500 c.c., NSU claimed that it should be rated at 500 c.c. The German tax authorities said that since there were three firing strokes per revolution of the triangular rotor it was a 1,500 c.c. engine. Since the output shaft rotates three times as fast as the rotor, it follows that the air intake volume is 500 c.c./revolution of the output shaft and on this air consumption basis it seems logical to equate it with a 1,000 c.c. four-stroke piston engine which has the same consumption. This last is the definition adopted for competitions by the FIA and so, in effect, the Ro80 (with two 500 c.c. rotors) must be regarded as a 2-litre car.

For taxation, however, the Germans have now adopted a new rule that any car not operated by a piston engine (e.g. electric cars) will pay 22 DM per annum for every 200 kg. of all-up weight. The Ro80 has a kerb weight of 1,210 kg. (2,668 lb.) with a full 17¾-gallon tank and the designed payload is 450 kg. This gives a maximum weight of 1,660 kg. and it therefore falls into the 1,800 kg. class which pays 9 x 22 = 198 DM per annum (about £17). In due course this tax system will be applied to all German cars and may be introduced throughout the whole Common Market in the next two to three years.

General design

Since NSU had never built cars in this size or price capacity before, the Ro80 started from a clean sheet of paper with no existing parts to incorporate. Their smaller piston-engined cars are air-cooled and rear-engined; NSU believe strongly that the bulk of the weight should be on the driving wheels and that the engine and transmission must therefore form a single unit. Since this Wankel engine is water- and oil-cooled they decided that it should be

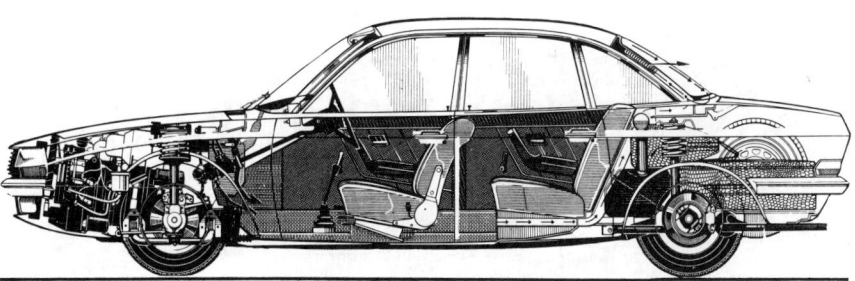

Figure 1: *These two drawings illustrate the compactness of the power unit (which is effectively of 2-litre size) and particularly its lowness.*

Serious contender

This picture emphasizes the rising dart-like profile adopted after extensive wind-tunnel testing.

front-engined, and therefore front wheel driven, for convenience of radiator installation. To some extent the size and performance of the car were fixed by the requirement to carry five people in comfort and by the belief they held in those days (in common with many others) that 100 b.h.p. was a practical limit for safety and good handling with f.w.d. Now from their own and other people's experience they know that this is not true and in years to come one may expect to see the present 115 b.h.p. (net) output increasing.

In adopting MacPherson front suspension and semi-trailing wishbones at the back one might guess that the NSU designers were trying to limit the unknown by using a tried and trustworthy arrangement which has given outstanding results on BMW and Porsche in Germany as well as Triumph in this country.

In our road impressions which follow this description, we have remarked that the engine is not sufficiently different in feel to be a major factor in assessing the car from a driving point of view. That doesn't mean that it is unimportant to the general concept of the car; it is extremely low (21½ in.), very short (20 in.) and very light; with all ancillaries, but without the transmission, it weighs only 265 lb. The whole power plant including torque converter, gearbox, differential, final drive and front disc brakes scales 470 lb. which is no more than many bare piston engines of equivalent power. These factors have allowed an extreme forward mounting (see Fig. 1) which gives maximum passenger accommodation within the wheelbase without making the car excessively nose-heavy (weight distribution is about 60/40) and without raising the bonnet height. Even so, low speed steering on radial tyres was considered unacceptably heavy and power assistance was therefore specified as standard and not, as some competitors prefer, as a desirable extra. One other engine feature, which we shall mention again later, is a tendency to irregular firing on the overrun (like a two-stroke) and it was this which dictated the use of an automatic or semi-automatic transmission with a hydraulic torque converter.

To NSU, as to some other engineering-orientated companies, the word "styling" is an anathema; the shape, they feel should be a fall-out from the proper satisfaction of the car's functions. So it has a very low projecting front fitting tightly over the engine and radiator to give maximum visibility and minimum aerodynamic drag. Nearly four years of testing was done in the large 125 m.p.h. wind tunnel at Stuttgart Polytechnic and the result is a car with a drag coefficient of 0.355—most modern saloons are some 30-40% higher than this. The high boot is not just for maximum luggage capacity but because any attempt to lower it put the drag up immediately; the rising dart-shaped profile puts the centre of pressure back where it belongs for optimum stability in cross winds—at the centre of gravity just behind the neutral steer line. Other points worth noting include the absence of projections from the smooth body contours, the pressure plates which keep the screenwipers in contact with the glass at very high speed and recessed rain channels, instead of the usual roof gutters, which probably help to account for the exceptionally low wind noise.

Figure 3: *For interest we have plotted power and torque figures (net) for the NSU and the Rover 2000 TC on the same graph. The comparison, however, is not entirely fair since the latter engine has a 10:1 compression ratio and needs more expensive higher octane fuel. At the same ratio (9:1) the Rover loses about 5% torque and 6% maximum power.*

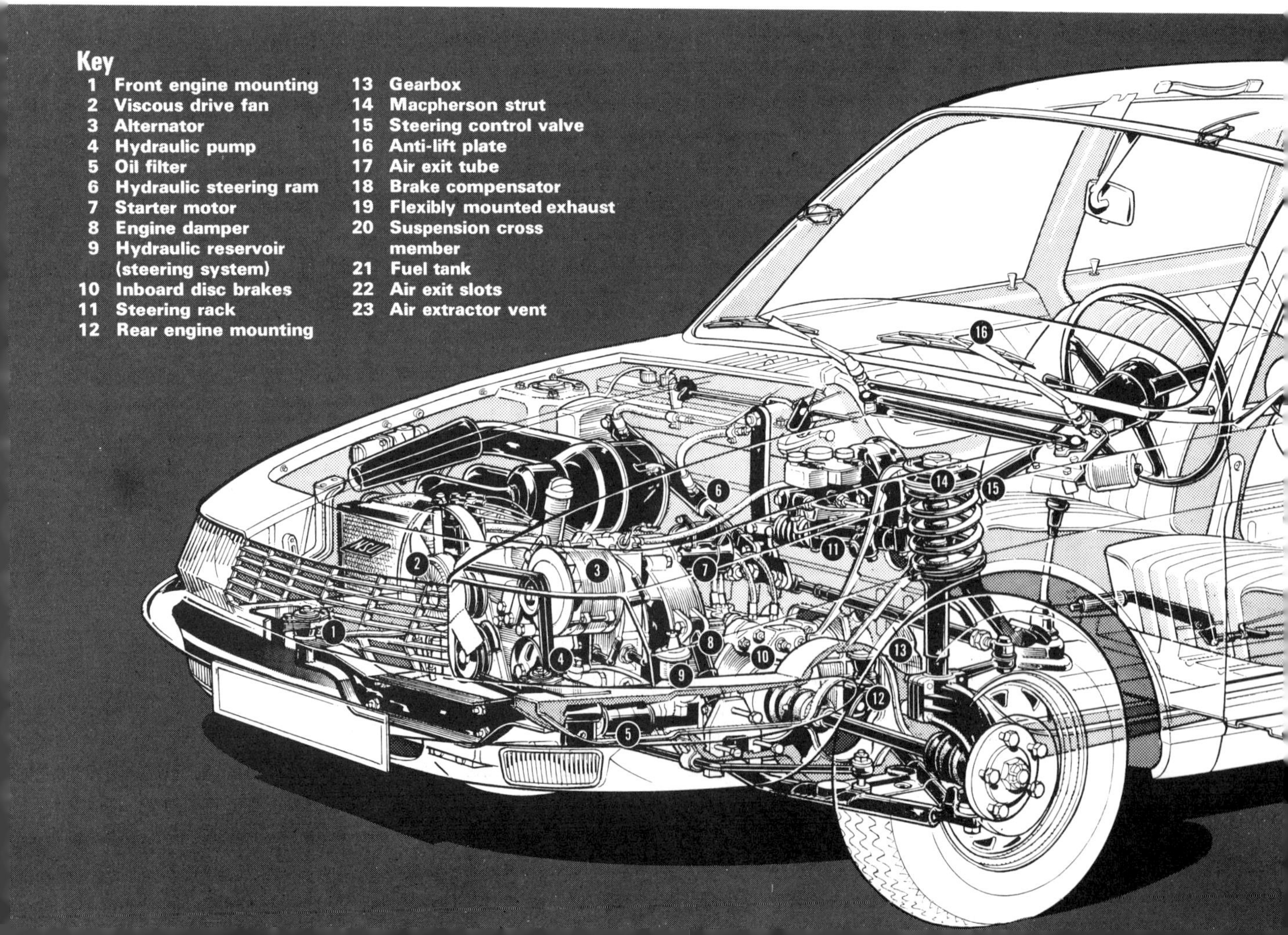

Key

1. Front engine mounting
2. Viscous drive fan
3. Alternator
4. Hydraulic pump
5. Oil filter
6. Hydraulic steering ram
7. Starter motor
8. Engine damper
9. Hydraulic reservoir (steering system)
10. Inboard disc brakes
11. Steering rack
12. Rear engine mounting
13. Gearbox
14. Macpherson strut
15. Steering control valve
16. Anti-lift plate
17. Air exit tube
18. Brake compensator
19. Flexibly mounted exhaust
20. Suspension cross member
21. Fuel tank
22. Air exit slots
23. Air extractor vent

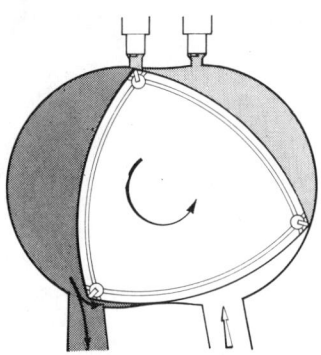

Figure 4: *The burnt gases (l.h. chamber) have just started to exhaust at high pressure through the exhaust port; induction is occurring in the right lower chamber; between the two there exists a direct leakage path until the apex seal passes beyond the exhaust port.*

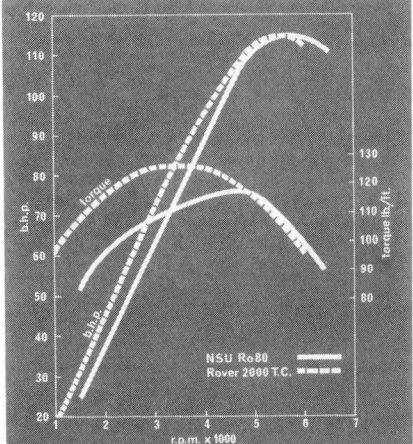

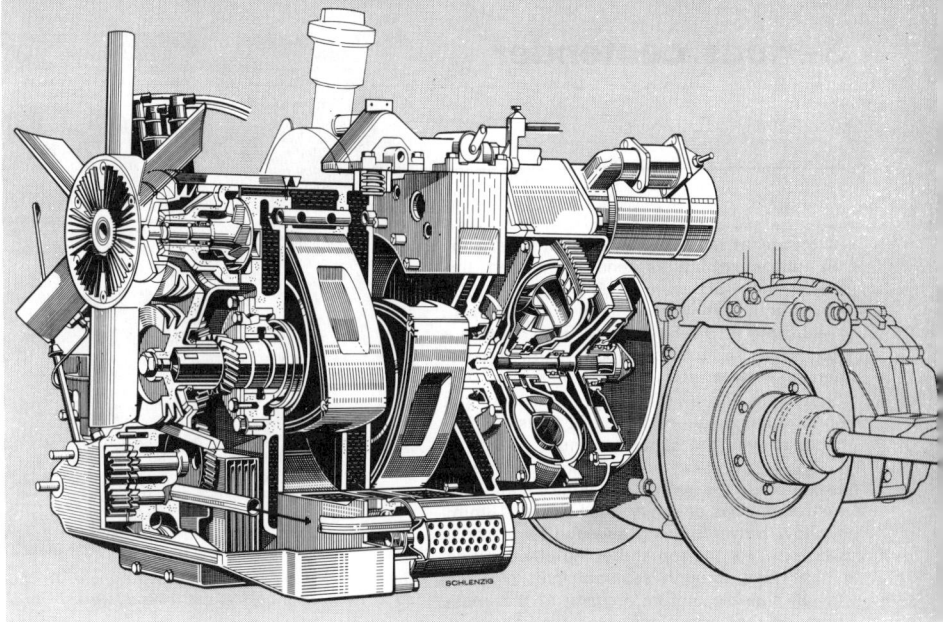

Figure 2: *Cross section through the engine showing the two triangular rotors with recessed combustion chambers, the torque converter and servo clutch at the rear, and the ancillary drives and viscous-coupled fan at the front.*

Power unit

This twin rotor unit (Fig. 2) first appeared in public at the Frankfurt Show two years ago and on that occasion and subsequently we have written quite a lot about it. In principle it has not changed either from this prototype or from the one rotor Spider engine but details and materials have altered under intensive development and a comparison is now possible with the Japanese Mazda Cosmo engine of identical capacity (*Motor*, July 29, 1967).

Both engines use aluminium alloy rotor housings. NSU would prefer to use cast iron for cheapness and rigidity but its thermal conductivity is inadequate so that local temperatures run too high—particularly around the sparking plugs. Here the resemblance ends; the Cosmo has a hard chrome plated rotor bore and carbon apex rotor seals for which a wear life of about 60,000 miles is claimed. NSU have given up carbon seals because they consider them too easy to fracture, particularly under detonation. They use cast iron seals running in a rotor bore with a nickel and silicon carbide surface electrically deposited. These seals are spring-loaded against the housing but, of course, as they pass the "constriction" of the epitrochoidal bore their normal centrifugal loading is reversed; above 7,500 r.p.m. the reverse acceleration is sufficient to overcome the spring force and the seals collapse inwards giving an increase in blowby and consumption. The rev limit is set at 6,500 r.p.m. for fuel economy and because there is no advantage in performance from exceeding this speed, but higher r.p.m. will not lead to mechanical failure or rapid increase in wear.

Both engines now use two plugs per cylinder; in the Cosmo they fire 5° apart but in the NSU simultaneously because the slight improvement in power is not considered worth the extra complication. One plug position is better for cold starting, the other for maximum power running and together they speed up combustion which helps to lower plug temperature. Plugs have been a problem—they are located in the hottest part of the engine and have in the past been unable to cope with the heat range involved in extremes of running. With better cooling and better plugs their life is now normal even on multi-grade oils with a high ash content. There are two coils and two contact breakers.

The Mazda engineers are strong believers in the use of side inlet ports and peripheral exhaust ports. In this way they get port timings which improve low speed torque and smoothness. Although admitting this, NSU believe that it leads to an unacceptable loss

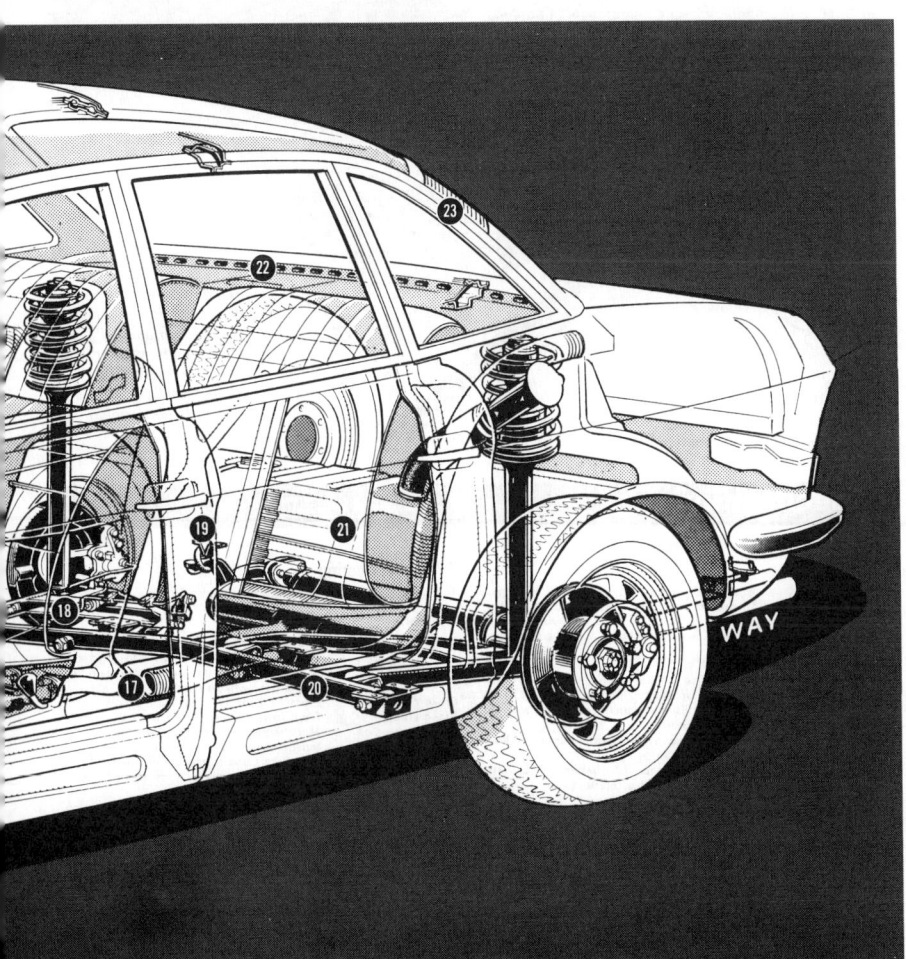

WAY

Serious contender

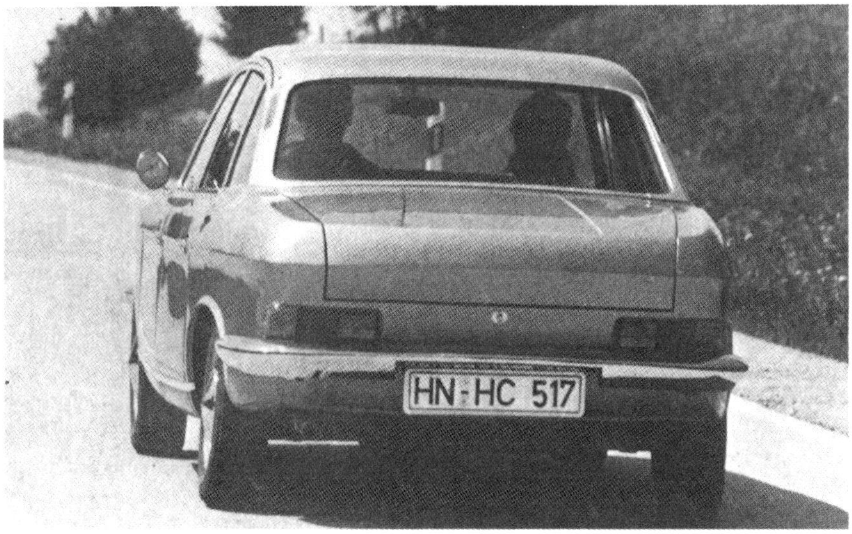

Rear wheels have a slight negative camber. The boot is deep and the rear seat can be folded forward so that very long objects can extend forward into the car.

of torque at all higher speeds and certainly the published figures tend to support this view—the NSU gives 115 b.h.p. at 5,500 r.p.m. with a maximum torque of 118 lb.ft., the Cosmo 110 b.h.p. at 7,000 r.p.m. with a torque of 96 lb.ft. at 3,500 r.p.m. A comparison between the NSU and the Rover 2000 TC engine (fig. 3) throws an interesting light on torque figures—both are of 2 litres nominal capacity with the same maximum power.

There is nothing unusual about carburation except that the twin-choke Solex compound instrument has one very small choke (18mm.) for low power running and one large choke (32 mm.) for the top end of the power range. These feed through separate inlet pipes as far as possible, before merging at the intake port, so that good low speed running is encouraged by high gas speeds in the small passage. The exhausts from each rotor are kept entirely separate.

Many engineers think that the future of the Wankel engine hinges on its ability to meet American pollution regulations and they point to the high surface to volume ratio of the combustion chamber as an adverse factor. NSU do not share this view at all; the engine can be tuned to come inside the CO limits without any modification at all. To meet the hydrocarbon regulations it needs an exhaust air pump at present but very little work has been done so far on pollution. Better combustion is being obtained by research on the combustion chamber shape and they feel that very soon it will be possible to meet all the limits by modifications only to the intake side—for example, by some such system as the Zenith Duplex. Their ambition is to do considerably better than the California cycle demands and they believe that this can be done almost as well by carburation as by fuel injection.

Fundamentally, the engine is very cheap to make—the target figure is about 60% of the cost of a six cylinder unit of equivalent power. At the moment this has not been realized because of the high cost of grinding the exceptionally hard inner coating of the epitrochoidal housing but this is being reduced by new machines and by more accurate manufacture which leaves less final grinding.

As the drawing shows, the engine drives through a hydraulic torque converter to a vacuum operated single dry plate clutch and thence to a three-speed all synchromesh gearbox behind the hypoid bevel final drive and differential. This semi-automatic transmission, by Fichtel and Sachs, gives two-pedal driving; take-off from rest is by means of the torque converter and gear changing is done by the driver using a normal floor gear lever. As soon as his hand touches the gear lever knob, a microswitch contact operating through relays brings the vacuum servo into operation to disengage the clutch. You can either change gear freely for normal motoring or you can select a single appropriate gear in town traffic and stay in it. The rest is conventional with constant velocity universal joints on the front drive shafts.

The hydraulic torque converter is very effective in damping out overrun transmission snatch (which was prominent on the single rotor Spider) and this is why the car is not offered with the alternative of a conventional gearbox. Irregular combustion in these conditions is caused by excessive exhaust dilution of the intake charge for reasons which are illustrated in Fig. 4; intake pressure is extremely low on the overrun whereas combustion pressure, at the instant that the rotor tip uncovers the exhaust port, is still high. When the apex seal is part way across the port there is a direct exhaust leakage path from the high to the low pressure area. This effect, of course, is not eliminated by using side inlet ports.

No oil cooler is necessary for the converter because it is designed for rather less slip and

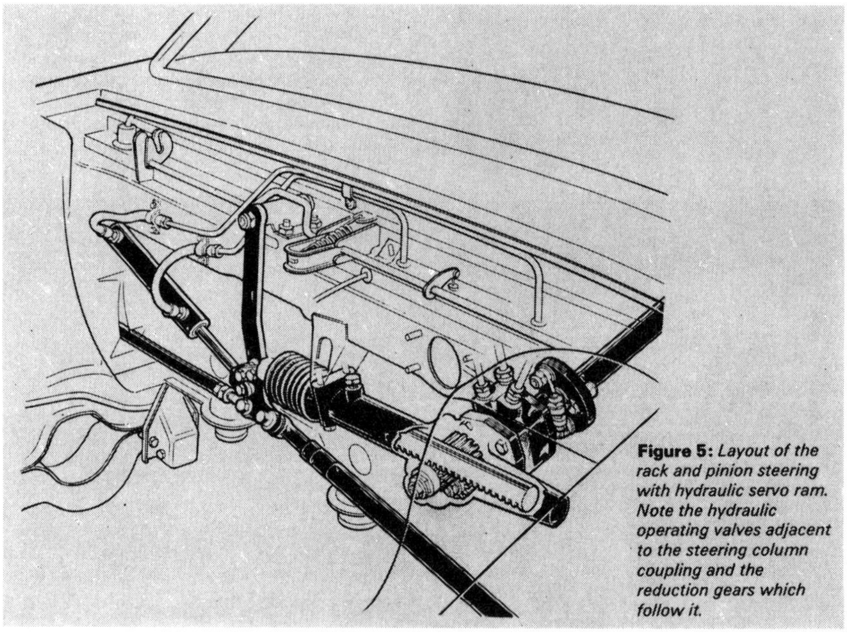

Figure 5: *Layout of the rack and pinion steering with hydraulic servo ram. Note the hydraulic operating valves adjacent to the steering column coupling and the reduction gears which follow it.*

Specification

Engine

Cylinders	2 co-axial rotors with two main bearings. Oil-cooled rotors, water-cooled rotor housing
Cubic capacity	2 x 497.5 (equivalent to 1,990 c.c. piston engine)
Compression ratio	9:1
Carburation	Two double choke compound Solex 18/32 HHD with accelerator pumps
Ignition	By twin coils and double contact breaker to two plugs/rotor
Cooling	Water cooling system with thermostat and viscous drive fan
Electrical system	12 volt 66 amp. hr. battery, 490 watt alternator and 2 b.h.p. starter
Maximum power (net—with all accessories)	115 b.h.p. at 5,500 r.p.m.
Maximum torque (net)	118 lb. ft. at 4,500 r.p.m.

Transmission

By hydraulic torque converter, single dry plate clutch vacuum operated and 3 speed all-synchromesh gearbox

Overall ratios	3.827, 5,869 and 9.984; reverse 10.226

Effective Gearing

Top gear	18.8 m.p.h./1,000 r.p.m.

Chassis

Brakes	ATE-Dunlop discs all round with dual line application, vacuum servo and load compensator. Handbrake operates in duo-servo drums (rear wheels only) of 6.3 in. dia.
Brake dimensions	Front 11.2 in. dia., rear 10.7 in. dia.
Brake areas	Front pads 30.2 sq. in., rear 12.9 sq. in.
Front suspension	MacPherson strut with anti-roll bar
Rear suspension	Independent by semi-trailing wishbones, coil springs and telescopic dampers
Wheels and tyres	Pressed steel with 5J rims and 175 HR-14 Michelin XAS tyres
Steering	ZF power-assisted rack and pinion

Dimensions

Length overall	15 ft. 8¼ in.; wheelbase 9 ft. 4½ in.
Width overall	5 ft. 9¼ in.; track 4 ft. 10¼ in. front and 4 ft. 8½ in. rear
Height (unladen)	4 ft. 7½ in.
Kerb weight	22 cwt. unladen, 23¾ cwt. with full tank

torque multiplication than usual; above 2,200 r.p.m. it becomes effectively a coupling rather than a converter so that most hard driving is in the range where heat generation is small (and efficiency high).

Chassis and suspension

Looking at the Ro 80 in the broadest possible way it is light, very low (4ft 7½in.) and has large wheels and tyres of very high cornering power spread right out to the corners—the wheelbase is long and the track exceptionally wide. These features and the all-round independent suspension give the clue to its first class road behaviour.

The rigid integral chassis/body construction is shown quite clearly in the main drawing. MacPherson front suspension has been adopted, of rather similar layout to that of the Peugeot 204 and Honda N500. Front wheel drive complicates the design of this kind of suspension because the strut must start above the drive shaft and finish at the rather low scuttle level but by careful detail design enough height has been found to allow a total wheel travel of 7.4 in. The coil springs are offset from the axes of the strut (as on the latest Fords) to reduce bending and "stiction" in operation.

The whole ZF steering system (Fig. 5) was arranged for bulkhead mounting in order to achieve maximum safety in a head-on accident. A vane type pump driven by two V belts delivers hydraulic fluid under pressure to the valve mounted behind the rack and pinion; according to the pressure on the wheel, the valve directs the fluid to one side or the other of the piston in the servo slave cylinder which is connected to the same drop arm as the rack

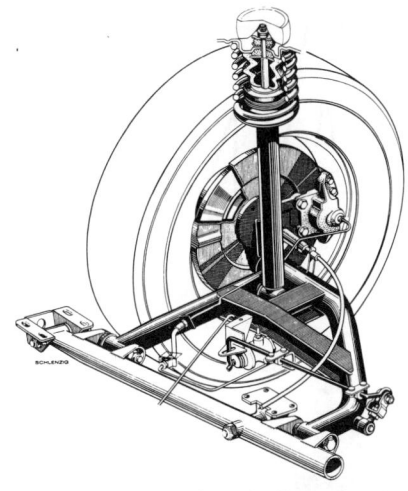

Figure 6: *Rear suspension and rubber-mounted cross member. Inside the wishbone frame can be seen the brake distribution valve, operated by a link and torsion bar, which modifies the rear braking according to load.*

and pinion. It will be noticed that the rack and pinion has a spur gear drive which drops the bottom end of the column several inches for convenience of installation. Overall gearing is 18.3:1 giving 3¾ turns from lock to lock.

It will be noticed in the drawings that a hydraulic telescopic damper is connected from the chassis to the clutch housing on each side of the engine; the purpose of this is to damp road excited engine movement on the flexible mountings which otherwise causes unpleasant "shakes" on rough roads.

Rear suspension (Fig. 6) is by semi-trailing wishbones mounted on axes which lie in the horizontal plane but which are inclined in plan view at an angle of about 80° to the centre line of the car giving a low rear roll centre. Originally these were mounted directly on the body structure but road noise transmission proved too high and a flexibly mounted cross member has now been interposed between them. Total suspension movement at the rear is just over 10 in. which allows for a considerable variation of laden weight without danger of bottoming.

Braking is by very large discs all round with inboard mounting at the front. The system has been designed with an eye to safety and a tandem master cylinder is used operating two independent circuits—one working on all four wheels and the other on the front wheels only through the second cylinders of the twin cylinder calipers; the heaviness of these calipers is another good reason for mounting them inboard. So the failure of one circuit leaves at least the front brakes in operation and, with a nose-heavy car, this should suffice for over 75% of normal efficiency.

The servo is direct acting on the master cylinder and a compensating device operates on the rear brake line pressures to limit the braking applied to the rear wheels in accordance with the load they carry. This system, rather similar to that used by Fiat, has a hydraulic control valve mounted on the chassis near the offside rear wheel and linked to the trailing suspension arm by a light torsion bar. Rear suspension attitude is therefore the variable which it senses and brake proportioning is adjusted for static and dynamic load variation.

All the usual instruments and controls are provided including a headlamp flasher; a switch allows all four direction indicators to flash simultaneously as an emergency warning sign.

Driving impressions

NSU have an unrivalled experience with the Wankel rotary engine and little or none with cars in the medium sized, medium priced category since their recent history is one of gradual progress from motorcycles and scooters into the small car field. Yet, paradoxically, when you have driven the Ro 80 for a few hours you realize that the car itself is in many ways outstanding whereas the engine, although it matches the high standard of the whole vehicle, is relatively unobtrusive.

Engines, of course, should be unobtrusive in sound and feel but this rotary unit is unobtrusive in character as well; most people would notice little difference in behaviour or performance compared with a good six cylinder design although they could hardly fail to be impressed by its remarkable smoothness at very high r.p.m. Acceleration is adequate but not extravagant—the subjective impression is that the Ro 80 belongs in the 2-litre category typified by, say, the Rover 2000 or Citroen DS saloons and this is confirmed by a standing quarter mile

time in the region of 20 seconds.

But as a completely effortless motorway car we can think of nothing which excels and few cars which approach it. The genuine maximum speed in neutral conditions is probably about 110 m.p.h. but on downhill sections of the Autobahn we did exceed this with great ease and on several occasions 200 k.p.h. (125 m.p.h.) appeared on the speedometer. At this speed there is virtually no wind noise at all so that you are left with little but road noise from the tyres and a hum from the engine which merges into the background unless you listen carefully. Whether production cars can retain the same standard of door and window sealing as this hand-built prototype remains to be seen but the general effect is to make 100 m.p.h. motorway cruising feel rather slow and 70 m.p.h. quite ludicrous. Some 30 miles flat out in no way disturbed the engine.

We criticized the single rotor Spider engine because of its high idling speed (1,400 r.p.m.); the Ro 80 will tick over quite happily at 600-700 r.p.m. but was, in fact,

set up to a little over 1,000 to prevent stalling under manoeuvring conditions, when loaded by the torque converter drag in gear plus the hydraulic pump load of the power steering. At low speeds the engine is quiet but not inaudible—there is a whine when accelerating which comes partly from the gearbox but partly from the train of gears which drives the ancillaries; production cars will have modified tooth profiles to quieten them. The tendency for "two-stroke snatch" on the overrun is completely absent from this car—thanks to engine changes and to the torque converter, the overrun is extremely smooth.

Our previous feeling that semi-automatic transmissions have a considerable future was strongly reinforced after driving the NSU. You have the essential feature of two-pedal control for taking the hard work out of city driving and, in exchange for the slight extra effort of moving the gear lever into whichever of the three gears you want, you retain total control over the gearchanging programme and save yourself quite a lot of money into the bargain. In this case the synchromesh is excellent so that the lever moves smoothly and easily from one position to another and the lower gears give sensible maxima approaching 50 and 80 m.p.h. respectively. The only disappointing feature is rather leisurely acceleration from rest to about 10 m.p.h. Steering, roadholding and braking all fall in the exceptional class for a five-seater saloon. We doubt whether anyone could really detect that the steering is power-assisted except by its lightness for parking

or driving slowly; it just feels like a first-class rack and pinion mechanism —accurate, reasonably direct, positive and directionally stable at all speeds. This is matched by handling and roadholding in the best front wheel drive tradition and by extremely high cornering power as you would expect from a car weighing just over 22 cwt. and running on 175-14 Michelin XAS tyres; you can make the tyres squeal but it is difficult to make them break away.

Because the centre of gravity is so low and the track so wide, roll is negligible. The ride is very comfortable both in the front and back seats although no attempt has been made to emulate the softly floating characteristic of some modern touring cars; road noise has been reduced to a satisfactory level but there is still some room for improvement here. The same might be said of the ventilation system because all the right components are there—fresh air inlets at both ends of the facia and extractor ducts in the rear quarters—but the actual throughput of air is rather disappointing and certainly not adequate to allow closed windows in hot weather. With the front windows wound partly down the wind noise remains very low but one feels that the car deserves ventilation which will allow them always to remain shut for the motorway cruising to which this NSU is so supremely well adapted.

Whether this car represents a turning point in Wankel history will depend largely on how the engine behaves in service. If it fails it won't be because the rest of the car isn't worthy of it. **M**

NSU WANKEL COM

Secret of Ro 80's performance a
semi-automatic torque cor
Front disc brakes are m
unsprung weight. Mo
front and rear
safety ma

S OF AGE

Refined model of rotary-combustion engine, plus tasteful Ro 80 design, mark Germany's newest quality car

GRIFFITH BORGESON

dynamic design is compact powerplant, incorporating
oupled to gearbox through single dry-plate clutch.
oard for cooling and splash protection plus reduced
struts act as spring/shock elements. Energy-absorbent
struction, plus short steering column, add important
el tank is protected by placement ahead of rear axle.

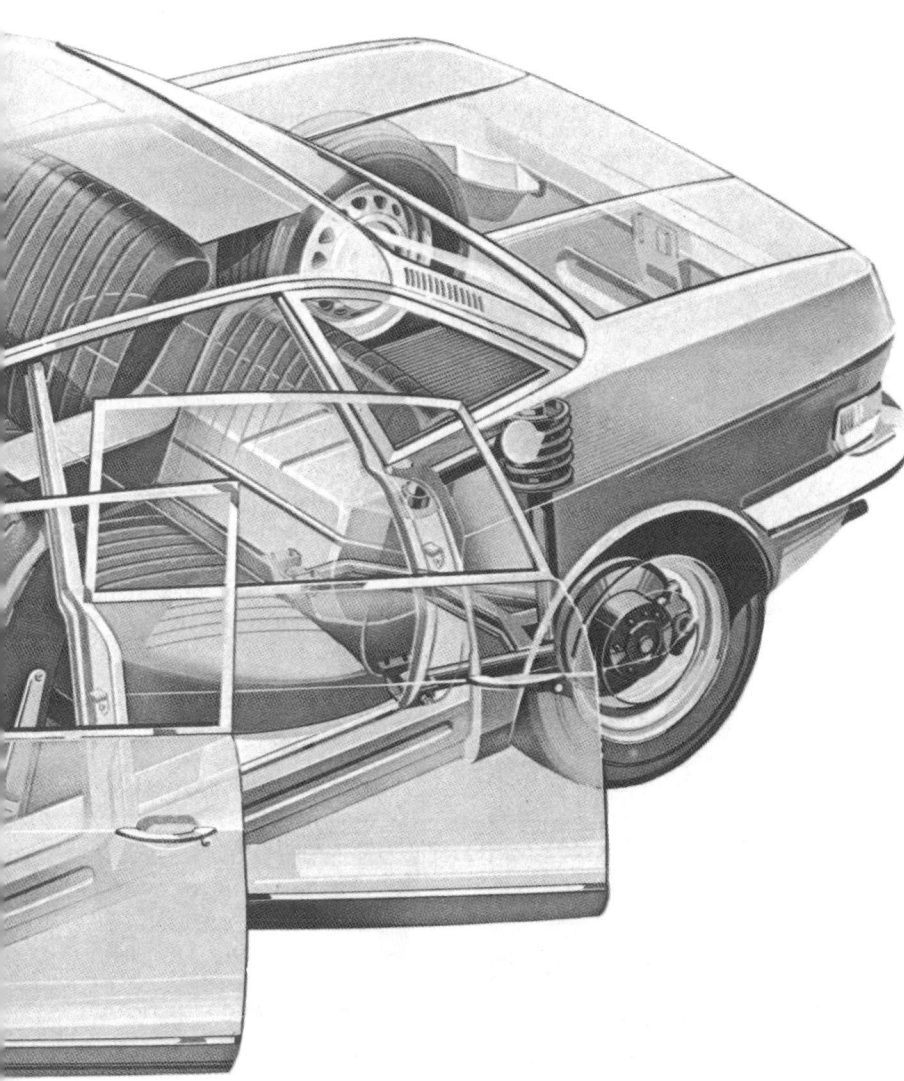

Ro rhymes with *go* and NSU's new Ro 80 goes like a 110-mph gale, at least. That it also is as silent as a zephyr is one of the striking features of its rotary-combustion (RC) engine. Its other major virtues are outstanding freedom from vibration, low weight, notable compactness, and significantly fewer moving parts and lower manufacturing costs than those of comparable, conventional, piston engines.

But the Ro 80 is no economy car. On the contrary, it was tailored to take its place among Europe's luxury compacts, such as the BMW 2000 and the Mercedes-Benz 230S, cars which in Germany straddle the $3500 price bracket. It joined this upper middle-class elite a couple of months ago; but American motorists probably will have to wait until late 1968 for the chance to sample and buy the Continent's newest quality car.

Its predecessor was the NSU Wankel Spider, the world's first RC-engined car, which was introduced late in 1963 and cautiously began its production life the following year. Its single-rotor engine developed only 50 bhp but the little Spider was light, nimble, and an adventurous ball to drive. Still, it was a hybrid, a not-too-happy mating of a radical powerplant with the chassis which had been engineered for the piston-engined NSU Prinz. But the new, twin-rotor, 128.5-bhp Ro 80 is an all-of-a-piece machine, designed from scratch to bring out the best that the Wankel engine has to give. Unlike the rear-engined Wankel Prinz, its engine is at the front of the vehicle and forms an integral structure with its front-drive powertrain. It marks the coming of age of the Wankel engine as an automotive power source and the emergence of NSU as a manufacturer of cars of genuinely distinguished quality.

This evolution has taken place with

NSU WANKEL

remarkable speed. It was just 13 years ago that NSU, then one of the world's largest and best motorcycle manufacturers, took its stand in favor of the Wankel concept. Almost simultaneously NSU recognized the approaching decline of the European motorcycle industry and 10 years ago began converting to automotive production. This began with modest little 2-cylinder cars; then a 4-cylinder line was added and today NSU produces some 100,000 cars per year. As little companies go, it is big — bigger than Porsche, BMW and even Auto Union. In the important Italian market it sells about twice as many cars as Volkswagen. None of this was done without brains, hard work and daring.

Along with this swift growth NSU has dared to invest millions in the future of the Wankel. For years this brought no tangible results and there was no shortage of critics to predict that the idea never would come to a practical end. They were surprised when the Spider appeared. Although it was a first try and essentially a curiosity, it ran. It ran well enough that considerably over 2000 of the little cars were sold. It ran well enough, in fact, to win its 1000cc GT Class in the German Rallye Championship last year. But before the first Spider had been sold, NSU had the confidence and daring to plunge into the design of a much bigger and better car to come. Of course it was the Ro 80.

The new car was a crowd-stopper at the opening of the international show season at Frankfurt last September, and for an assortment of reasons. One was its sky-high level of quality, which hardly anyone had expected from this specialist in small, inexpensive machinery. Another was its styling — a provocative combination of cool conservatism with a highly authentic and functional aerodynamic flair. And last, but inevitably most important, was what everyone had been expecting — the biggest and best NSU-Wankel engine to date.

During their brief history there has been an interesting trend in the manner in which these engines have been promoted. It can be best described, perhaps, as a progressive de-emphasis of the Wankel's radical nature and of the claims made for it. It entered life as a revolutionary upstart that needed only some sorting out to give rise to a new automotive era. Not all of these hopes have been fulfilled. Then, too, NSU learned what older heads long have known: the public will turn out in droves to be titillated by novelty, but when they put hard cash on the line they cling to the tried and true.

These factors undoubtedly have been basic to the product philosophy which has shaped the Ro 80. The engine no longer is billed as a technological breakthrough but as a logical extension of and improvement upon 4-cycle principles which have stood the test of time. And the body package,

which easily could have been given a very daring form, instead was targeted straight at the solid citizen. Like rebels who have gone before, NSU opted to go square. In doing so it created a notably excellent overall automobile. It was this, and not just the introduction of a bigger and more perfect Wankel engine, that most impressed the sharp-eyed critics at Frankfurt. Many expressed downright amazement at what NSU has achieved.

The Ro 80's body was admired universally and many considered it beautiful. It was designed by NSU's own internal staff, without benefit of experts from the outside. At the very least, it is clean, tasteful and attractive.

As an exercise in functional design it merits very high marks. Certainly no car in the world can claim better visibility for all occupants, and few are as good. The compact size of the engine permits a variation on the Dart theme that is as practical as it is pleasing to the eye. It makes possible a windshield that is immense, relative to the size of the car.

Over the years NSU has held every motorcycle speed record from 50cc to the absolute, and has some of the world's best know-how in the aerodynamics of ground vehicles. This experience was applied with the most scientific care to determining the form of the Ro 80 body. According to measurements made in the wind tunnel of the University of Stuttgart, it has a drag coefficient of 0.36 — one of the very lowest in the passenger-car industry. The car's truly excellent aerodynamic qualities are reflected in fuel economy, speed, silence and — very importantly — in directional stability. The car is almost totally insensitive to crosswinds.

Comfort for four passengers and a child is up to a very high standard although some rear-seat leg room is

Ro 80's clean exterior lines, which pay off with quiet ride at speed, attest to wind-tunnel influence in start-from-scratch design. Interior layout is functional, safety/comfort conscious.

NSU Ro 80 SPECIFICATIONS

ENGINE: Twin-rotor NSU/Wankel, liquid cooled. Displ. 1990cc. 128.5 bhp. Torque 117.2 lbs.-ft. @ 4500 rpm. C.R. 9:1. TRANSMISSION: Semi-auto. torque converter. Front-wheel drive, constant-velocity U-joints. STEERING: Rack & pinion, power assist. BRAKES: All-disc (front inboard). SUSPENSION: Independent, coil spring. BODY: 4-dr., 5-seat sedan, unit construction. DIMENSIONS: Wheelbase 112.5, length 188, width 69, height 55½, track 58.5 front, 56.5 rear. Fuel tank 22 gals. Curb wt. 2668 lbs. PERFORMANCE: 0-60, 12.3 secs., ¼-mi. 19.8. Top speed 115.

sacrificed in the interest of luggage space. Interior appointments are rich and handsome and safety provisions comply with latest American standards.

In its handling characteristics the Ro 80 can only be ranked as a true Gran Turismo machine. Again in the motorcycle field NSU was a brilliant innovator of frames and suspension systems (from which Mr. Honda benefitted), and this know-how was not wasted when the Ro 80 was designed. Its very long-strut, fully independent suspension system gives the car very much the character of a competition thoroughbred. Its ride is superb: taut, firm, yet supple. It becomes very slightly choppy only when crossing tar strips but even this may be ironed out as the radial-ply tires are more accurately matched to the machine. Cornering side-bite is really excellent.

In the steering department the Ro 80 sustains the same high standards of performance. Its rack-and-pinion steering is quick and absolutely positive. The front-drive car carries 63% of its weight on the front wheels, making a hydraulic assist mandatory, but this does not detract from an ideal degree of steering "feel." The supershort steering column does not extend forward of the firewall, so that the possibility of it being a factor in crash injury approaches the vanishing point.

The Ro 80 is a contender for the honor of being one of the best-braked cars in the world, not excluding racing cars. Its main braking system is all-disc, with the front discs mounted inboard for reduction of unsprung weight. Each front disc carries two calipers, each rear disc, one. Locking of the rear wheels under hard braking is prevented by a control device which limits rear-wheel braking effort relative to the weight which is supported by these wheels at any given moment. The hand-brake system is entirely independent and utilizes drum brakes at the rear. Entirely independent brake lines are provided for these two systems and each has its own oil reservoir and oil level indicator. Each also has a warning light on the instrument panel and these light up automatically in case of failure of either of the braking systems. The brakes are very powerful and resistant to fade.

A semi-automatic torque converter transmission comes as standard equipment on the Ro 80. NSU calls this system its "Selective Automatic"; Porsche uses a 4-speed version of the same Fichtel & Sachs transmission, which it calls "Sportomatic." The advantage of the system is that it does away with

the clutch pedal, while preserving floor-shift manual control. Gears are changed by a flick of the lever.

The list of the Ro 80's plus features is long, but these will serve to indicate where NSU has arrived after 10 brief years in the industry. And it's a good thing for NSU because superb new cars are popping up all over. They even have tried-and-true engines.

The Ro 80 engine is not identical in behavior to the conventional automotive powerplant, nor will it ever be. It offers a different sort of driving experience which in some ways is better and, in others, worse.

From the performance standpoint the great advantages of the Ro 80 are its truly exceptional smoothness and silence. The faster the car is driven the more pronounced these characteristics become until, in the upper half of the speed range, the car glides along the road almost uncannily, the only sound being the faint, smooth hum of the engine and the muted tramp of the suspension at work. This behavior, which gives the feeling of having a turbine or electric motor under the hood, makes speed seem strangely and agreeably effortless. And, as long as it is operating in the beefier band of its torque curve, the Ro 80 is as eager a performer as most of us could ask for in a spirited town and cross-country machine.

But the torque curve is steep and the engine has a strong appetite for revs. It does not have the low-rpm throttle response and performance of a piston engine; it needs at least a couple of thousand rpm before it begins to pull strongly. This means that, until this point is reached, acceleration is on the sluggish side, even with the throttle wide open. This is the one trait of the Wankel engine which requires some getting used to and which suffers by comparison with good piston engines. It is not as good for getaway from standstill or for acceleration in the lower rpm range; and at idle it lopes and its noise level is a bit obtrusive. But as a road machine it is very good and as an expressway cruiser it is in a class of its own.

Has the Wankel any other bugs in terms of today's state of art? From the beginning, critics have insisted that the "insuperable" problem inherent in the principle would be sealing its rubbing surfaces. But according to many firms, on three continents, this problem has been thoroughly solved to the point where the life expectancy of rotor seals is not inferior to that of conventional piston rings. We are told

that the one-time problem of chatter marks on the cylinder bores has been totally overcome, along with problems of lubrication. As for exhaust-emission control, NSU emphasizes that the solutions which apply to conventional engines work equally for the Wankel. What is its normal service life? NSU says that rotor seals should be replaced every 60 to 80 thousand miles, depending upon conditions of use. The standard guarantee in Germany for new cars is 10,000 miles or six months. NSU confidently has trebled that guarantee for the Ro 80.

NSU's plans call for the modest production of 50 Ro 80s per week, with exports outside of Germany not to begin until at least six months after the new car's September introduction. A service network has been established in Germany, of course, and a training program has been instituted for service personnel from most of the hundred-odd countries in which NSU cars are sold. But a global service organization for the Ro 80 will not be created overnight and this is a growing pain that both the new car and its customers will have to live with for a while. But if the Wankel engine still is exotic, it won't be for long.

As we have reported recently in these pages, NSU and Citroen of France have been hatching a master plan aimed at the European Common Market which is just around the corner. During our conference with NSU's management late last August, we were told of the joint production plans of the French giant and the much smaller German firm.

The new company, which for the present is being called Comobil/Comotor, is owned equally by the two firms. It will manufacture economy cars, using the NSU Wankel engine in single-rotor form. NSU will build the engines at a rate of up to 1000 per day, starting in 1969, and Citroen will build the balance of the machine. Aside from having one rotor instead of the two, the new engine will be very closely similar to that of the Ro 80 and a majority of parts will be interchangeable between the two.

It is in such large-volume production, of course, that the Wankel engine's promise of significantly lower manufacturing cost can be realized. The Ro 80, plus the recently introduced Mazda Cosmo in Japan, plus the "ready-for-production" RC Curtiss-Wright, plus the huge Citroen-NSU program, all point rather strongly to the fact that the Wankel engine, once a novelty, has arrived. /MT

Rack and pinion safety steering with hydraulic servo assistance

Dual-line braking system Four disc brakes with servo and hydro-mechanical proportional brake control

Fuel tank: 18 (IMP) gallons in the safest place on the car, immediately ahead of the rear axle

Wheelbase 9ft. 4½ in.

Overall length 15 ft. 8 in.

Twin rotor NSU/Wankel RC engine 113.5 BHP
Liquid cooled
Selective-Automatic transmission
Front-wheel drive

Kerb weight (DIN) 2668lb.
Specific power output 95.5 BHP/ton
Acceleration 0 to 60 mph 12.4 secs.
Normal fuel consumption 25.2 mpg

Window area 30 sq.ft.
Luggage space 20.5 cu.ft.
Tyres 175 SR 14

The NSU Ro80

By PATRICK McNALLY

THE new NSU Ro80 saloon is a totally revolutionary design as it is the first all-new production car to utilise the Wankel rotary engine. Although the twin rotor engine was the starting point of the design, the rest of the car, too, is of advanced specification, with front-wheel-drive, four-wheel disc brakes and all-independent suspension.

The body lines of the Ro80 are unusual, perhaps even futuristic, and although they may not be to everybody's taste the overall effect is good and the lack of unnecessary chrome embellishment is to be applauded—the clean lines dictated by the design should not date. Wind tunnel tests show a very low coefficient of drag (.355), surprisingly little for such a large saloon—this would also seem to indicate that the technicians at Neckarsulm have got their arithmetic right. The car is said to be very stable in cross winds, but this is probably as much to do with the FWD as the shape. Power comes from the twin-rotor rotary combustion engine. It develops 130 bhp SAE at 5500 rpm with 117.2 lbs/ft torque on a 9 to 1 compression ratio. Each rotor displaces 500 cc per shaft revolution. The engine is water- and oil-cooled and, as the oil is used also for lubrication as well as to cool the rotors, an oil cooler is incorporated in the lower part of the timing case. Two cross-draught Solex carburetters together with a dual ignition system—two spark plugs per rotor—ensure satisfactory combustion. A normal coil ignition system is fitted to the Ro80 and not the condenser discharge system used on the NSU Spider. A 12-volt system is used with a 490 watt alternator and a conventional starter motor. The engine is mounted ahead of the front axle, while the automatic transmission drives the front wheels. A torque convertor is used in conjunction with a single dry plate clutch to transmit the power to the three-speed automatic gearbox. The gear ratios are 2.056, 1.208, and 0.788 to 1, with a final drive reduction of 4.857. Power is taken via a differential to a pair of drive shafts fitted with constant velocity joints.

The main advantage of using a rotary engine as opposed to a conventional piston design is noise level. However good it is, the conventional piston engine gets noisier as the engine speed increases; in contrast the NSU Wankel RC unit gets quieter the faster it runs—a very definite advantage. At one time it was thought that the Wankel engine was suffering from insuperable snags. There was talk of chatter marks on the epitrochoidal bore surface, apex seal wear and high oil consumption, but all these have now been ironed out and NSU are so convinced of the quality of the engine that they have decided to guarantee it for three times the usual period. Other advantages are that it weighs about two-thirds the weight of a reciprocating piston engine developing the same bhp, and it costs less to produce.

The all-independent suspension is provided by McPherson struts on the front, with single bottom wishbones and an anti-roll bar. The positive location of the bottom wishbones constitutes a further development of the McPherson suspension system, which in its original form relied upon a single link and the anti-roll bar for location. The anti-roll bar in this case fulfils only its original function of preventing excessive roll. The rear wheels are controlled by trailing arms and long-stroke suspension struts. Coil springs and hydraulic dampers are used all round. A four-wheel disc-brake arrangement is employed, with the front brakes inboard on either side of the transmission. The rear wheel braking is controlled by a hydro-mechanical device permitting the application of maximum braking at the rear end only in proportion to the loads supported by the rear wheels. The brakes themselves are ATE Dunlop with 11.18 ins discs on the front and 10.71 ins on the rear. A servo is used. The steering is by rack and pinion with hydraulic servo systems and overall ratio of 18.3 to 1, giving 3.7 turns from lock to lock. The steering unit itself is unconventionally placed high on the scuttle behind the instrument panel. Pressed steel 5J × 14 wheels are used with radial 175 SR × 14 tyres. Many of the usual extras are standard on the car.

NSU Ro 80

New front-wheel-drive sedan engineered from the ground up for use with a 2-chamber Wankel engine

BY GÜNTHER MOLTER

Looking down on engine it can be seen that twin-chamber Wankel uses two carburetors, two coils and four spark plugs.

THE NEW NSU Ro 80—the first complete car to be engineered from the ground up to meet the special requirements of a rotary piston engine—will be introduced to the public at the Frankfort Motor Show. On the same day, production of the new sedan will begin at the NSU factory in Neckarsulm.

NSU has more experience with rotary-engined cars than any other manufacturer. The first practical application was the installation of a 500-cc NSU-Wankel unit powering a conventional NSU Prinz 4-seater. This was done simply to show that it was possible to power an automobile by this novel kind of engine. Next the engine was put into a Sport Prinz and this was followed by production of the Sport Prinz with a rotary engine. This model was used to gain experience not only in producing such a car and training service personnel but also to learn how the design would stand up in the hands of average drivers. When this had been accomplished, NSU was ready to produce a new model specifically designed around the use of the rotary engine.

From the outside, the new car gives not a hint that it is not equipped with a conventional reciprocating engine. The body, which was designed by a graduate of the *Schule für Formgestaltung* at Ulm who works for NSU, is slim and sporty. The proportions of the car are pleasing and its aerodynamic appearance is confirmed by a very low C_W (drag coefficient), 0.355, lower than that of many sports cars. The engine, a water-cooled NSU-Wankel with two chambers

---

The author in the NSU Ro 80. Car is larger than it appears in photos and is actually longer than Rover 2000 or Volvo 144.

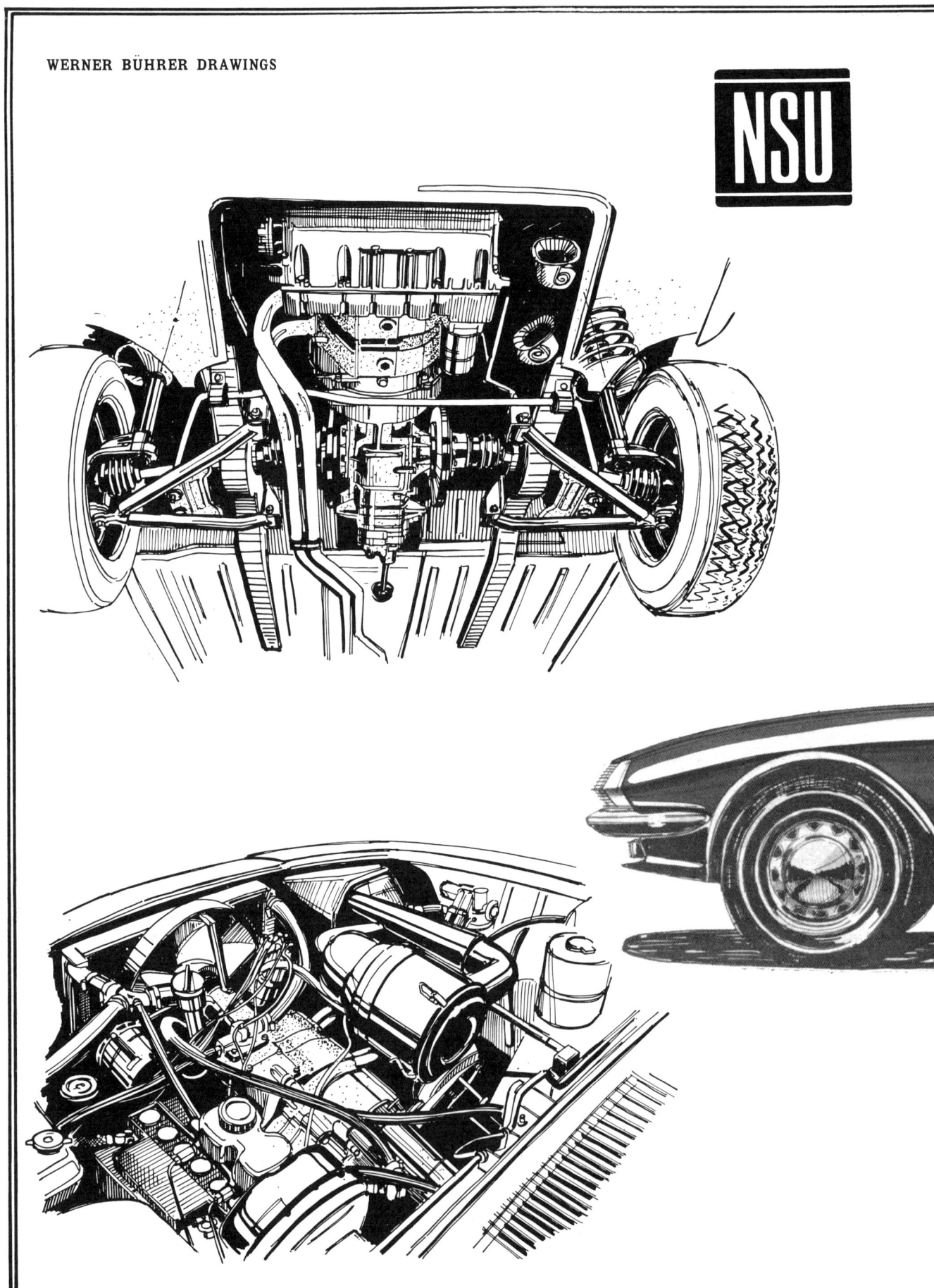

NSU Ro 80

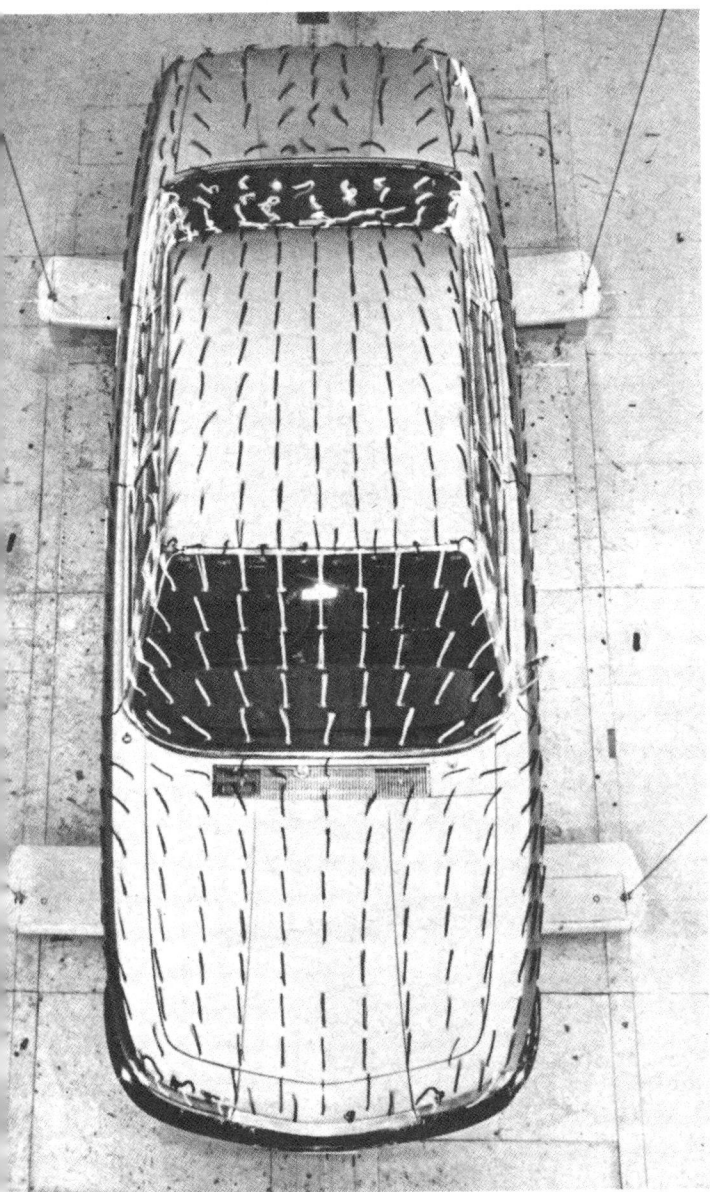

NSU Ro 80 during wind tunnel tests. Small number of tufts disturbed demonstrates aerodynamic cleanness of the new sedan.

NAMING THE Ro 80

WHERE DID THEY get the name for the NSU Ro 80? The factory code name for the project was T 80 but this wasn't thought to be suitable because T 80 reminded Germans of T 34 and the T 34 was a Russian tank of World War II. T 80 was also the designation of the Mercedes-Benz record car that was ready to go but never run because of the outbreak of WW II. "Rotary" seemed to be the right name for the car but the international Rotary club had prior claim. "Delphin" was also proposed but the French equivalent, "Dauphin," was too close to "Dauphine," a model built by Renault. Rota was also considered, but there is an Austrian steel plant named Rotax, so in the end NSU settled on Ro 80 and that's its name.

of 497.5 cc each, is rated at 115 bhp (DIN) at 5500 rpm and develops 117 lb-ft of torque at 4500. It is mounted in front of the front axle and drives the front wheels through a Saxomat semi-automatic transmission.

The suspension is independent at all wheels and these are shown very clearly in the Werner Bührer drawings on the previous page. ATE-Dunlop disc brakes are used on all four wheels, and these are servo-assisted and have a limiting valve in the rear circuit. The brakes are inboard at the front and outboard at the rear. Steering is by rack-and-pinion and is also servo-assisted.

In basic dimensions, the Ro 80 has a wheelbase of 112.6 in.; it is 69.3 in. wide, 55.5 in. tall and has an overall length of 188.2 in. This is a good-sized car and slightly larger than typical 2-liter sedans as the Rover 2000 (wheelbase 103.4, overall length 178.5), Volvo 122S (102.4 and 175.0), BMW 2000 (100.4 and 177.2) or Mercedes-Benz 200 (106.3 and 186.2). The unladen weight of the car is 2600 lb and the factory gives the top speed as more than 110 mph.

Driving Impressions

MY FIRST impression on getting into the car was that it is a comfortable sedan with sporting character. There are four doors, of sufficient size to permit easy entrance. There are bucket seats in front and these are very well shaped and comfortable. The driving position is excellent.

There are two pedals—the Saxomat transmission requires no clutch pedal, of course—and the shift lever is floor mounted. The Saxomat, which is built by Fichtel & Sachs, is a 3-speed semi-automatic and in my opinion is not the best possible choice for the car though NSU representatives say it was chosen because the Ro 80 should offer some "sports-like feeling." Its operation is simple enough (when your hand touches the shift lever, the clutch is disengaged; then you move the lever to select the gear you want and the clutch re-engages when you take your hand off the lever) but it offers neither the convenience of the fully automatic transmission nor the sporting character of a fully synchronized 4- or 5-speed manual gearbox.

In all other respects, I liked the car very much. Road holding is excellent and the ride is very comfortable. Unlike some front-wheel-drive cars, there is not the slightest tendency to change from understeer to oversteer if the throttle is let off in the middle of a turn. The brakes are excellent and the steering response is more like a sports car than a medium-sized sedan.

It is necessary to make use of the gearbox to obtain the best performance from the Ro 80. Although the engine is smooth-running from idle, I have the impression that it would prefer to stay over 3000 rpm. From idle up to about 2000 rpm, it seems just a little lazy. The factory representatives assured me that this was a mistaken impression but as we were not able to take any acceleration figures, I remain unconvinced.

The engine is very smooth and turbine-like and there is no noticeable vibration, which is the hallmark of the rotary piston engine. For a 995-cc engine, the performance is excellent: In the higher rpm range it is quieter, and has less vibration and far better performance characteristics than a reciprocating engine of the same size.

The Ro 80 is undoubtedly intended as the first in a line of NSU cars with larger, more powerful engines. A 2-liter engine with fuel injection would offer more torque at low rpm and this may be the direction the NSU-Wankel engine development will take in the future. But first we will have to see what degree of acceptance the Ro 80 enjoys in a price range that includes formidable competition such as the BMW 2000 and Mercedes-Benz 200.

For Americans, the Ro 80 is a technically interesting car to be read about but not seen, as the exhaust emission characteristics of the Wankel engine are such that the new smog control laws will prevent its being sold in the U. S.

Car of the year—or decade?

Wankel engine smooth and quiet; performance good, economy poor; very quiet at speed and handling outstanding; well made, roomy and very comfortable.

IT is hard to see how anything else but the NSU Ro80 could have been nominated as Car of the Year by our Dutch contemporary, *Auto Visie,* through their international panel of judges. The enterprise and expertise alone behind the Ro80 project would almost have been sufficient to clinch the title: that the car has also turned out to be so outstandingly good makes the decision inevitable.

The Ro80 (Ro for rotary engine, 80 for the drawing board design number) was a venture on which NSU staked their future as it involved not just a radical power plant but an entirely new breed of NSU, a marque hitherto typified by relatively cheap but well engineered rear-engined vehicles; the know-how behind them has undoubtedly rubbed off on the Ro80. That it was designed from scratch round the engine, unhampered by tradition, compromise, fashion or rationalization, probably has a lot to do with its success. The Wankel gamble has certainly paid off—at least on a fairly expensive luxury car like this for which frugal economy is not of prime importance.

To recap, the twin rotor engine sits low and well forward in a big, roomy all-independently sprung five seater body, and drives the front wheels through what must now be considered a conventional form of semi-automatic transmission. Enhancing its technical specification is dual circuit, all-disc brakes and rack-and-pinion steering—both power assisted. At first, you are aware of the engine only because it is a natural focal point for attention: later, it is the car as a whole that you realise is so impressive and that the Wankel is but an unobtrusive part of it. The steering, handling and roadholding are probably better individually and almost certainly collectively than those of any other luxury car we have tried. So it is not only very safe but, on the right road, very exhilarating to drive. It is also an extremely comfortable car; despite firmish suspension it rides very well, the seats are good, the inside very spacious, the noise level low—especially at speed

—and the heating and ventilation quite efficient. And like many German cars, it is beautifully made (even if the door buttons did stick on our car) and very fully equipped.

After a relatively short period of development, the Wankel engine has already surpassed in smoothness and refinement, particularly at high speeds, the standards established for an equivalent piston engine, and at least equalled them on performance—as the Ro80's brisk acceleration and top speed of 112 m.p.h. confirm. But despite assistance from the low-drag body, fuel consumption remains fairly heavy, though with development still little beyond the threshold stage, there will presumably be improvements here, particular with progress on special fuel injection systems.

The other disappointment—which we hope was peculiar to the test car—was the rather unrefined and noisy transmission which did not work nearly so well as we felt it should. As there are no Ro80 Press demonstrators available yet in Britain, the whole of this test was done in Italy on a new, low-mileage car provided for us by the factory. Later on, we hope to try another one to re-assess the transmission—provided, that is, that customer demand does not continue to deflect all cars away from us. Even though import duty inflates the Ro80's price to £2,250 in Britain, it is still very competitive even without its novelty value: in Germany, it is considered such a bargain that NSU can't keep pace with the orders.

Performance and economy

The engine is started just like any other, using plenty of choke when cold—though it can be pushed home again almost immediately once the engine is running. A chokeless, full-throttle burst before warming up can stall the engine but it coped without hesitation or splutter on a steep garage ramp on half throttle and no choke, 10 seconds after starting up on a bitter morning.

Each of the two rotors has three firing strokes per revolution but as the output shaft rotates three times as fast as the rotors

PRICE: £1,828 10s plus £420 5s purchase tax equals £2,249

NSU Ro80

there are two firing strokes per drive shaft revolution—the same as for a four-cylinder, four-stroke piston engine, or a two-stroke twin. On the basis of air consumption, therefore, the 497 c.c. chambers of the Ro80 can be equated to an ordinary engine of 2 litres so the Corsair 2000E or Rover 2000 would be comparable piston-engined cars. Probably because there are no mechanical valves to chatter, the sound is that of a two-stroke in the low and middle reaches of its impressive rev range; and probably because of what we suspect was over-rich carburation, it would hunt with a rhythmic beat when idling at about 1,200 r.p.m. Up to 3,000 r.p.m. it does not sound unusually silky (probably because of the separate exhausts), even though there is virtually no mechanical vibration. But the higher the revs the smoother it becomes, in both sound and feel, until at 6,000 r.p.m. and well beyond it seems just like a turbine—a comparison heightened by the fan's viscous coupling which starts to slip at about 4,750 r.p.m. so that its whirring remains constant while the engine note gets higher. Certainly at really high speeds, no four-cylinder four-stroke is in the same league and even a much bigger V-8 with which we were able to make immediate comparison was, if a little less busy, no smoother.

It is this uncanny effortlessness that makes 100 m.p.h. seem so easy and deceptive: on the flat, dead-straight almost cornerless

Autostrada from Rimini, the Ro80 felt as though it could hold indefinitely the breeze-assisted 117 m.p.h. recorded in the performance data. That such a speed is possible at all on a modest 115 b.h.p. stems largely from the low aerodynamic drag of the body which was not so much styled as engineered in a wind tunnel—and has a remarkable drag coefficient of 0.355 to prove it. Power/weight ratio rather than streamlining, though, is what governs acceleration and while the Ro80's is quite brisk, it is less outstanding: from 0—50 m.p.h. it falls between that of a Rover 2000 and a 2000 TC but at high speeds it approaches the latter more closely.

This is not to say that the performance is weak at low speeds as any deficiency in torque is compensated for by the torque converter which, on full throttle, will always keep the engine above 2,500 r.p.m. so you can slog from 20 to 40 m.p.h. in high gear in 8.3 seconds—about the same time taken by the 2000E which has unusually good torque and flexibility at low speeds.

The rev-counter is red-lined at 6,500 r.p.m. but NSU said that 8,000 r.p.m. was quite safe, at the expense of oil consumption and rotor tip wear if used persistently. We compromised with 7,250 r.p.m. during performance testing and kept to the 6,500 r.p.m. limit for road work with a resultant oil consumption of about 400 miles per pint. Wankels do not need to be run-in like piston engines so high speeds early in the car's life are not damaging.

Judged by standards applying to fast, roomy, five seaters, the steady speed consumptions in top gear are quite reasonable really, dropping from 33 m.p.g. at 30 m.p.h. to 17 m.p.g. at 90 m.p.h.:

Performance

Conditions

Weather: Cool and dry, wind 5 m.p.h. for acceleration, higher for max. and fuel consumption.
Temperature approx. 45°–50°F.
Surface: Dry tarmacadam.
Fuel: Premium 93 octane (R.M.). 3 star rating.

Maximum speeds

	m.p.h.
Mean of opposite runs	112.6
Best one-way kilometre	117.1
2nd gear } at 6,500 r.p.m. (see text)	80
1st gear }	47

Acceleration times

m.p.h.	sec.
0-30	5.1
0-40	7.1
0-50	9.8
0-60	14.2
0-70	18.6
0.80	24.6
0-90	33.1
0-100	44.3
Standing quarter mile	19.7

m.p.h.	Top sec.	2nd sec.
20-40	8.3	6.5
30-50	9.7	7.0
40-60	11.2	7.8
50-70	13.2	8.0
60-80	14.5	9.3
70-90	17.0	—
80-100	21.1	—

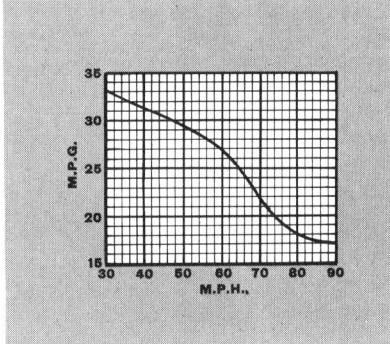

Fuel consumption

Touring (consumption midway between 30 m.p.h. and maximum less 5% allowance for acceleration) ... 20.2 m.p.g.
Overall ... 15.3 m.p.g.
(= 18 litres/100 km.)
Total test mileage ... 1,250 miles
Tank capacity (maker's figure) ... 18 gal.

Brakes

Pedal pressure, deceleration and equivalent stopping distance from 30 m.p.h.

lb.	g	ft.
25	0.40	75
50	0.76	39½
60	0.89	34
Handbrake	0.32	94

Fade test

20 stops at ½g deceleration at 1 min. intervals from a speed midway between 30 m.p.h. and maximum speed (= 71 m.p.h.)

	lb.
Pedal force at beginning	30
Pedal force at 10th stop	30
Pedal force at 20th stop	30

Steering

Turning circle between kerbs:

	ft.
Left	32¼
Right	35½
Turns of steering wheel from lock to lock	3¾

Speedometer

True	30	40	50	60	70	80	90	100
Indicated	33	45	55	65	77	86½	96	106

Distance recorder ... accurate

Weight

Kerb weight (unladen with fuel for approximately 50 miles) ... 23.5 cwt.
Front/rear distribution ... approx. 60/40
Weight laden as tested ... 27.25 cwt.

Parkability

Gap needed to clear a 6ft. wide obstruction parked in front:

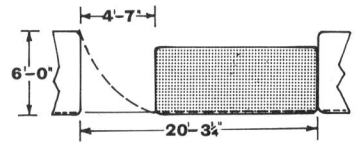

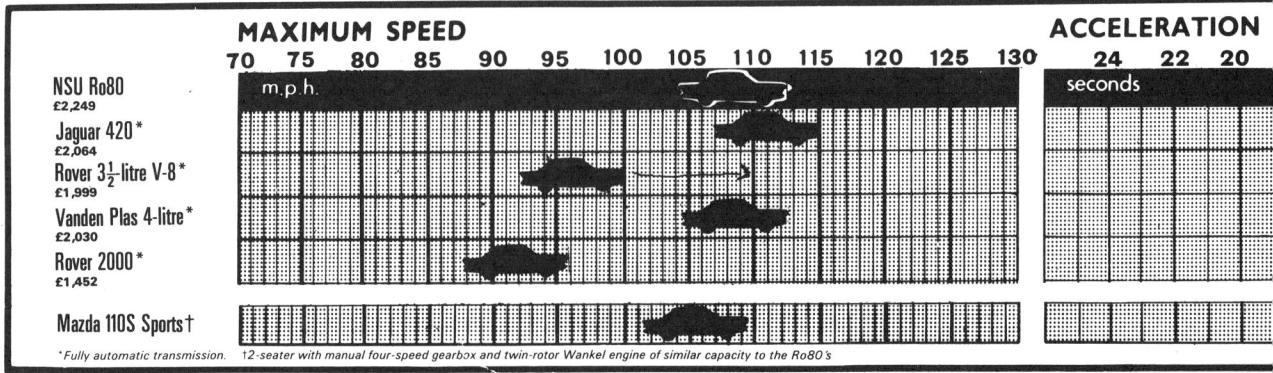

	MAXIMUM SPEED	ACCELERATION

NSU Ro80 £2,249
Jaguar 420* £2,064
Rover 3½-litre V-8* £1,999
Vanden Plas 4-litre* £2,030
Rover 2000* £1,452
Mazda 110S Sports†

*Fully automatic transmission. †2-seater with manual four-speed gearbox and twin-rotor Wankel engine of similar capacity to the Ro80's

The Ro80's unusual low-front high-tail styling is the result of wind-tunnel testing.

the Jaguar 240, for instance, is thirstier throughout and the Corsair 2000E not very much better. These figures suggest that the Ro80 is capable of returning an overall consumption of between 16 and 22 m.p.g., though ours was only 15.3 m.p.g.—largely because the car encouraged such fast driving. As there are no overall speed limits in Italy we cruised at 100 m.p.h. on the autostrada so the engine was always working pretty hard. But it was probably second gear that did the damage: the torque converter (itself a fuel drinker) gives the car lively acceleration and hillclimbing between 0 and 85 m.p.h. so on the mountain secondary roads of central Italy it was used nearly all the time. Coupled with the rich running and high idling speed—neither of which we felt like adjusting since the linkage of the twin Solex carbs is not straightforward—it is hardly surprising that the final figure was poor.

A little of this thirst is offset by the engine's tolerance of 92 octane (3-star) petrol, though on anything less it pinks badly, even on quite a light throttle and at high speeds—detonation like this would eventually destroy the rotor seals. The big 18-gallon fuel tank allows a good range of 360 miles at 20 m.p.g.

Transmission

A hydraulic torque converter is sandwiched between the engine and a vacuum operated dry-plate clutch and three-speed all-synchromesh gearbox, the clutch mechanism being activated by a touch-sensitive micro switch in the gear lever knob. Similar arrangements are used with considerable success by Fiat, Simca and Volkswagen as cheap alternatives to fully automatic transmission: NSU use it for different reasons. One is that the torque converter compensates for the engine's modest pull at low speeds; another is that the fluid coupling cushions any over-run snatch far better than a solid one—an important consideration for a smooth running luxury car.

In both these respects it works very well and we know from past experience that this form of transmission can be easy and effortless to handle, very smooth and even quite fun. Nevertheless, this one was disappointing and not a patch on the

Continued on the next page

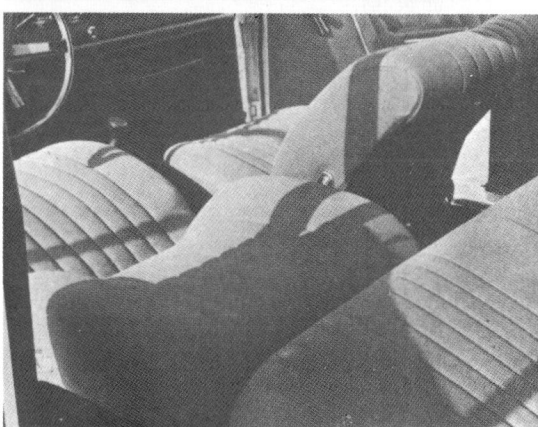

The comfortable front seats have three-way adjustment and will lie right back to make a bed.

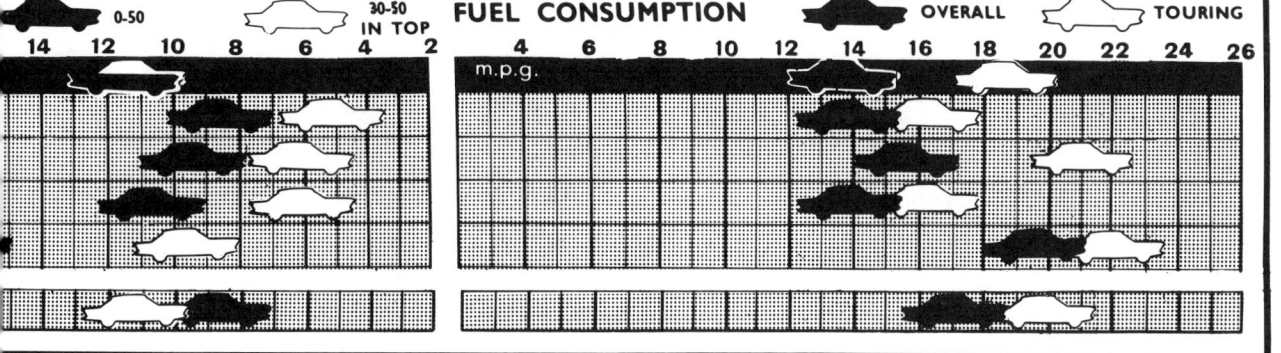

The high tail and side scallop were evolved in a wind tunnel to improve streamlining: an added bonus is that it makes the boot very deep.

We could not take our test boxes to Italy but this load of test kit and personal luggage went inside the boot with room to spare.

NSU Ro80

nominally identical transmission on the prototype car we drove last September on which it was difficult to make a bad change: without a lot of practice, it was sometimes hard to make a good one on this car. The servo mechanism would slam: the clutch in with a jerky thump if engine revs were not matched perfectly to road speed when the gearlever was released. The fast idling speed exaggerated this fault when selecting a gear at rest though the jerk could be prevented by applying the brakes first. The synchromesh on second gear was also very weak, that you had to ease the lever through to avoid a crunch. Such deliberation did not upset the timing of normal upward changes because the engine takes time to lose revs between the widely spaced ratios. But for downchanges, it was necessary to double-de-clutch, revving the engine, as you might with a manual box, after releasing the clutch knob to ease the load on the synchro cones.

Of course, with this system, it is not necessary to do much gearchanging. The car will start in top gear quite easily, albeit rather slowly at first, and for all normal driving, second and top between them can cope with practically anything. If it didn't affect the fuel consumption so much, second gear alone would be ideal for all townwork, eliminating the need for gear changing altogether.

Safety check list

Steering assembly

Steering box position	Good—well back on scuttle
Steering column collapsible	No
Steering wheel boss padded	Yes, heavily
Steering wheel dished	Slightly

Instrument panel

Projecting switches	Yes—but they are large-faced and guarded by padded rail. Heater knobs are small, hard and projecting
Sharp cowls	No
Padding	Yes—on screen pillars, and above and below facia

Windscreen and visibility

Screen type	Toughened
Pillars padded	Yes
Standard driving mirrors	Interior, and exterior on door
Interior mirror framed	Yes
Interior mirror collapsible	Yes—by snap-on clips
Sun visors	Crushable—but they don't twist sideways

Seats and harness

Attachment to floor	On slides bolted to floor
Do they tip forward?	No
Head rest attachment points	No
Back of front seats	Upholstered but not padded
Safety harness	Not fitted to test car
Harness anchors at back	Yes

Doors

Projecting handles	Window winders
Anti-burst locks	Yes
Child-proof locks	No

Handling and brakes

With 60% of the car's not inconsiderable weight on the front wheels the steering was considered too heavy during prototype testing so the rack-and-pinion gear now has a hydraulically operated ram to help the driver. Not only is the result the best power steering we have tried but also the only one that does not betray itself in the slightest degree. Kick-back has been eliminated without affecting feel. But it is not just the lightness and precision of the steering that makes the Ro80 perhaps the world's best handling saloon. The car's behaviour is so impeccable on twisting mountain roads that without highly skilled or suicidal provocation it is impossible to slide the back wheels: eventually, the front ones will start to run wide with understeer but, even on a wet road, you have to be pretty brave to reach this situation. Arriving at an unexpected corner too fast, you just wind on more lock and glide round, as securely as a weight swung on the end of a string, without any obvious understeer, scrub, fuss or drama. Lifting off the power, as most mortals would in such a situation, does not induce any unruly tuck-in or oversteer (as on some front-wheel drive cars): in fact the Ro80 is almost totally insensitive to throttle opening. Turning the steering wheel is the only way to make it change direction for even in a strong cross wind, it is completely stable. It rolls very little and does not lurch or rock over a hump-and-bump taken at speed. It seemed to us that the roadholding and cornering powers, coupled with the ease of control, were so much higher than the average driver would ever contemplate, or the support of the seats would permit in comfort, that the Ro80 must rank as one of the safest cars ever built.

The power steering takes all the effort out of parking and,

The rounded nose, protected by a wrap-round bumper, compensates when parking for a poorish turning circle. The auxiliary lights below the bumper act as good kerb spotters, leaving long-range work for the bigger lamps above. The XAS Michelin tyres are standard equipment.

Two fingertip stalks operate the washers, wipers, horn, dip, flasher and indicators. Note the safety crash pad on the steering wheel boss.

although the turning circle is not particularly tight, the rounded front corners compensate for the poor lock when edging out of a tight gap—as the parkability figure of only 4ft. 7 in. confirms (see diagram).

On the road, the all-disc German Dunlop brakes—inboard at the front, outboard at the back—felt splendid as they responded smoothly and progressively to light, if not featherweight, pressure on the wide pedal. They were also immune to fade, not only in our standard 20-stop test but also under the more severe demands of braking for hairpins when rushing down a mountain pass. However, the best recorded stop of a little under 0.9g was a bit disappointing while panic braking to lock all the wheels gave even poorer results. Bear in mind, though, that these tests were not done on MIRA's high-friction surface. There was also a pronounced juddering (possibly caused by wind-up in the drive shafts) that set in just before the car came to rest in a hard stop.

Comfort and controls

Concentrating all the major mechanical parts up in the nose of the car has left most of the unitary body/chassis free to carry people and luggage. The passenger compartment is so unusually long that four six footers can stretch their legs with room to spare —or five if need be as there is no transmission tunnel to get in the way at the back. Both front seats have generous fore-and-aft movement and fully reclining squabs which can fold right back to make a bed. There is also an additional adjuster which slides the seats bodily along an inclined ramp to alter the height. So whatever your shape or size, the driving position behind the smallish, low-set, vertical steering wheel is relaxed and commanding. Thigh and lumbar support is excellent and although the prominently curved squabs and non-slip cloth upholstery in our test

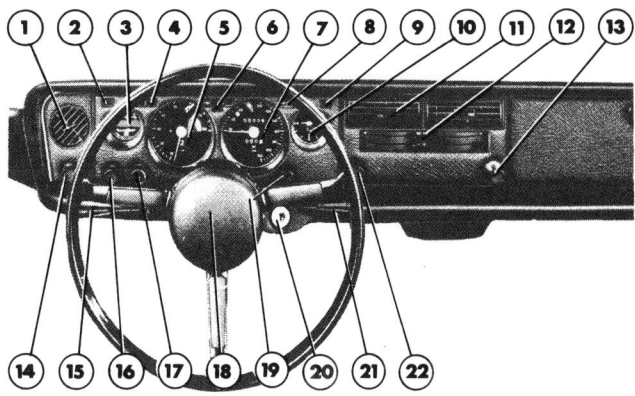

1, cold or warm air vent. 2, parking tell tale. 3, fuel gauge and engine temperature. 4, indicators and main beam tell tales. 5, rev counter. 6, warning lights for low petrol, handbrake/low fluid, and oil/water. 7, speedometer with total and trip distance recorders. 8, choke and ignition warning lights. 9, rear window heater warning light. 10, clock. 11, pair of cold air vents. 12, temperature, distribution, air volume and fan controls. 13, cigar lighter. 14, lights. 15, flasher, dip and indicators. 16, rear window heater and fog lights. 17, four-way flasher. 18, crash pad. 19, panel rheostat and trip re-set. 20, ignition/starter/steering lock. 21, wipers/washers/horn. 22, choke.

Specification

Engine

Cylinders	2 co-axial oil-cooled rotors with two main bearings in water-cooled housing
Cubic capacity	2 x 497.5 c.c. (equivalent to 1,990 c.c. piston engine)
Valves	None
Compression ratio	9:1
Carburetters	Two double choke compound Solex 18/32 HHO with accelerator pumps
Fuel pump	Mechanical
Oil filter	Full flow
Max. power (net)	113.5 b.h.p. at 5,500 r.p.m.
Max. torque (net)	117 lb. ft. at 4,500 r.p.m.

Transmission

Hydrokinetic torque converter coupled to 3-speed synchromesh gearbox with s.d.p. clutch operated by vacuum servo energized by gearlever switch.

Top gear (s/m)	0.788:1
2nd gear (s/m)	1.208:1
1st gear (s/m)	2.056:1
Reverse	2.105:1
Final drive	4.857:1
M.p.h. at 1,000 r.p.m. in:—	
Top gear	18.8
2nd gear	12.3
1st gear	7.2

Chassis

Construction	Unitary

Brakes

Type	ATE—Dunlop discs all round with dual line application, vacuum servo and load compensator. Handbrake operates on duo-servo 6.3in. rear drums.
Dimensions	11.2in. front; 10.7in. rear.

Suspension and Steering

Front	Independent by MacPherson struts with coil springs and an anti-roll bar.
Rear	Independent by semi-trailing arms and coil springs.
Shock absorbers:	
Front and rear:	Double-acting telescopic.
Steering gear	ZF power-assisted rack and pinion.
Tyres	175-14 Michelin XAS
Rim size	5J

Coachwork and Equipment

Starting handle	No
Jack	Screw pillar
Jacking points	Under body sills
Battery	12-volt negative earth, 60 amp hrs capacity
Number of electrical fuses	8
Indicators	Self-cancelling flashers
Screen wipers	Electric two-speed
Screen washers	Electric

Sun visors	Two
Locks:	
With ignition key	Front doors
With other keys	Boot and glove compartment with separate key for fuel filler cap
Interior heater	Fresh air heater and demister with separate cold air ventilation. Heated back window.
Upholstery	Cloth or plastic
Floor covering	Carpet
Alternative body styles	None

Maintenance

Sump	12 pints SAE HD 10W/30
Gearbox/final drive	3½ pints SAE 90 Hypoid
Steering gear	ATF oil and Mobil transmission oil
Cooling system	15 pints (1 drain tap)
Chassis lubrication	none
Minimum service interval	5,000 km. (about 3,000 miles)
Contact breaker gap	0.015 in.
Sparking plug gap	0.024-0.0028 in.
Sparking plug type	Beru 280/1862
Front wheel toe-out	zero
Camber angle	30°
Castor angle	0°
King pin inclination	8° 30'
Tyre pressures:	
Front	28lb./sq.in.
Rear	24lb./sq.in.

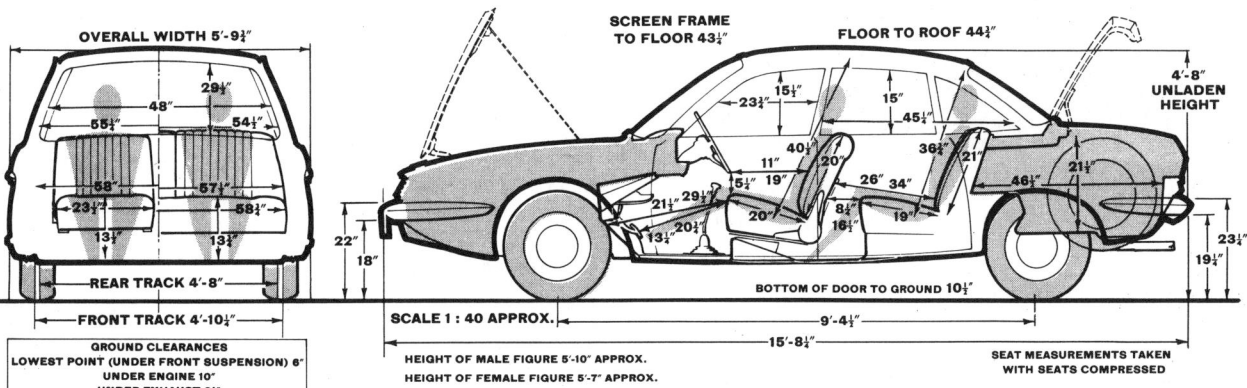

OVERALL WIDTH 5'-9½"
29¼"
48"
54½"
55½"
53"
57½"
23½"
58½"
13½"
13½"
REAR TRACK 4'-8"
FRONT TRACK 4'-10½"

GROUND CLEARANCES
LOWEST POINT (UNDER FRONT SUSPENSION) 6"
UNDER ENGINE 10"
UNDER EXHAUST 6¼"

SCREEN FRAME TO FLOOR 43¼"
FLOOR TO ROOF 44¼"
4'-8" UNLADEN HEIGHT
15½"
23½"
15"
45¼"
40½"
36¼"
11"
20½"
21"
5½" 19"
26" 34"
46¼"
21¼"
21½" 29½"
20½"
20"
8½" 16½"
19"
13¼" 20½"
23¼"
19¼"
22"
18"
BOTTOM OF DOOR TO GROUND 10½"

SCALE 1 : 40 APPROX.
9'-4½"
15'-8½"

HEIGHT OF MALE FIGURE 5'-10" APPROX.
HEIGHT OF FEMALE FIGURE 5'-7" APPROX.

SEAT MEASUREMENTS TAKEN WITH SEATS COMPRESSED

NSU Ro80

car provided quite good lateral support, we could have done with still more when really exploiting the car's cornering powers.

Subjected to such spirited chauffering, a passenger is better off in the back seat where the folding central armrest and roof-top handle provide better grabs than the door pull alone on the front door. No doubt seat belts would help too, but our car didn't have any.

The pedals are a little offset to the right and although the brake is wide left foot braking brings your knee up against the steering wheel. The brake is also much higher than the accelerator so you cannot side-step without lifting your foot from one to the other. The handbrake, which operates special drums on the back wheels, is tucked handily between the seats but if you sit well back the gearlever is too far forward, particularly when reaching for second. In this position the passenger's legs are less likely to touch the gear knob (and thus release the clutch)—but it can still happen, and is quite alarming if you are accelerating hard at the time.

The exceptional stability of the car's ride greatly enhances the comfort of the furniture inside. As already mentioned, the body scarcely rolls at all and even when driving fast through an S-bend there is no uncomfortable sway on changing lock. Nor does the body pitch on wavy surfaces, or yo-yo over an unexpected hump, because the firm damping catches the car in mid bounce and lowers it gently. Several modern saloons can match its bump smothering qualities on poor secondary roads, but even when the going was very rough, rude jolts were few—though the tyres can often be heard thumping. On certain coarse surfaces, they will also rumble but, even so, the Ro80 is in general a quiet car. The engine itself, though by no means silent, is never obtrusive, except for a certain low-speed exhaust resonance that can only be detected from the back seat. You are more aware of the high-pitched whine and sizzle from the transmission which, even at speed, is thrown into prominence by the very low level of wind noise—another bonus reaped from proper streamlining which includes burying the rain channels rather than allowing then to stand proud. In contrast, the heater fan running fast is absurdly noisy, drowning all other sounds.

Volume, temperature and distribution controls permit fine regulation over the powerful heater. Apart from the usual under-scuttle and screen outlets, there are vaned swivellers at each end of the facia which can be used either to demist the side windows or to take the chill off your face. Sited in the middle of the facia are two rectangular cold air vents which, through adjustable vanes, can aim fresh air into almost any part of the car. Their one big fault is that they have a common volume control and cannot therefore be adjusted individually.

As there are extractors by the back window—which is electrically heated, incidentally, by embedded wires—front quarter-lights have been eliminated, leaving the side windows uncluttered. It is the exceptional depth of the windscreen, though, coupled with the very low bonnet, that makes the inside so light and airy and the forward look-out so good, despite fairly thick screen pillars. The deep sun visors offer good protection against glare but, surprisingly, they don't twist round to cover the side windows. By sitting up you can just see the back corners for reversing and, with three side windows, there are no three-quarter rear blind spots. Although the lights do not match those of, say, the Lancia Flavia or Citroën DS, they are still better than average, especially when the built-in fog-lights are used as kerb spotters. The gearlever automatically turns on the rather dim reversing light.

Fittings and furniture

If you are sitting low and well back the big safety pad over the steering wheel boss partially masks the otherwise clear white-on-black rev-counter and speedometer (though the covered sectors are not really important). Like Mercedes and Porsche, NSU have evolved finger-tip switchgear for all the most needed minor controls. The left-hand stalk works the indicators, dip and flasher, that on the right the two-speed wipers, electric washers and strident three-tone horn. You are likely at first to dip with the washers and hoot with the flashers but, when your reactions eventually become automatic, the system is excellent. Other controls—for the four-way emergency flashers, rear screen heater, lights, choke, cigar lighter, trip re-set and panel lights—are stripped across the dash. Although all the warning lights seem a bit bewildering at first the facia illumination is very effective, the needles, danger sectors and heater symbols being picked out in colour. None of the other switches is labelled.

Like most German cars, the inside is exquisitely finished in modern materials though the cloth seats in our car (other upholstery is available) would be impractical for many people. There is a useful illuminated oddments locker (which also houses the car's eight fuses behind a transparent cover) and a smallish parcel net beneath. Maps can be kept in flexible pockets on the back of each front seat. We could not check the size of the boot objectively but suffice to say that it is very large and can be reached from inside the car by removing the back seats squabs—useful for carrying an awkwardly long load. Both the boot and bonnet are automatically lit up when the side-lights are on: inside, there are two lights—one, rather dim, housed in the safety snap-on stalk of the dipping mirror, and the other above the back seats. Other equipment includes coat hooks, grab handles, an arm-rest on each door, three ashtrays, a cigar lighter and polished aluminium kick strips.

Maintenance and accessibility

The forward-hinged bonnet is released from inside the car and supported on a long, feeble prop. Although the engine sits very low in the chassis nearly all its ancillaries are very easy to reach—including the brake pads, as the inboard discs are on each side of the final drive unit. There is no chassis lubrication to do but servicing is needed every 5,000 km, just over 3,000 miles—though most of this involves just routine checks. The engine oil and filter can be left before changing for around 12,000 miles. There is a useful toolkit and the pillar-screw jack is quite easy to work. **M**

1, radiator filler. 2, twin coils. 3, alternator. 4, oil filler. 5, viscous fan coupling. 6, distributor. 7, twin carburetters. 8, dip stick. 9, hydraulic reservoirs. 10, brake servo. 11, battery. 12, starter motor. 13, rotor housing. 14, screen washer bottle.

MAKE: NSU. MODEL: Ro80. MAKERS: NSU Motorenwerke, Neckarsulm, West Germany. CONCESSIONAIRES: NSU (Gt. Britain) Ltd., Harbour Way, Shoreham-by-Sea, Sussex.

Maintenance summary

Every 3,125 miles: check power steering oil, fluid levels, cooling system, brake pad thickness, plugs, contact breaker and timing, engine and gearbox oil.
Every 6,250 miles: check play in clutch, oil linkages, change plugs, clean fuel pump and air cleaner, check rear drums.
Every 12,500 miles: change engine oil and filter, change gearbox oil, adjust handbrake.

In 1978 the Ro 80 may have a little competition.

We've spent 17 years developing this car. For the next ten our competitors will be wondering how. Because we've incorporated some pretty advanced ideas in the Ro80. By any standards.

Take the revloutionary Wankel engine. Twin rotors in an epitrochoidal bore. That's two rotors going round and round, instead of four or more pistons going up and down: unprecedented smoothness.

And this smaller engine takes up less space. So there's extra room for five inside, as well as all their bags in the boot.

Surprisingly, this big boot helps the car go faster. It's all part of the beautiful, aerodynamic shaping.

In the Ro80 you feel relaxed because you feel safe. At any speed. Front wheel drive, power assisted disc brakes and all round independent suspension give reassuring stability, always.

In fact it's never been easier to handle such power. There isn't even a clutch pedal. Just a Selective-Automatic transmission. With butter-smooth gears.

To help you out of tight corners there's servo-assisted steering. To keep you in at tight corners, Michelin XAS radial tyres. And the Ro80 offers a very personal comfort. Fully adjustable seats. Heating and fresh air ventilation. Fine carpeting. And wide windows (a de-mister at the back.) The sensible things.

All to be had at a sensible price. £2232 (recommended retail price including P.T.).

This has been just a glimpse of the future.

There's more to the Ro80. Much more. Enough to make you despair over cars as they are today. But unless you buy the Ro80 there's nothing you can do except wait.

It'll be ten years before the others catch up.

Send me full details of the revolutionary NSU Ro80

Name...

Address...

....

If you wish to receive details of other NSU cars tick the appropriate box.

| SUPER PRINZ £599 ☐ | 1200c £780 ☐ |
| 1000c £680 ☐ | 1200TT £840 ☐ |

NSU

ROAD TEST
by John Bolster

NSU Ro80

Superb roadholding and a new sound

THE NSU Ro80 is very much in the public eye, since it has been chosen as the car of the year by the international jury appointed by *Auto Visie*. It is of great interest because it is the first Wankel-engined saloon designed to sell in large quantities, and in Germany it is remarkably cheap for such a large car. It also stands out for the excellence of its chassis design.

The Ro80 looks smaller than it is, but its overall dimensions are considerable. It has, for example, a wider track than the Rolls-Royce and an overall length of 15 ft 10 ins. It is low built and relatively light for its size, the structure having many advanced safety features. The screen pillars and roof bracing are of double box-section steel, giving great strength in the unlikely event of overturning, but these strong pillars do not cause blind spots as they are sited outside the driver's normal field of vision.

Front wheel drive has been adopted in conjunction with the MacPherson suspension geometry and Rzeppa universal joints, with large inboard disc brakes. At the rear, there are trailing arms and the discs carry

small central drums for the hand brake. The rack and pinion steering has a reduction from the column by spur gears, and it has a double-acting plunger-type servo. The engine is carried extremely far forward, but it is very light.

The transmission is through a fluid torque converter and a single dry plate clutch to a fully synchronized 3-speed gearbox. The normal central gearlever incorporates a switch, which releases the clutch through an electrically controlled vacuum servo, giving two-pedal control.

The Wankel engine has been deliberately designed for long life rather than ultimate performance and it therefore peaks at the moderate speed of 5500 rpm, the red marking on the rev counter dial starting at 6500 rpm. A special single distributor operates with two coils, and vintage-sized 18 mm sparking plugs have been adopted, for Wankels are notoriously hard on their plugs. The Solex carburetters have four butterflies between them, the two large ones opening fairly late in the accelerator pedal movement.

Instant starting in all weathers is a feature, using a normal manual choke. The exhaust gas is blue at first, for the Wankel has a controlled admission of oil into the fuel line which varies with throttle opening. This is not normally perceptible after the engine has reached its working temperature, but the oil consumption is appreciably heavier than that of a typical four-stroke.

Very comfortable seating and a screen of immense depth soon make the driver feel at home. There is literally no vibration at any speed but there is a subdued sound from the transmission and from the phasing gears of the rotors. This whining is almost drowned by the jet-type whistle which is emitted when the main throttles open. Curiously enough, this is not so noticeable at high speeds but it is very obtrusive during hard acceleration in the lower gears. The volume is not great, but the high pitch is rather disturbing and I feel that further silencing research is needed. This applies particularly to typical English conditions, but during the much faster driving which is normal on the Continent, the Ro80 is

26

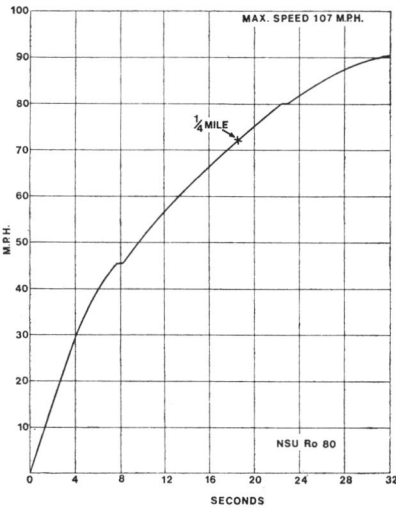

MAX. SPEED 107 M.P.H.

¼ MILE

NSU Ro 80

SECONDS

SPECIFICATION AND
PERFORMANCE DATA

quieter than most cars. There is some road noise on bad surfaces.

The mean maximum speed is 107 mph and 110 mph is frequently seen under normal road conditions. At 107 mph, the rev counter was indicating 6250 rpm, which is well below the red marking. Unfortunately, the speedometer was more than 10 per cent fast, an exaggeration which this car does not need. Second gear, with its easy 80 mph maximum, is very useful on winding roads or in traffic.

It is to be hoped that an orthodox 4-speed gearbox will eventually be offered. The present transmission suits the car very well, but for the enthusiastic driver it lacks finesse. The gearlever is delightfully light in action and the changes go through well if the movements are not made with excessive haste. Any of the three gears may be used for a standing start, second giving a reasonable getaway, though first is naturally quicker. By using left-footed braking, the engine can be accelerated to pull hard against the converter and then, on releasing the brake, wheelspin can be produced. A normal start is rapid, the car moving off rather sedately, though the acceleration is much more vivid than it seems. It is sometimes difficult to engage a gear from rest.

The roadholding is superb and the car is very well sprung. The suspension never feels too soft, but the ride over any surface is excellent, assisted by the very comfortable seats. There is very little roll and the car simply rushes round corners, understeering slightly and always feeling completely stable. As would be expected from the shape and the weight distribution, the behaviour in crosswinds is most impressive. The power-assisted steering is just about perfect, being light at all times but with plenty of feel.

Braking is powerful with low pedal pressure and, in a very real emergency, I was able to stop the car in an unbelievably short distance. At higher speeds when driving hard, I sometimes tended to lock the front wheels when I had left my braking rather late, but I soon became accustomed to the potency of the inboard discs. The handbrake is safe for parking on steep gradients.

If one regards the Ro80 as being equivalent to a 2-litre piston-engined car, the maximum speed is highly satisfactory and the acceleration is more than reasonable, having regard to the size of the body. The fuel consumption is definitely heavier than would be expected of an orthodox machine, however. This is not entirely due to the Wankel engine, for a torque converter always increases the thirst for fuel, but the fact must be faced that a fast driver will pay out at the rate of 17 mpg and his wife will probably not do better than 20 mpg. This sounds heavy, but in fact the extra cost of a year's running will not amount to much compared with the 23 to 25 mpg of other 2-litre cars; in any case the Ro80 has an 18-gallon fuel tank.

This NSU is very well made and finished, with extremely full equipment. The heating and ventilation systems have many controls and can be adjusted to give exactly the right results. The headlamps are more effective when dipped than those of some Continental cars but on main beam they lack ultimate range, probably due to the transparent fairings that cover them. There is something very modern about the interior treatment and perhaps the muted sound of jet aircraft is all part of this.

The NSU Ro80 gives a combination of roadholding and riding comfort which is unsurpassed, and has power-assisted steering which is equally outstanding. Its unconventional Wankel engine adds greatly to the interest of driving it and some may find its high-pitched song of battle inspiring. Cruising at 90 mph in luxury over almost any sort of road surface, it gives one a glimpse of what motoring in the future will be like.

Car tested: NSU Ro80 four-door saloon. Price, £2249 5s including PT.

Engine: Twin-rotor Wankel, equivalent capacity 1990 cc. Compression ratio 9:1; 113.5 bhp (net) at 5500 rpm. Twin Solex double-choke horizontal carburetters. Bosch distributor and twin coils.

Transmission: Hydraulic torque converter; single dry-plate clutch operated by switch on gearlever; three-speed all-synchromesh gearbox with central change. Ratios (without torque converter multiplication): 0.79, 1.21 and 2.06:1. Hypoid bevel final drive, ratio 4.86:1. Articulated half-shafts with Rzeppa joints driving front hubs.

Chassis: Combined steel body and chassis. Independent front suspension by MacPherson struts and lower wishbones with helical springs and anti-roll bar. ZF power-assisted rack and pinion steering with double reduction. Independent rear suspension by trailing arms and helical springs. Telescopic dampers all round. Disc brakes all round, inboard in front, with vacuum servo. Pressed-steel five-stud ventilated disc wheels fitted Michelin 175-14 ins radial-ply tyres.

Equipment: Twelve-volt lighting and starting with alternator. Speedometer, rev counter, water temperature and fuel gauges and clock. Heating demisting and ventilation system with heated rear window. Two-speed windscreen wipers and washers, reversing lights, fog lamps, flashing direction indicators with hazard warning and cigar lighter.

Dimensions: Wheelbase, 9 ft 4.7 ins; track, 4 ft 10.5 ins (front), 4 ft 8.5 ins (rear); overall length, 15 ft 10 ins; width, 5 ft 9.5 ins. Weight, 1 ton 3 cwt 84 lb.

Performance: Maximum speed, 107 mph. Speeds in gears: second, 80 mph; first, 46 mph. Standing quarter-mile, 18.6 s. Acceleration: 0-30 mph, 4 s; 0-50 mph, 9.8 s; 0.60 mph, 13.4 s; 0-80 mph, 22.4 s.

Fuel consumption: 17 to 20 mpg.

FIRST ROAD TEST THE REVOLUTIONARY '69 NSU WANKEL Ro 80

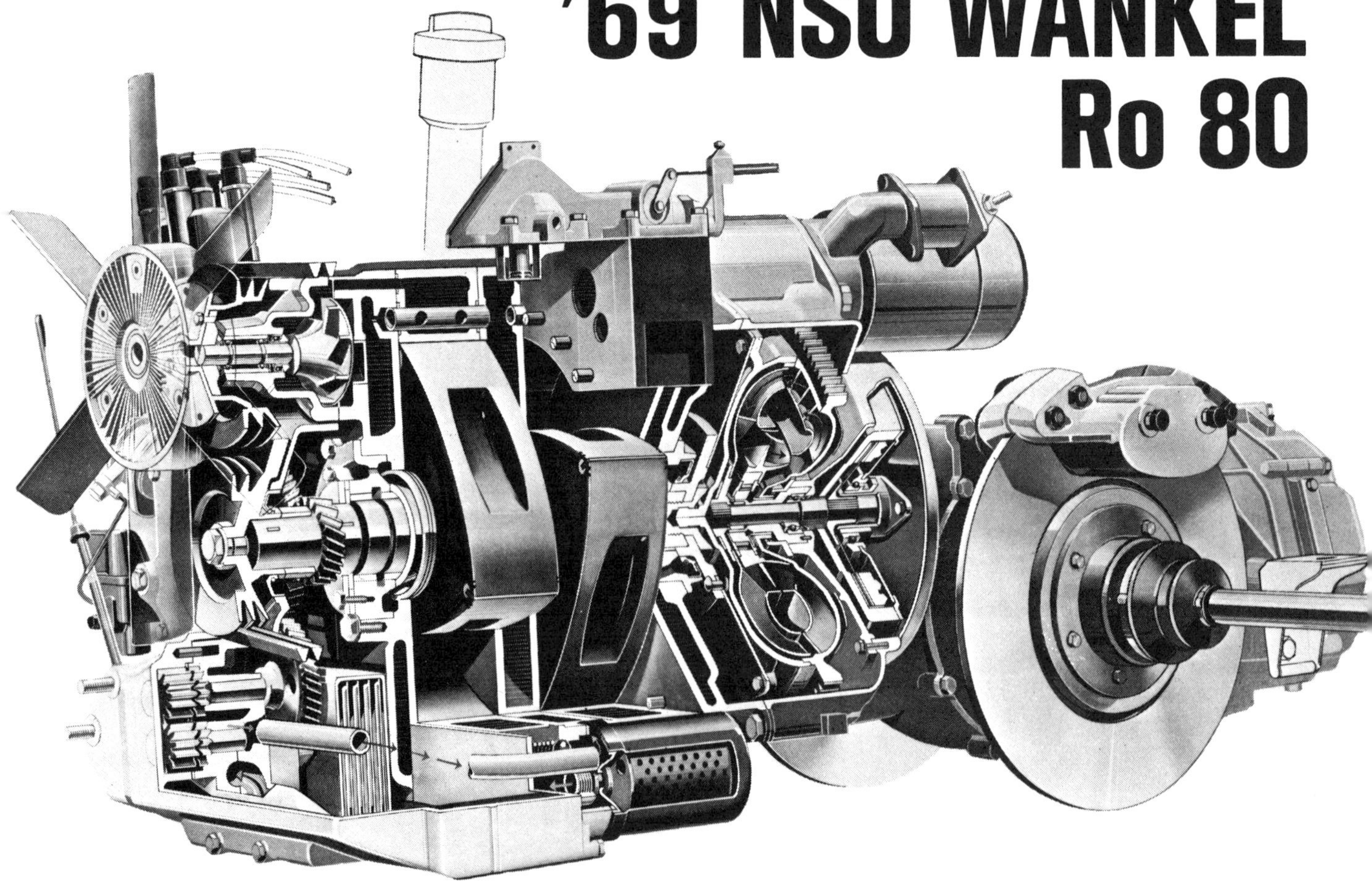

The Ro 80 has a savage, brutal appearance which is enhanced even more by the optional aluminum alloy wheels. Its lines are timeless and virtually guarantee that it will become a modern classic.

The Ro 80's wedge shape is most evident when viewed from the rear. The car is larger than photographs lead one to expect.

The Car of the future; is it here now?

Build a better mouse trap and the world will beat a path to your door," states the adage, and in the case of NSU's Ro 80 it holds true only with reservations. While auto buyers in Germany have swamped the relatively small factory with Ro 80 orders, the rest of the automotive industry has very reluctantly accepted the fact of the rotary-piston Wankel engine's existence, with the exception, perhaps, of some of the more than fifteen licensees of NSU's Wankel patents. As more progress began to be made, though, more licensees came into the fold, including Daimler-Benz, Alfa Romeo, and Rolls-Royce .

With the introduction of NSU's single-rotor-Wankel-engined Spider in 1963 and its subsequent production a year later, original skepticism turned into credibility, though still of a very limited nature as the NSU Spider was little more than a play-

thing for knowledgeable auto fans — and a research vehicle, in both senses of the term, for NSU's engineering department.

By the time of the Ro 80's introduction during the summer of '67 all of the operational and production problems had been completely solved and the finished product confronting the international automotive press was, in effect, the 'better mouse trap';

The pistons have been eliminated along with their connecting rods, the entire valve train and timing gear. Overall engine size with respect to the power developed is compact, and the absence of reciprocating motion makes for almost turbine-like smoothness in the higher speed

Testing a car with a rotary-piston engine is an entirely new experience

gives exactly 60 mph in the second range, which, incidentally, is the term NSU prefers in place of 'gear,' and 90 in third range, which is also the top gear of the three-speed transmission.

Top speeds in the indirect ratios at the 6500 rpm limit are 45 mph in first and 75.7 mph in second, whereas going one-third into the red and touching 7000 revs yield 49 and 81.3 mph respectively. A steady 5000 rpm

At a steady 100-mph cruising speed the Wankel unit turns over at 5600 revs, fully 900 rpm below the red line. Acceleration has fallen off at this point, which may be considered as a normal cruising speed for the car on the open highway. It takes 37.5 seconds to attain the 'ton.'

At 100 mph, with the windows closed, the loudest sound is the

The rear doors do not open through a wide enough angle, complicating entry and exit. The front seat-backs recline fully. There is a wide central armrest at the rear.

The wedge-shaped body is the result of lengthy wind-tunnel experiments and is one of the factors responsible for excellent aerodynamics and high-speed handling. In an 80-mph corner all four wheels retain their adhesion. Lean is hardy noticeable from the inside of the Ro 80.

rumbling of the tires! The wind noise is very subdued and the engine hums at a low tone. During acceleration it sounds for all the world like a turbo-jet, and this sound must be common, in all probability, to all purely rotating powerplants. At the 'ton' all occupants can converse in low tones, which is a credit not only to the exquisitely silent engine, but to the car's excellent aerodynamics as well.

The standard zero-to-sixty time, holding the car on the brake and revving the engine to 2000, came to 11.8 seconds. Accelerating normally, as one would do in everyday driving from an 800 rpm idle with first engaged, amounted to 12 seconds flat.

Naturally, the car is at its best when shifting normally through all three ranges, but when making use of the lazy method and starting from rest in the upper two ratios, it must be remembered to tromp smartly on the throttle and not be afraid of a rapid rev build-up, as the engine requires revs. It comes in very smoothly at the 2000-rpm figure and accleration in second and third, if anything but brisk, is still adequate.

The engine normally idles at 1200 rpm in neutral, when warm. It starts instantly from cold on the manual choke, which is pushed in one notch as soon as the engine is running. Despite the relatively rapid idle it is a bit rough in neutral and very reminiscent of a two-stroke unit. Immediately upon engaging a gear the revs drop to 800, but, surprisingly, the engine does not become any rougher. The sound dampening is very good for there's very little noise on the inside, but quite a bit when standing next to the hood, and the burble emanating from the twin tail pipes sounds very much like that of a highly tuned sports engine.

As soon as the revs build up slightly and the car gets under way every hint of roughness disappears and the engine becomes incredibly smooth. The progressively operating power steering requires very little effort yet imparts a very natural road-feel to the driver, being relatively direct with its 3 ¾ turns from lock to lock. The brakes, also servo assisted, are not feather-light, which is a blessing on a fast car. They are very effective, a panic stop from 60 mph is accomplished within 164 feet straight and true.

Handling is faultless. Especially impressive was the bird-dog line held at 100 mph in extremely gusty conditions with hands off the wheel. This is due to a combination of front-wheel drive, excellent balance and good aerodynamics. The Ro 80 is equally at home in corners. The tendency of the preproduction prototypes for

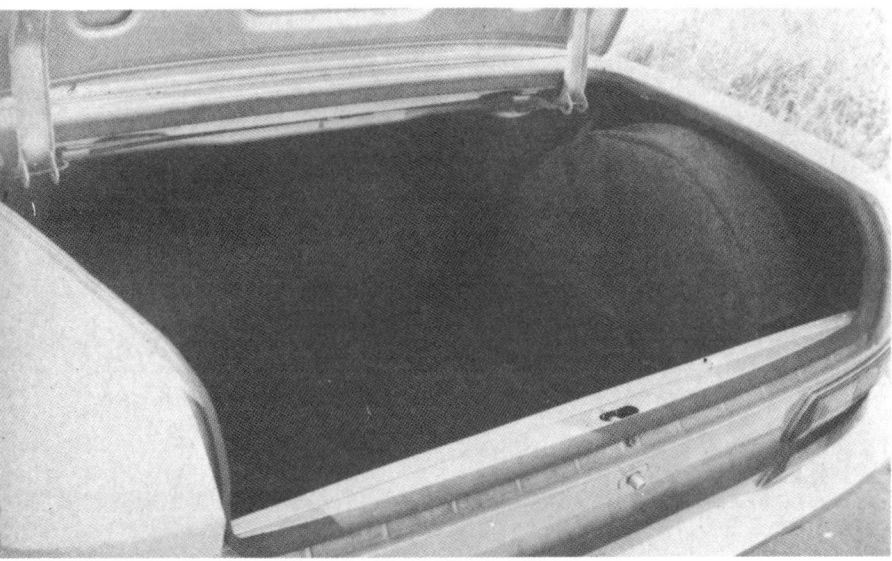

Positive, straight-line braking is a simple matter from all speeds. A rear-brake limiting valve, dependent upon load, is an aid in providing maximum retardation values.

The fully carpeted trunk is deep due to the car's front-wheel-drive conception. The spare has a separate cover. Tool kit is provided.

oversteering in fast, sharp corners has all but disappeared and the Ro 80 may be considered as being a neutral handler. There is absolutely no tendency to plow, as most front-wheel-drive cars do.

If one does, on occasion, overestimate a corner, it is only necessary to take the foot off the gas and steer through. The Ro 80 is equipped with Michelin XAs asymmetrical radial ply tires with inner tubes. Naturally, these contribute a good part of the handling ability.

All-around visibility is excellent and all windows are green tinted for protection against glare. Both the accelerator and the large brake pedal are suspended and the shift lever is floor mounted. It has a standard three-

speed and reverse gate and an extra transmission parking detent to the left and upwards. The parking brake is placed between the seats and behind the shift lever.

Seating is very comfortable and there are upholstery choices of either cloth, vinyl or natural leather. The flat floor is carpeted throughout, as is the spacious trunk which has the spare vertically mounted at its right and under a separate cover. There is a tool kit and chassis jack beside the spare. Rear-seat backs may be snapped out of position and placed flat onto the bench. thereby extending the trunk space for the stowage of long and bulky items such as skis or fishing rods.

Two Solex 18/32 HHD side-draft

carburetors are employed, again being identical with the Spider engine's unit. Regular gasoline of 88 octane rating is used and this is absolutely adequate. Compression ratio is 9:1 power output comes to 115 DIN bhp/130 SAE bhp at 5500 rpm and the maximum torque of 117.1 lb.-ft. is developed at the relatively low speed of 4500 rpm.

Ate-Dunlop disc brakes are employed all 'round, the front pair being mounted inboard for minimal unsprung weight and maximum cooling. These are vacuum-servo assisted and a dual circuit system is utilized. The primary circuit supplies all four brakes while the secondary one acts on the front discs only, since 70% of the Ro 80's braking effort is accomplished at the front end. The parking brake actuates two auxiliary drums, one at either rear wheel.

The front suspension consists of McPherson struts and lower wishbones, plus a stabilizer bar. At the rear a horizontal H tube with its sides angled forwards at 10° has two lower,

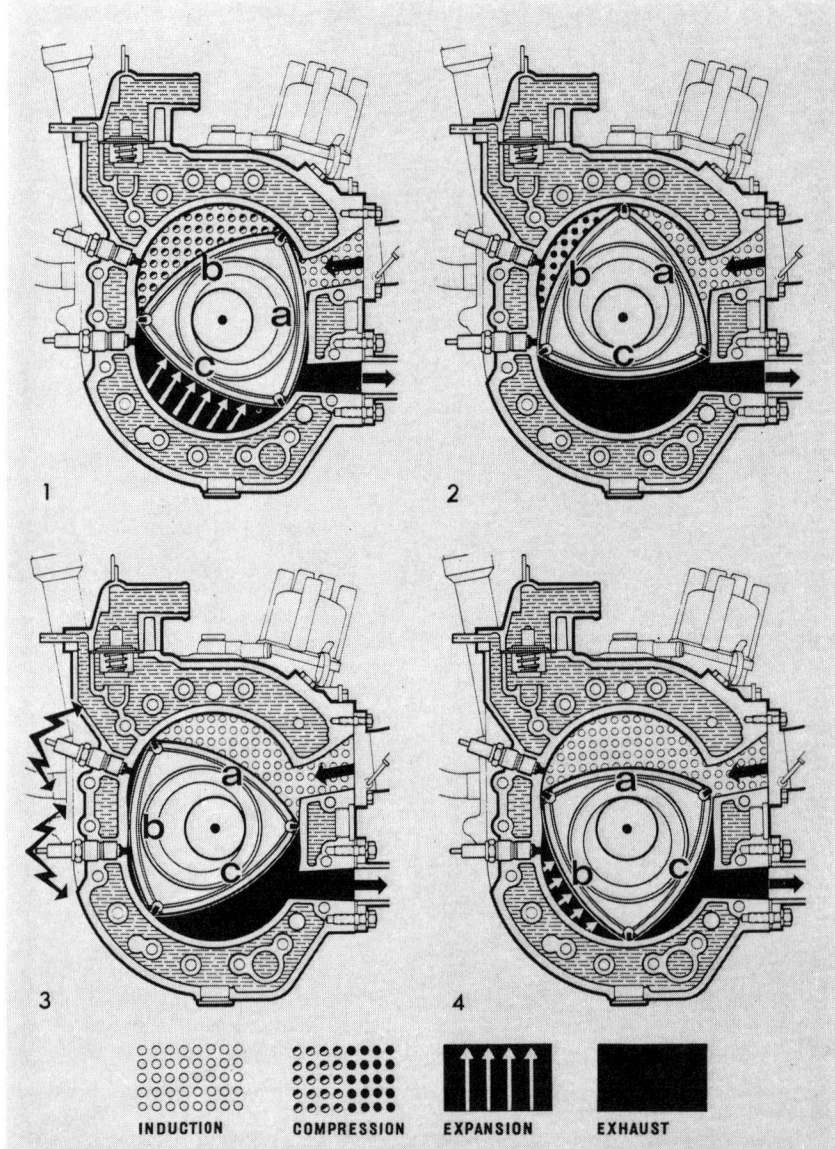

1

2

3

4

INDUCTION	COMPRESSION	EXPANSION	EXHAUST

A fuel-filler-cap lock is standard and there is a separate key for it. Another key fits the trunk and glove compartment, while the third is for ignition and door locks.

The optional alloy wheels may be standard equipment for Ro 80s delivered to the U.S.

trailing A-arms attached to it, these being, conversely, angled outward through 10°. As at the front, coil springs with coaxially mounted shock absorbers are used, the springs being mounted relatively high in the rear body section and attached to the lower A-arms via long struts. The shocks are double-acting hydraulics all around.

Steering is accomplished via a ZF rack-and-pinion unit with progressive, hydraulic power assist. The steering-wheel shaft is very short, terminating just ahead of the firewall. Radial ply tires of 175 SR-14 dimensions are specified as standard equipment and, indeed, the chassis design has been laid out with radial plys in mind.

The body/chassis is of unitized

construction with a platform frame as the basis. However, the entire front section is bolted on for ease of panel replacements. There are three separate sections: two side sections and a central piece incorporating the radiator grill. The hood is front hinged and provides easy access to the engine compartment, but it has a tendency to vibrate at speed on uneven surfaces.

The body form has been aerodynamically engineered in wind-tunnel experiments and the very small mass of the twin-rotor Wankel engine makes the ultra-low hood possible while still allowing the engine to be placed ahead of the front wheel centers. This provides for a weight distribution of 63/37 empty, front and rear, and 51%/49% fully loaded —

ideal for a front-wheel-drive conception.

The very large windshield sweeps backward at an angle of 54° and, combined with the low hood-line, provides really excellent visibility. The body lines sweep upward at the rear to terminate in a trunk line higher than the hood, while the sill panels under the doors are slightly rounded. Large, rectangular headlamps and standard-equipment fog lights below blend well with the horizontal grille and wrap-around front bumper, and the horizontal motif is repeated at the rear, with the blinker, tail light and back-up lamp combined in a strip on either side, above the rear bumper which is also of the wrap-around variety.

In addition to this, the Ro 80's body has a savage, brutal beauty — there is certainly nothing subtle about it — yet in contradiction to

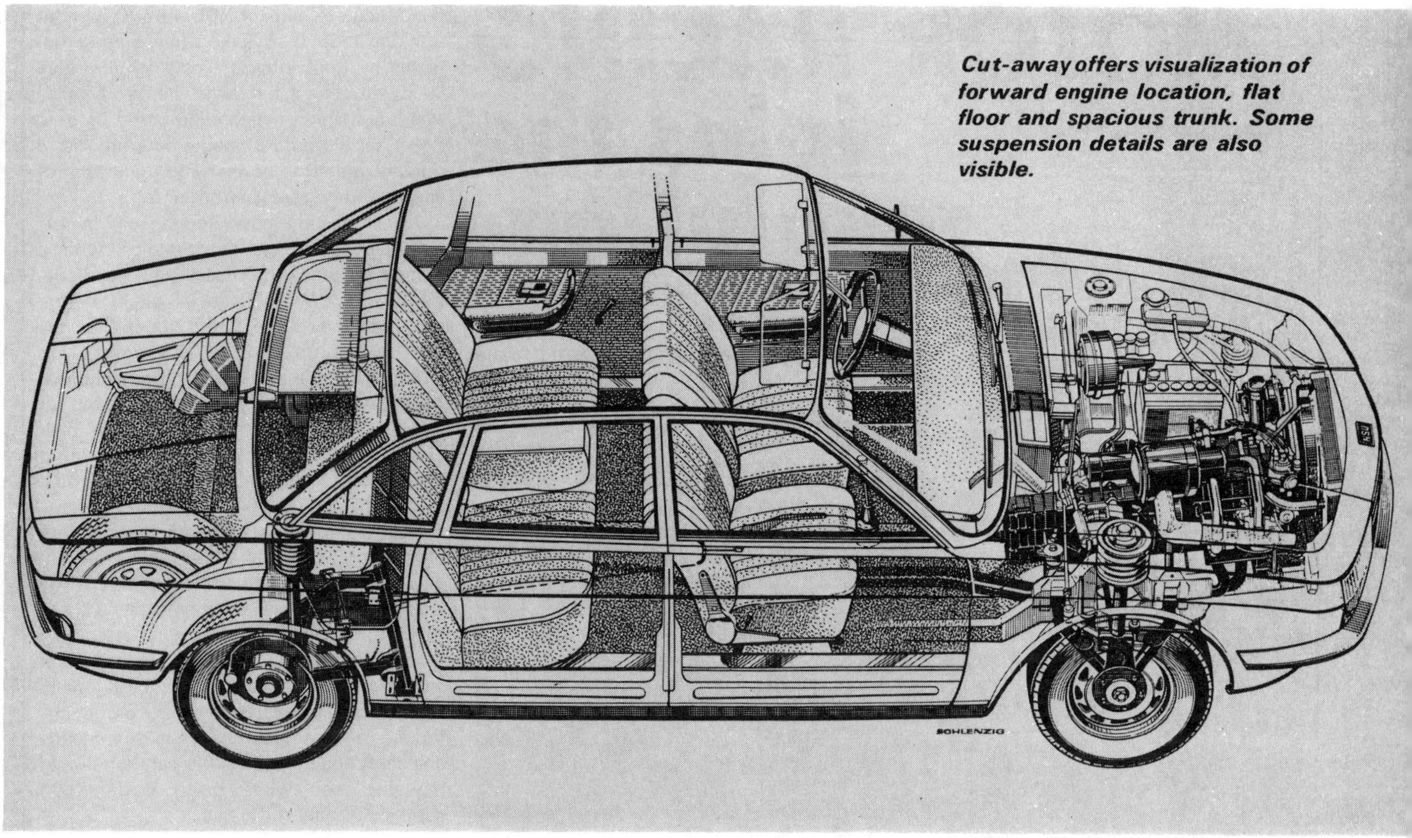

Cut-away offers visualization of forward engine location, flat floor and spacious trunk. Some suspension details are also visible.

this, the car appears to be much smaller than it actually is! It may be safe to say the Ro 80 will become a modern classic, for its body lines alone would suffice for this distinction. With the very advanced mechanical conception thrown into the bargain, it seems almost a certainty, for the Ro 80 has the stuff from which automotive legends are made. ♠

The twin-rotor Wankel engine is almost buried underneath the accessories. The oil filler cap is at the lower left while the filler cap of the radiator-header tank is at the lower right and above it are the twin plastic containers for the dual-circuit system's brake fluid. Behind them is the circular vacuum reservoir.

Ro 80

Data in Brief

DIMENSIONS

Wheelbase (in.)	112.6
Length (in.)	188.1
Height (in.)	55.5
Turning radius (ft.)	19.3

WEIGHT, TIRES, BRAKES

Weight (lbs.)	2664
Distribution	
Front	63%
Rear	37%
Tires (radial)	175 SR × 14
Brakes (front and rear)	disc

ENGINE

Displacement (cu. in.)	60.69
Displacement (cc.)	995.0
Maximum horsepower at rpm	130/5500
Maximum torque at rpm	117.1 lb. ft./4500
Fuel required	regular

SUSPENSION

Front	McPherson strut/coil
Rear	coil

ACCELERATION

0-30 mph (seconds)	4.4
0-40	6.4
0-50	9.4
0-60	11.8
0-70	16.2
0-80	21.4
0-90	26.9
0-100	37.5
Standing start ¼ mile (sec.)	19.0
Speed at end of ¼ mile (mph)	77.6
Top speed (mph)	111.9

BRAKING

From 60 mph (ft.)	164

MOTOR RACING joins the revolution-

and finds that the Wankel engine is only one 'different' feature of the impressive NSU Ro80.

Left: *Instruments are sensibly shaped and easy to read, though the control knobs and warning lights take a little learning.*
Below: *Heart of the matter. The Wankel rotary engine really comes into its own at high revs, when it is as smooth as a turbine.*

It's difficult to think of NSU's Ro80 without thinking about the Wankel rotary engine that drives its front wheels. That's until you've lived with it for a few days. Then, you realise that it is such an outstanding car in its own right that it would probably be a hit with a donkey under the bonnet and a juicy carrot suspended two feet in front of it.

It's interesting how German car manufacturers seem able to come up with a winner just when they desperately need one. Remember BMW's financial plight before they introduced the 1500, which became the 1600, 1800, and 2000? Today they're laughing all the way to the Deutschbank. And now, NSU, who have been fighting for survival for a long time, stand their best chance to date through the all-round excellence of their revolutionary (if you'll excuse the pun) Ro80.

Not that it will make them a fortune, with production pegged to a maximum of 80 per day (the current rate is 50 per day). The Ro80's very high development costs will see to that. But the pay-off could well come when NSU introduce their intermediate car later this year, which will embody many Ro80 features, but be driven by a conventional four-cylinder 1.7 litre overhead-camshaft engine. This is the car that should pay the rent, while the prestige Ro80 supplied the jam and cream.

What makes it (the Ro80) such a good car? It is no single feature, but a combination of many, some fundamental, others quite minor, but no less pleasing for all that.

Specification

Body-chassis: All-steel, integral construction.
Engine: Wankel rotary with twin co-axial rotors. Displacement 497.5 cc twice per revolution (equivalent to 1,990 cc reciprocating-piston engine). Compression ratio 9 to 1. Maximum power 128.5 bhp (SAE) at 5,500 rpm. Maximum torque 117.2 lb-ft at 4,500 rpm. Twin-choke Solex 18/32 HHD carburettors fed by mechanical fuel pump.
Transmission: Vacuum-servo-operated single-dry-plate clutch, torque converter and three-speed all-synchromesh gearbox with floor shift. Ratios: 1st 2.056 to 1; 2nd 1.208 to 1; 3rd 0.788 to 1; reverse 2.105 to 1. Final drive by hypoid bevel, 4.857 to 1.
Suspension: Front, independent with MacPherson struts, wishbones, telescopic dampers and anti-roll bar. Rear, independent with coil springs, trailing arms and telescopic dampers.
Steering: Rack and pinion, servo-assisted, 3.7 turns lock to lock. Turning circle 38¾ feet.
Brakes: Front, 11.2 inch discs. Rear, 10.7 inch discs. Additional drum-type parking brake on rear wheels.
Wheels and tyres: 14 x 5J steel wheels with Michelin XAS 175SR14 radial-ply tyres.
Weights and measures: Approx kerb weight 24 cwt; length 188 inches; width 69 inches; height 55.5 inches; wheelbase 112.5 inches; ground clearance 5.5 inches; front track 58.5 inches; rear track 56.5 inches; fuel tank capacity 18 gallons.

Performance

Acceleration:

0-30 mph	5.2 sec
0-40 mph	7.0 sec
0-50 mph	10.0 sec
0-60 mph	14.0 sec
0-70 mph	18.6 sec
0-80 mph	24.8 sec
0-90 mph	34.4 sec

Speeds in the gears:

1st	47 mph
2nd	80 mph
3rd	110 mph

Overall fuel consumption on test: 21.6 mpg.

NSU Ro80.

Though the Wankel engine is a big talking point, its impact on the driver is considerably less than the means through which it transmits its power. NSU have taken the best features of automatic and manually operated transmission, and combined them in a system which they describe, accurately, as selective automatic.

The major components are a three-speed all-synchromesh gearbox with floor shift, a torque converter, and a single-dry-plate clutch, operated by vacuum servo which in turn is energised by a microswitch in the gear knob. The result: a choice of three gear ranges, any one of which can be used at any time, including pulling away from rest, and which offer maxima of 47, 80 and 110 mph.

Up and down shifts can be made simply by moving the lever from one position to another, the clutch being automatically disengaged as the gear knob is touched, and re-engaged the moment the knob is released. Consequently, there is no clutch pedal, which leaves the brake pedal free for left or right foot operation.

The only things you have to remember are not to rest your hand on the gear knob before or after you shift gears (otherwise, you lose your drive), and to either brake slightly or increase engine revs in order to get a completely smooth down shift (without one of these precautions, a quick shift from third to second, or second to first, is liable to provoke a bit of a jerk in the transmission).

The combination of two-pedal control (hence left-foot braking) and immediate manual control of the gearbox makes the Ro80 an exhilarating car to drive rally-style, and there can be few if any cars of its size which feel so utterly safe when being driven hard over twisty roads, particularly when the going gets rough.

Full engine braking is available, so the usual technique when in a hurry is to use one of the two lower gear ranges, allowing the engine to make full use of its high-revving capabilities. It is at the top end of the rev range that the Wankel engine really comes into its own, because if anything it seems quieter and smoother at the red line of 6,500 rpm (which incidentally can be exceeded by a considerable margin) that it does, at say, 5,000 rpm. At worst the rotary has the smoothness of a good six-cylinder, but at best it feels as vibrationless as a turbine.

In developing a state of tune for the Ro80, NSU engineers have gone for quite a high maximum bmep, or power, at the expense of low-speed torque, as a result of which the car suffers a little in initial acceleration from rest. But bearing in mind that it takes over five seconds to reach 30 mph, the remaining acceleration times shown in our data panel speak well of the car's accelerative ability once on the move. NSU's research and development department are currently working on an improved

induction layout for the Wankel engine which will not only help to raise the torque curve between the torque converter's stall speed of around 2,500 rpm, and the current speed of maximum torque, namely 4,500 rpm, and at the same time boosting power throughout the rev range.

Cold starts were instantaneous throughout the test; warm-up if anything was quicker than with a conventional engine, and the choke could be dispensed with almost straight away. Despite the dual exhaust system, the engine beat smooths out at around the tick-over speed of just over 1,000 rpm, and of course with the minimum of moving parts there is also the minimum of mechanical noise.

It was this unusually low level of engine noise which caused the transmission hum on the test car to become a major annoyance, particularly on a neutral or trailing throttle. We were told that this was due to the use of too generous machining tolerances in the construction and matching of gears, and that

The Ro80 in its right-hand-drive form, which incorporated several modifications. The previous single-headlight fairings have been replaced by twin headlights and the fog lamps, previously white, are now amber. The screen is now tinted blue and the sun visors are recessed into the roof lining which is now fireproofed and in a new, more luxurious material. The kick plates are wider and wrap round the whole of the door sill.

this had since been overcome (our test car was many months and 17,000 miles old). We subsequently had the chance to drive two 1969 models (identifiable by their dual headlights) and both of these had almost silent transmissions.

If there is a better system of servo-assisted rack and pinion steering on a current production car we have yet to sample it. Were it not for the fact that a front-wheel-drive car of some 3,000 pounds laden, and carrying about 60 per cent of the weight on the front wheels, could not possibly have such light steering without power assistance, we would not have believed that a servo unit had been fitted. It retains all the feel and accuracy of a good, well-damped rack and pinion, but of course requires only a fraction of the effort when in a tight spot. Furthermore, the steering effort required varies in a subtle way as the front wheels go about their work, so that the driver can judge very accurately the degree of understeer as he goes through a corner.

During normal motoring the understeer

remains quite modest, but as the car is pushed towards its limit of adhesion (which is difficult to find on anything but a very slippery road) it builds up progressively in conjunction with considerably more body lean than is evident from inside the car. A momentary lift-off, of course, will immediately tighten the line, and the adhesion with Michelin XAS tyres is so good that even backing off when close to the limit produces nothing more violent than a grudging sideways shuffle by the rear tyres before they grip again.

The Ro80 is quite a softly sprung car, yet the suspension movement is well damped to eliminate any nauseating float or pitch. Pot holes and other rough stuff are heard more than felt, and straight-line stability remains impeccable over quite atrocious surfaces. In fact, through its combination of steering, handling, ride comfort and braking performance (we were unable to induce fade) this must rank as one of the all-time greats in this era of safety consciousness.

In attending to the needs of passengers, NSU have given as much thought to those who travel in the rear as to the driver and the person alongside him. People who rode in the back of the Ro80 rated the sumptuous, high-backed, and sensible angled seat as the best they had ever sat in. The individual front seats are equally impressive, the driver being given a relatively high position behind the wheel, which, in conjunction with unusually deep front and rear screens and generous side windows, helps to accentuate the excellent all-round visibility. The only slight detraction is the tendency for the rear screen to mist up in humid weather, despite the elaborate ventilation system—a problem which NSU have overcome by fitting a double demisting element in the screen as standard equipment.

The car's interior is tastefully trimmed in matt black, all prominent surfaces being well padded, and the carpets backed by thick felt. The circular instruments are lined up ahead of the driver, and surrounded by a bewildering number of controls and warning lights of various colours which have to be learnt at length. Fortunately the lights are multi-coloured—yellow for fog lamps, green for indicators, blue for headlamp main beam, orange for fuel reserve, red for hand brake and dual-circuit warning, another green for choke, another yellow for ignition, another red for battery charge, and a third yellow for the rear screen demister. Then there are all the usual control knobs and levers to be found in any fully equipped car, plus no fewer than eight ways of regulating the temperature, distribution, direction or volume of the heating and ventilation system, which on 'all systems go' puts out almost enough heat to cook the Sunday joint. When you buy an Ro80 you have to sign a pretty hefty cheque, but at least you're buying the lot!

The NSU Ro80 is, and is always likely to be, an expensive car. But for the moment it is unique (and not just because of its engine). So as you write out that cheque, take comfort from the thought that you're finally putting one across the Joneses!

DESCRIPTION—NSU Ro80

Technically, one of the most interesting of modern cars, the Ro80 bristles with unusual features. It was introduced in the autumn of 1967 but has undergone little change since.

It is powered by NSU's twin-rotor Wankel engine. Each of the two stages—cylinders is not really appropriate in this case—has a swept volume of 497.5 c.c. Combustion takes place once per revolution in each, making it equivalent to a reciprocating-piston engine of 1,990 c.c. displacement.

Each stage breathes through its own compound twin-choke Solex carburettor. Ignition is by two coils, each with its own contact breaker. Two special Beru sparking plugs are used for each combustion chamber.

Transmission is semi-automatic. Power is transmitted through a torque convertor and a servo-operated dry plate clutch to an all-indirect 3-speed gearbox. All forward gears have baulk-ring synchromesh and the gearbox features a transmission lock. Final reduction is by hypoid bevel and front wheel drive is employed. Tyres are Michelin XAS 175–SR 14 on 5in. wide rims and the overall gearing in top gear is equivalent to 18.6 mph per 1,000 rpm, with the torque convertor locked.

Front suspension is of the MacPherson strut type, featuring coil springs and an anti-roll bar. Trailing arms are used at the rear, in conjunction with telescopic spring /damper units. Servo assistance is provided for the rack and pinion steering gear.

Brakes are disc on all four corners, those at the front being situated at the inboard end of the driving shafts. Disc diameters are 11.2 and 10.7in., front and rear respectively. Incorporated in the rear discs are 6.6in. dia. drum parking brakes. Vacuum servo assistance is provided and two separate hydraulic circuits are used. One actuates one pair of front caliper pistons only whilst the other actuates a second pair of front caliper pistons and the rear caliper pistons.

DESCRIPTION—CITROEN ID20

DS and ID Citroens continue with only minor changes the body style and mechanical layout which were introduced so far ahead of their time 13 years ago; but the later 4-cyl. engine is much more responsive and free-revving. Capacity is 1,985 c.c. from almost square bore/stroke dimension of 86-85.5mm, and compression is 8.75 to 1 for the DS and ID20 models. The ID19 is similar but with lower compression, and the DS21 has larger bores, to give 2,175 c.c. The engine drives the front wheels, and there are power-assisted inboard disc brakes at the front, drums at rear, and independent front-rear hydraulic circuits. Steering is by rack and pinion with power assistance (optional on ID19), and common to all big Citroens is all-independent suspension by pressurized hydropneumatic spheres, with automatic height control. Another option is, surprisingly, manually operated gear change; standard transmission is with automatic clutch and hydraulic gear change. Manual change was fitted to the test car.

Michelin XAS tyres are standard on all models size 180–380mm.

2 CAR TEST

CITROEN ID20
NSU Ro80

Our electric fifth-wheel speedometer is used for all performance testing. It is independent of the car's speedometer and is checked for accuracy against distance with a stop watch each time it is used.

A unique feature of the Citroen is swivelling headlamps connected to the steering. They are lit only on main beam

COMPARISON

On the surface it would seem strange to compare cars with a price difference as large as £545, but we chose these two because of their similarity in layout and size, and because they have the same swept volume of engine (1,985 c.c. for the Citroen, 1,990 c.c. for the NSU). Price for price, the more logical competitor for the NSU is the Citroen DS21 Pallas (£2,121 against the NSU's £2,279) and this would be appreciably faster than the ID20 because it has an extra 15 bhp.

In addition, the NSU was a very early demonstrator with over 30,000 miles to its credit. We are running it for a few months to gain experience of the rotary power unit.

During the period of this double test we also tried the latest right-hand-drive demonstrator which was a much nicer car in almost every respect.

Performance—NSU Ro80

Without exceeding the recommended rev limit of 6,500 rpm, the Ro80 accelerates from rest to 60 mph in 14.0 sec. From 0-80 mph takes 25.5 sec. These figures compare well with those returned by our original road test Ro80 early last year (13.9 and 24.8 sec respectively).

Thanks to the torque convertor, acceleration at low road speeds in a high gear is remarkably good. From rest to 20 mph, using top gear, takes only 5.9 sec; 40 mph comes up in another 8.0 sec—identical with the original test car. Although the acceleration drops off progressively as the speed increases, the 60-80 mph time is still a commendable 15.2 sec—0.8 sec better than the original car.

Maximum speed is also well up to scratch, a mean of 106 mph and a best one-way of 108 mph being recorded. The speedometer, incidentally, is wildly optimistic, the latter figure representing a reading of 190 kph, equivalent to 118 mph.

In our report on the original Ro80 we criticized its overall fuel consumption figure of 18.2 mpg. During the course of this latest test, the very disappointing overall figure of 16.4 mpg has been returned. Oil consumption, at around 250 miles per pint, also adds significantly to running expenses. In its defence, however, it must be admitted that it was habitually driven hard and that the lower price of 92-octane petrol helps to keep down costs.

Performance—Citroen ID20

Despite having a claimed power output of only 91 bhp, compared with the DS21 Pallas' 106 bhp, the ID20 performed surprisingly well. From rest, 60 mph comes up in 14.2 sec and 80 mph in 28.4 sec. Equivalent figures for the Pallas tested at the end of 1965 (with 6 bhp less than the latest version, please note) are 14.4 and 28.2 sec, but its 0-90 mph time of 42.0 secs pips the ID20 by 1.7 sec.

Despite lower gearing, the ID20's in-the-gears acceleration is inferior to that of the DS21. In top, 20-40 mph takes 14.2 sec (Pallas—12.6 sec); 40-60 and 60-80 mph take 16.0 and 18.2 sec respectively (Pallas—13.5 and 17.7 sec).

A mean maximum speed of 100 mph was recorded, with a best one-way figure of 105 mph. The DS21 topped this comfortably, with 107 and 108 mph respectively. The ID20's speedometer error is no worse than average,

104 mph being indicated at a true 100 mph.

One of the Citroen's biggest attributes is its ability to travel fast without consuming an excessive quantity of petrol. The overall figure returned during the test was 23.8 mpg—a very good performance for such a spacious car, driven hard. Oil consumption too, is modest (around 1,000 miles per pint).

Performance Differences

In terms of sheer performance, there is less to choose between the two than one expects. True, the Ro80 is some 6 mph faster, but the ID20 actually has a slight edge up to 60 mph through the gears. Thereafter, the NSU has the advantage, but not until around 80 mph does it become at all significant. Their performances over a standing ¼-mile illustrate this. The Ro80 takes 19.7 seconds, reaching 72 mph in the process, the ID20 is marginally quicker (19.6 seconds), reaching 70 mph.

Above: Handbrake and restart check on the MIRA test hill.
Below: Long-wave pitching test, one place where the Citroen has the edge on everything

Yet their characters differ enormously. Although both have excellent high-speed cruising qualities, one is very aware of the Citroen's big-four thumping away (comparatively speaking) just ahead of the bulkhead. The Ro80's engine, on the other hand, is uncannily silent and smooth. The fact that it is ahead of the transmission may help, but there is no doubt that the Wankel's lack of reciprocating parts is largely responsible.

It is unrealistic to compare in-the-gears acceleration times for the two, as the Ro80's torque convertor, with its 2.2-to-1 multiplication capacity, gives it an enormous advantage. Strangely enough, it still feels sluggish—more so than the Citroen. This could be due to the monstrous hum of the engine, together with complete absence of any form of surging.

The Ro80's dry plate clutch is vacuum operated, the servo being triggered by a micro-switch built into the gear lever knob. On the well-used test car, it is far too easy to beat the clutch and thus cause clashing of the dog-teeth. Weak synchromesh may also be a factor. A later car, tried shortly afterwards, did not suffer from this fault. In fact, the quality of the gearchange was exceptionally good.

There is a tendency to use the Ro80's gearbox as one would in an ordinary car. This is quite unnecessary and does little to aid performance. It is far better to follow NSU's advice —treat each gear as a performance range. First need only be used for restarting on steep gradients. The Ro80, incidentally, excels at this, treating the 1-in-3 gradient at MIRA with contempt. Intermediate is the gear to use normally in urban areas. Top is obviously an open-road gear.

The Citroen uses a perfectly straightforward all-synchromesh, column change 4-speed gearbox. The quality of the change is very good and the ratios suit the car well. It is also commendably silent in operation.

Ride and Handling—NSU Ro80

On public roads, one rarely even approaches the handling limitations of the Ro80. Its behaviour is virtually neutral and with adhesion little short of phenomenal. The light, precise power-assisted steering is completely devoid of ''fight'', yet has ample feel.

Its track handling, although still above average, is less impressive. Exuberant cornering results in a great deal of understeer—enough to cause complete front-end breakaway on a good, dry surface. Lifting off, even under these extreme conditions, produces no drama. The car remains under complete control and excess speed soon scrubs off.

The ride, especially at higher speeds, is well above average and the road noise, both thump and tyre roar, well subdued. MIRA's washboard produces most unpleasant vertical scuttle shake, even at speeds far removed from the critical one. The suspension copes fairly well with the *pavè* and long-wave surfaces.

Seating is good—definitely above average —but front seat lateral support is not really adequate for spirited driving.

Ride and Handling—Citroen ID20

The ID20's handling characteristics are broadly similar to those of the Ro80. It is, however, rather less sporting in character, the accent being primarily on comfort. Front wheel drive and a forward weight distribution bias result in a stable, understeering character. Under normal conditions it understeers rather more than the Ro80. Its power-assisted steering lacks the sensitivity and sporting feel of the Ro80's, but one gets used to this.

Although it understeers strongly when pushed hard, the front end never quite breaks away (dry surface). There is considerable body roll but this causes no discomfort. Lifting off on a fast corner results in a gentle decrease in the turning radius—a useful safety feature. Its only

Above: Extreme cornering behaviour show up a lot about the car's inherent characteristics and often explains the way it feels when travelling normally

Above: One of the MIRA special surfaces is this section of authentic Belgian pavè. Front-drive cars are always much more stable on it than rear-drive cars

Above: With all its accessories, the Wankel engine takes up almost as much space as a piston unit. Dual ignition is provided for each chamber. Right: Interior of the Ro80

handling oddity is a tendency to wallow if a sizeable bump is encountered when cornering hard.

The Citroen's unique hydro-pneumatic suspension system provides quite an exceptional ride over almost all types of surface. Some roads—notably those of a nobbly nature—do not show it to good advantage but a drive along MIRA's test surfaces soon makes it abundantly clear that there is little, if anything, to compare with it. The way it copes with the long-wave pitching surface is quite uncanny. It also copes very well with the *pavé* but is less happy on the washboard. The excellent seats further augment the comfort provided by the suspension.

It isn't perfect—the hydraulic pump is quite noisy in operation and the car suffers from quite marked temporary changes of attitude when accelerating or braking. Comfort is unimpaired but the rather poor rear view mirror is even more difficult to use.

Brakes

Disc brakes are fitted all round on the NSU so it is understandably a little better on braking than the Citroen, which has discs at the front only, drums at rear. Good, progressive action is appreciated with the NSU, and pedal loads are relatively light. On the Citroen a round "mushroom" pad is fitted having virtually no travel and being set very much below the level of the accelerator. The result is that it is rather difficult to adjust braking progressively, and one tends to stop rather snatchily, especially when the car is still unfamiliar. But on both cars the brakes are good, and there was no fade during repeated hard braking on the circuit.

Handbrakes are good—impossible to reach under the facia on the Citroen with safety belts fastened—but both cars could be parked confidently on 1 in 3.

Noise—NSU

Cruising speed is very high with the NSU because the engine remains wonderfully smooth and quiet right up to maximum speed. At 80 or 90 mph it is an outstanding motorway car, no more than a subdued hum being audible from the engine, and the wind noise level is extremely low. On the test car the door seal may have deteriorated slightly, as there was some noise from the region of the pillar on the driver's (left) side; it was obtrusive to the driver, yet scarcely noticed from the passenger seat.

In the gears there is rather more fuss from

the engine, mainly exhaust and induction noise, rising and falling in traffic as engine speed goes up and down in response to throttle changes. If it had positive drive instead of a torque convertor, and engine speed geared directly to car speed rather than throttle opening, there might be less impression of fussiness at low speeds.

Noise—Citroen

In its original form the Citroen used to be very high-geared, and have that wonderful "seven league boots" feeling, striding along at 90 mph without any impression of effort. In the search for more performance it has become much more fussy, and the engine noise level all the time is disappointing; although it never reaches the stage of thrashing or sounding over-revved, the engine always sounds busy, and at 80 mph in top it feels ready for a higher gear. There are also tiresome chuntering noises intermittently when the pump cuts in to keep up the hydraulic pressure.

With such a streamlined shape, wind noise is also disappointing, and there is even a lot of wind rush through the fresh air vents if they are fractionally opened. Undoubtedly the NSU is the quieter car by a long way, and the Citroen is relatively fussy and busy.

Fittings and furniture
NSU

In the NSU Ro80 the interior layout is essentially functional, but trimmed tastefully and in extremely neat fashion. The facia is all covered in padded pvc., and seats are also in pvc. They are comfortable, and have reclining backrests, but do not match up to the luxury of the Citroen seats. They also lack the curvature necessary to give adequate lateral grip in really hard cornering.

The switches are laid out in an orderly fashion but a number of them have combined functions which have to be memorized, particularly as most of them have no identity at all. A red switch is fitted for the hazard warning lamps. Both cars, incidentally, have parking lamps. The NSU has a straightforward Neimann steering column lock. Recesses in the roof lining above the screen take the visors, on the back of each being a vanity mirror. The driver's vanity mirror even sports a safety cover.

Wipers, washers and loud horns are worked by a column stalk on the right, while a

SPECIFICATION

CITROEN ID20
PRICE £1,734

		Maximum spee
rpm	mph	
4,950	100	Top
5,500	74	3rd
5,750	50	2nd
6,200	30	1st
		Acceleration

Ind. mph	sec	mph
31	4.0	0-30
41	6.7	0-40
52	9.8	0-50
62	14.2	0-60
73	19.8	0-70
83	28.4	0-80
94	43.7	0-90
19.6 sec	70 mph	Standing ½-mile
Top (3.82)	3rd (5.71)	mph
—	9.0	10-30
14.2	7.9	20-40
14.6	8.3	30-50
16.0	8.7	40-60
17.0	10.1	50-70
18.2	—	60-80

	23.8	**Overall mpg**
	25.0	**Typical mpg**
1,000		**Oil—Miles per pi**

FRONT ENGINE, FRONT-WHEEL DRIVE
ENGINE
Cylinders	4, in line, 5 main bearings
Cooling system .	Water; pump, fan and thermostat
Bore	86mm (3.39in.)
Stroke. . . .	85.5mm (3.36in.)
Displacement .	1,985 c.c. (121 cu.in.)
Valve gear	Overhead; pushrods and rockers
Compression ratio .	8.75-to-1 : Min. octane rating
Carburettor. . . .	One downdraught twin choke We 28/36 DLEAZ
Max. Power . .	91 bhp (DIN) at 5,500 rpm
Max. torque . .	104 lb.ft. (DIN) at 3,500 rpm

TRANSMISSION
Gear ratios	Top 0.79, Third 1.18, Second 1. First 3.25, Reverse 3.15
Final drive	Spiral bevel, 4.86-to-1

SUSPENSION
Front	Independent, hydropneumatic with height control interconnec with rear, parallel semi-leading an anti-roll bar
Rear	Independent, hydropneumatic s with height control, single tra arms

STEERING
Type	Citroen power-assisted rack and pi

BRAKES
Make and type . .	Citroen, inboard discs front, board drums rear with Citroen pressure servo
Dimensions . .	F. 11.6in. dia.; R, 10in. dia.

WHEELS
Type	Pressed steel disc, 5-stud fixing, wide rim
Tyres—make . .	Michelin
—type . .	XAS radial ply tubed
—size . .	180-15in.

SPECIFICATION

NSU Ro80
PRICE £2,279

Maximum speeds

	mph	rpm
Top	106	5,700
3rd	—	—
2nd	79	6,500
1st	46	6,500

Acceleration

mph	sec	Ind. mph
0-30	4.9	35
0-40	6.9	45
0-50	10.4	55
0-60	14.0	65
0-70	18.5	76
0-80	25.5	86
0-90	35.8	96
Standing ¼-mile	72 mph	19.7 sec

mph	3rd (5.87)	Top (3.83)
10-30	5.1	6.6
20-40	5.8	8.0
30-50	6.6	9.9
40-60	6.9	11.3
50-70	7.5	13.0
60-80	—	15.2

Overall mpg	16.4	
Typical mpg	18.0	
Oil—miles per pint		250

FRONT ENGINE, FRONT-WHEEL DRIVE

ENGINE

Cylinders	Twin rotor Wankel rotary engine
Cooling system	Water; pump, viscous-coupling fan and thermostat
Displacement	2 x 497.5 c.c. (2 x 30.4 cu.in.) per shaft revolution
Nominal capacity	1,990 c.c. (121.3 cu.in.)
Carburettors	Two Solex 18/32 HHD
Max. power	115 bhp (DIN) at 5,500 rpm
Max. torque	117 lb.ft (DIN) at 4,500 rpm

TRANSMISSION

Gear ratios	Top 0.79
	Second 1.21
	First 2.06
	Reverse 2.11
Final drive	Hypoid bevel, 4.86-to-1

SUSPENSION

Front	Independent. MacPherson struts telescopic dampers, anti-roll bar
Rear	Independent, trailing arms and vertical struts, telescopic dampers

STEERING

Type	ZF power-assisted rack and pinion

BRAKES

Make and type	ATE Dunlop disc front and rear, with TEVES vacuum servo
Dimensions	F. 11.2in. dia.; R. 10.7in. dia.

WHEELS

Type	Pressed steel disc, 5-stud fixing, 5in. wide rim
Tyres—make	Michelin
—type	XAS radial ply tubed
—size	175-14in.

Left: Interior of the Citroen ID20. Above: The four-cylinder engine on the Citroen is mounted well back and the spare wheel is in the nose with jack and toolkit

matching and confusingly similar stalk on the left works the headlamp flasher and indicators. The wipers leave large areas unswept at the upper part of the screen. The luggage boot is enormous, in spite of losing space to a useful 18-gallon tank.

Fittings and Furniture
Citroen

Interior fittings are not as luxuriously executed on the ID as the dearer DS or luxury Pallas models, but it is still an inviting interior with superbly comfortable seats. Padding is very soft, and the seats are well shaped, with easy adjustment and hand wheel control for reclining backrests. In keeping with the unusual design of the Citroen is its distinctive facia layout. There are ventilation grilles at each end, and a large glove compartment in front of the passenger. The speedometer is a clumsily-marked oblong quadrant; switches are scattered about in rather disorderly fashion, but positions can be memorized and whichever switch is needed is then found easily, because they are so well spaced.

Easy provision is made for radio, on the left of the facia, and there is a large ashtray drawer. The interior mirror is too small and mounted much too low, where it is badly affected by the frequent changes in attitude of the car allowed by the ultra-soft suspension. Visibility is good, but it is difficult to judge the extremities of the forward quarters beyond the sloping bonnet; large rubber overriders protrude at the front and cushion the blow of any careless parking bumps. A steering column lock is fitted, but the lock is immediately beneath the steering column and difficult to reach; it is also rather awkward that the key has to be pulled against a spring before it can be rotated the final turn which allows the key to be withdrawn. An electrically-heated rear window is standard.

Quite the most excellent feature of the Citroen, after its suspension, is its directionally controlled quartz-iodine headlamps. The outer lamps are fixed, but the inner lamps swivel in response to the steering, and the resultant night driving visibility is a revelation whenever the road is clear of oncoming traffic and main beams can be used.

The boot opening is rather small, but the compartment is really deep and extends well forward; the fuel tank is ahead of it, well out of the way of any rear collision.

Personal View

It came as a surprise to find this later Citroen not as good a motorway car as I had remembered, so its slightly cumbersome bulk in town does not pay off with advantages for restful high-speed travel. If I were to have the ID20, and an overdrive could be ordered for it, it would certainly be on my list of extras. In this respect it is a little disappointing, but the superb ride and insulation from the road are as good as ever I remember. If I were operating a car hire service and had to choose between these two, it would be the Citroen without a doubt, and then I would know that my passengers would be so impressed with the comfort that there would be more business to follow.

But I don't operate car hire, in fact I doubt whether I cover as many as 100 miles a year with adult passengers in the back. What I do value, is effortless motorway cruising at the 85-90 mph which we must hope the next Minister of Transport will legalize, and for this the NSU is much more suitable. Much as I would value the Citroen's superb long range headlamps and round-the-corner illumination, the hard truth is that if you live in the southeast and are on the road mainly at civilized hours you don't get much chance to use main beams, there being so often something coming the other way. So this praiseworthy feature, too, would be a little wasted on me. The NSU's better handling would remove any final doubts from the decision.   JSMB

Personal Opinion

Seldom have I found such difficulty in choosing between two cars. It finally boils down to a question of money. Since operating costs would be of vital importance, the Citroen's considerably better economy would tip the scales in its favour. There is also comfort in the thought of £545 in the bank.

Ignoring financial considerations and comparing brand new examples of each, I might well settle for the Ro80. Its superbly effortless cruise, accurate steering and tenacious road-holding appeal immensely, as does its first-class braking system.

On the other hand, the ID20 undoubtedly scores as far as ride, seating and lighting are concerned. But its engine feels rather harsh compared with the perfectly smooth Wankel unit of the Ro80. This is particularly true at speeds over 70 mph.   DRT

NSU Ro80

SCG ROAD TEST

NSU HAS BUILT A BETTER CITROEN! For those who thought we were unfairly critical of the Citroen DS-21 in our May test — go out and try to buy an NSU Ro80. Practically every fault we magnified in the Citroen — terminal ugliness, indeterminate fender limits, amorphous seats and suspension, trashy dash, unsynchronized servo-systems, etc. — have all been overcome without losing the imaginative

engineering flavor. You'll have to *pay* a little more, maybe as much as two grand more, when you are able to get your hands on one, but in the bargain you also get one of the most technically audacious engines since the Webly-Vickers sleeve-piston 40/80, the WANKEL!

When we say *try* to get an Ro80, we mean legally. It seems that only about 20 old, used, very late '67 models got into the country before the Feds noticed how "hazardous to your health" they were and shut the door. That just goes to show how dumb the world's auto journalists were when they voted it the International Car of the Year — doesn't it? Anyhow, as of July 1969, the car has been modified to American specs — smog burners, round lights, rubber switches, filter tips, fallout shelter and clearance lights — and is now safe for human consumption. As it was, most of the cars in the U.S. were owned by auto corporations who bought them to take apart and see what makes them hum.

Well, while NSU was preoccupied with qualification, we went out and borrowed an old dangerous model from a real chrome-plated auto nut, Tom Ivey, who has gone through three Miuras trying to find his boat to Valhalla. Tom's Ro80 is a little more than

stock, however, as it is still flaunting its last concourse, so credit also goes to International Motors, Long Beach, who put up their repair shops as collateral, and Overseas Motors of Detroit, who let us play with a legal, flat-black version.

Lovely, aren't they? Next time you see a Citroen, try not to point and snicker; remember, beauty is in the eye of the title holder. And yet the Ro80 doesn't seem to sacrifice any aerodynamics to styling. Although we tested the Citroen before we could measure air drag, the Ro80 has the second lowest figure we've seen, 150 lbs.

at 70 mph versus 115 lbs. for the Lotus Elan+2, and NSU authoritatively claims a drag coefficient of .355. Conversely, it has about the most aero lift we've seen, but evenly distributed front and rear for minimum effect on stability.

Long before the impact of external appearance wears off, though, everyone wants to see what a real Wankel engine looks like. Not much, really, since all the old familiar peripheral gear is necessary, which conceals the fact that the block is just a slightly different shape — roughly cylindrical — and very small for its 128 horsepower. Even after you include torque converter, transmission, differential, inboard disc brakes and all the accessories: starter, alternator, pumps, radiator, etc., it seems there is a lot of wasted space. If the cavernous trunk weren't *quite* adequate, you could fit some bags in on top of the engine.

Now, about the value of the Wankel. How would you like the simplicity of an engine with only three moving parts? Fine, that's a good description of a single-cylinder 2-stroke — in theory — and that is where the Wankel shines — in theory. When you get down to the hard facts, there are a hundred thousand man-years of engineering development in the plain old recipro-

cating engine, and quite a few basic design problems left in the Wankel — like sealing the rotor, cost of manufacture and combustion chamber area/volume ratio. It is *not* going to replace the "hammer and crank," but like air-cooled engines, it happens to be a very fine powerplant in some applications. You might expect it to be much more reliable than your "old-fashioned" engine with pistons, rods, valves, rockers and sundry other items that go up and down or clankity clank, but we suspect that rotor tip wear might require a rebuild every 10 or 20 years.

The really big question about this engine is how do you hop it up? When it comes time to race, what . . . buy high-compression rotors, mill the housings, build 120° headers, set the timing from *what* dead center? Good luck, tinkerers of America.

Operationally, the car is about the same as any other. You still pour gas in one end and oil and water in the other, and the same sort of noises come out the exhaust pipe, even if there is rather less fuss coming from the engine room. Actually, engine noise is noticeable, but primarily because it is different — being more of a low pitched whine, or hum, apparently coming from the rotor gears. As for vibration, you have to go a long way to beat some of today's more precisely balanced reciprocating engines, which *cannot* be perceived to be running any more than the Wankel.

The only way your friendly parking attendant, Ben deFender, will ever know what an exotic machine you have, is that the clutch disengages whenever he touches the shift lever. "Whoo, man — spooky!" The drive train consists of a 3-speed manual transmission with torque converter and a servo-actuated clutch activated by a microswitch in the shift knob. You tend to learn very rapidly that the shifter is not a proper

PHOTOS / PAT BROLLIER, P. CONNOR

place to rest your hand, or even brush with your knee, since the clutch is either on or off, and a light sneeze will trip the switch. It's no trouble at all to learn to drive, as you soon tire of stomping on the floor when you shift — or more embarrassing — jabbing the brakes, which causes a somewhat jerky shift. Adapting back to a manual clutch is the tricky part.

Quarter-mile acceleration runs are . . . uh . . . uncommon. In normal operation, clutch engaged, engine idling, the poor thing doesn't have enough poop to *fall* off the line. However, once you get moving, the combination of torque converter and a strange torque curve give the eerie feeling of propeller drive — the faster you go, the stronger it gets, up to the point at which NSU suggests you shift. (See what we mean on the "acceleration-g" graph.) What happens above redline is a curious thought, but we'll wait for reports from the field. Shifting is another problem. The combination of indeterminate clutching and the

massive rotational inertia of two Wankel rotors, a torque converter, *and* a manual clutch, put a lot of fret on the synchros — enough to keep our best *completed* shift at about 0.5 seconds, and it doesn't take a lot of those to show up badly in your e.t. Surely, if we ôwned the car, we could have gotten much better times by using the electric clutch at the start and by experimenting (crashing) with the shifts. Performance is still adequate for street use, but consistent rumors are that they'll soon announce an optional 5-speed manual. Plus, John Blunsden reports that NSU opted for high peak horsepower at the expense of a steep torque curve, and is now working on the torque between 2500 rpm (converter stall) and 4500 rpm. Howdy y'doo it without a cam to time?

Stopping performance is only average, at 144 feet from 60 mph, or an average of 0.83 g, but not because of any deficiency in the brakes. The system is a one-up version of the Citroen — with air-scooped, in-board front discs, a more controllable power booster, load-compensated ratio adjuster, *plus* rear discs. The only drawback

is the relatively small 175 x 14 Michelin radials which are the limiting factor when all else goes well.

It's hard to believe the steering works at all, to see all the mickey-motion linkage on the firewall, where it is safely out of range of the "crush space." But work it does, with a hydraulically boosted rack-and-pinion that provides undetectable assist until it is needed, and for parking with muscles — is alive, alive-o. For more determinate work, though, such as flailing on the skidpad, the soft, comfortable suspension really lets you down.

Wishbones and MacPherson struts up front and independent trailing arms at the rear, combined with a lot of travel, don't do much for ultimate cornering capability, and at the limit of 0.65-0.70 g, the outside front tire is running on its sidewall. Stably, tho! As with all front-wheel-drive cars, you'll never get it to oversteer. We almost thought not to confess that the Ro80 is fwd, because with low torque on a high coefficient, there's no way of knowing which end has the pony. Except, perhaps, for the whompin' lot of understeer you get at the tiller with front drive and 61% front weight distribution to push around.

Since the great majority of you won't be racing the Ro80, we ought to give you an idea of just what a good touring car it is. The interior is impeccable, in the staid Teutonic tradition of BMW, Porsche and Mercedes. The dash is well laid out, with a very legible VDO tach and speedo, and is uncluttered with such things as control and warning light identifications to tell you what the hell each one means — or does. One bizarre switch seemed to do no more than turn on *either* the right or left parking lights. Figure that out! And, of course, the two levers on the steering column control the dimmers, turn signals, horn, 2-speed wipers and windshield washer. That's a safety feature, they say. It doesn't take your hands off the wheel — but it sure does take your mind off the road. But upholstery, seats, trim — all are comfortable, well designed and finely detailed — worthy of a far more expensive car.

At speed on a thruway the vehicle itself is so quiet and well-balanced that you are more aware of outside influences such as road condition. Not that a lot of them come through, but you are more apt to notice the ones that do. Visibility is extraordinary. A very low hood, very high windshield header and far ranging seat really bring the outside inside. Just don't maneuver too sharply — or you'll fall off your highchair.

So, NSU now has a luxury sedan, and a very advanced and refined one from both a technical and esthetic standpoint. It's not for nothing it was named International Car of the Year. Many people thought that this was because it marked the arrival of the Wankel as a competitive powerplant. Maybe it was, and maybe it did. But the Ro80 would have made it with a pair of donkeys under the hood. It's that good. 🏁

Ro80

PRICE

Base .... N.A.
As tested .... N.A.
With options ...... Electric sunroof, electric
aerial, radio, leather upholstery

ENGINE

Type .... 2-rotor Wankel, water-cooled,
aluminum block
Displacement .... 121 cu. in. (1990 cc)
Horsepower .... 128 hp at 5500 rpm
Torque .... 117 lbs.-ft. @ 4500 rpm
Bore & stroke .... N.A.
Compression ratio .... 9.0 to 1
Valve actuation .... None
Induction system .... Dual Solex 18/32 HHD
Exhaust system ..... Steel headers, 2 into 2
Electrical system .... 12-volt alternator
Recommended redline .... 6500 rpm

DRIVE TRAIN

Clutch .... Single dry disc, vacuum-servo
actuated, with torque converter

Transmission	Gear Ratio	Overall Ratio
1st Synchro	2.06	10.00
2nd Synchro	1.21	5.87
3rd Synchro	.79	3.82
Differential	Hypoid-bevel, 4.86 ratio	

CHASSIS

Frame .... Front engine, front drive
Front suspension .... Lower wishbone,
MacPherson strut, anti-roll bar
Rear suspension .. Independent trailing arms,
coil-shock units
Steering ...... Power assist rack and pinion,
3.7 turns,
overall ratio 18.3 to 1,
turning circle 39 feet
Brakes .... Dual-circuit, all disc,
load-compensated ratio,
11.2-in. dia. front,
10.7-in. dia. rear
Wheels ..... Steel disc, 14-in. dia.; 5-in. wide
Tires .... Michelin XAS, 175 SR 14,
pressures F/R: 32/26 (rec.), 36/30 (test)

BODY

Type .... Unit steel, 4-door, 5-passenger
Seats .... Front buckets, rear bench
Windows .... 4 manual, no vents
Luggage space .... Rear trunk, 21 cu. ft.
Instruments .. 220 kph speedo, 8000 rpm tach
Gauges: .... fuel, temp.
Lights: oil pressure, ammeter, brake fail

WEIGHTS AND MEASURES

Weight ...... 2870 lbs. (curb), 3100 lbs. (test)
Distribution F/R 61%/39%
Wheelbase .... 112.5 in.
Track F/R .... 58.5 in./56.5 in.
Height .... 55.5 in.
Width .... 69.0 in.
Length .... 188.0 in.
Ground clearance .... 5.5 in.
Oil capacity .... 6 qt.
Fuel capacity .... 22 gal.
Coolant capacity .... 7.5 qt.

MISCELLANEOUS

Weight/power ratio (curb/advertised) ... 22.2
Advertised hp/cu. in. 1.06
Speed per 1000 rpm (top gear) .... 18.8 mph
Warranty .... 18 months/18,000 miles

AERODYNAMIC FORCES AT 100 MPH

CORNERING CONDITIONS

CORNERING CONDITIONS

PERFORMANCE

Acceleration .... 0-30 (5.8 sec.) 0-60 (15.9 sec.)
0-quarter mile (20.3 sec., 71.3 mph)
Top Speed .... 110 mph (est.) at 5850 rpm (power limited)
Braking .... Distance from 60 mph: 144 ft. (0.83 g av.)
Number of stops to fade: not attainable
Stability: excellent
Maximum pitch angle: 0.8°
Handling .... Max. lateral: 0.65 g right, 0.70 g left
Skidpad understeer: 4.2° right, 5.0° left
Maximum roll angle: 5.5°
Reaction to throttle, full: more understeer; off: less understeer
Dynamometer .... Road horsepower: N.A.
Condition of tune: excellent

Speedometer: Kph	60.0	80.0	100.0	120.0	140.0	160.0
Actual mph	31.0	42.0	54.5	65.0	76.5	87.5

Mileage .... Average: 17.1 mpg
Miles on car: 45,550 to 45,750
Aerodynamic forces at 100 mph:
Drag .... 305 lbs. (includes tire drag)
Lift F/R .... 150 lbs./140 lbs.

TEST EXPLANATIONS

Fade test is successive max. g stops from 60 mph each minute until wheels cannot be locked. Understeer is front minus rear tire slip angle at max. lateral on 200-ft. dia. Digitek skidpad. Autoscan chassis dynamometer supplied by Humble Oil.

NEXT MONTH IS THE Ro 80's third birthday and we thought it would be nice to celebrate by borrowing one for a week or so and seeing how our 1968 CAR of the Year has matured.

The latest version, when it arrived, looked even nicer than the original, which in itself must surely be one of the most handsome as well as aerodynamically one of the most efficient saloons ever built. Recent modifications, minor and major, apart from a new range of dazzling colours, have been to the engine, the lighting system, the windscreen (which is now tinted as standard), the rear end (where a chromed handle for the boot has appeared, despite strong objections from the purist styling department!) and the interior (which has been extensively tidied up, and for which the fresh-air ventilation arrangements have been revised).

Lights on the Ro 80s sold in Britain differ visually from their German counterparts, although as far as we can make out there is no legal compulsion for this. Early cars had a six-lamp system with main and dipped beams housed behind complex glass fairings

which also formed the lenses. Fog-lamps were faired in beneath the bumper at either side. The thickness and proneness to distortion of the outer glasses combined with the need to cut away parts of the reflectors of the headlamps themselves to make this setup rather less than satisfactory. For most markets the factory's answer, when the time came to introduce a list of small modifications just before last year's Frankfurt show, was to substitute quartz halogen bulbs for all six lamp units, thus boosting the output enough to put the Ro 80's lighting equipment at least on a par with most of its opposition. Cars sold in Britain, however, had always had quite different arrangements, with four small circular units for dipped and main beams housed in specially cast nacelles which were painted the same colour as the bodywork. Although the smaller effective size of these circular lamps probably reduces their power, freedom from the distortions of the standard one-piece lens and from the peculiarities of the flattened and trimmed reflectors used in the original setup undoubtedly provides compensation. With halogen bulbs fitted as standard, this equipment in its

Latest Ro 80 front end, at least for British-market cars, incorporates four circular qi lamps plus rectangular qi driving lights. Interior has revised seating

latest form gives superb results, with brilliant output and very accurate control, making the fog-lamps more or less superfluous except for aesthetic and possibly aerodynamic reasons.

Just as significant as the switch to halogen headlamps has been the complete revision of the ventilation system. One of the few criticisms levelled at the Ro 80 during our CAR of the Year assessment was that the fresh-air arrangements were inadequate. For a saloon with such obvious aerodynamic merit (the drag factor, you will recall, is astonishingly low) it seemed almost inconceivable that the designers could have got their sums wrong when it came to locating the outlet vents in the rear pillars and determining their size. Yet that, apparently, is what had happened, and the latest car has important revisions to the internal trunking with a couple of very large supplementary outlet ducts in the sills of the rear doors. These extract via the gaps around the door shut-lines, a trick which has been exploited in other German cars and which again appears to work well. Neither is it the only modification. Two extra inlet vents have appeared in the neatly laid out Ro 80 dash, and for good measure the unique triple-curvature windscreen has been tinted so as to lessen the system's overload from direct sunlight in very hot weather. We tried it during one of the warmest days of Britain's only real summer in living memory, and at speed with all the windows closed the car continued to put through a noticeable but far from irritating draught of cool air which could be controlled to within fine limits both quantitatively and directionally. We are terrors for punishment and would not object to an even greater throughput, but then no saloon so far has satisfied us in this respect. The Ro 80 comes as close to adequacy as any, especially with the reasonably quiet booster fan in operation, but it takes time to master the central distribution controls so as to get optimum results in all weathers.

The other obvious internal change has been to the seating. NSU were quick to change their minds about the Ro 80's sales appeal as soon as it reached the market. At first their revolutionary new car was conceived as a sort of 20-years-on answer to the Citroën DS: a truly practical family machine, efficient, aesthetically satisfying, totally functional and therefore of more appeal as a piece

of luxury household equipme than as an enthusiast's toy. How ever, even at the time of our vis to the factory in connection wit the CAR of the Year award, D von Heydekampf, the charmin and very intelligent Uhlenhau type managing director of the ther independent Neckarsulm firm, ha begun to detect abnormal intere in the car among sporting drive the world over. Apart from causin him some concern because of th three-speed semi-automatic gea box, which was an integral part the design and couldn't be change however much the enthusias might dislike it, this had led him consider ways in which he coul capitalise on an unexpecte demand. One way, of course, was encourage owners to drive the ca hard—something NSU had n done before, but which they hav since followed through admirabl with some clever wording in th handbook and a promise that the would pick up the bill should har driving lead to engine damag during the first year of the car life. More practically, von Heyd kampf saw that certain psyche logical factors could enhance th car's image. Most important these was the seating, which is wh body-hugging buckets have r placed the comfortable but rathe wide and flabby family-car orig inals. These new seats make a tre mendous difference to the 'feel' the Ro 80, encouraging one to thro it into corners as a matter of cours rather than making one feel rathe daring in doing so. Yet they ar no less comfortable than th earlier type, and they are not reall any more restrictive since th range of adjustments, both latera and vertical, is just as great. The also have the merit of being softe than is normal for German luxury car seats, with a more pliable viny covering that proves its worth o a long journey.

Apart from one or two mino modifications to the trim, mos noticeable of which are the fittin of childproof locks, the identifi cation of dashboard switchgear b sensible symbols and the building in of the safety sun visors, an apart also of course from th famous boot handle (which in fac is hardly noticeable, let alone ob jectionable, but saves denting th lid when slamming it), the othe changes have been mechanical an largely confined to the engine. Fo some reason NSU have chosen no to talk about several of them, mos noticeably the switch to thyristo ignition and the elimination of on of the two sparking plugs previously used for each rotor chamber. The reason for this is probably that they were initially rather critical of their Japanese licensee Toyo Kogyo's decision to use a single plug per chamber in the twin-rotor Wankel engine first featured in their Mazda sports car. This engine was so widely praised, however, for its low speed torque and freedom from idling knock that NSU engineers took a second look at the idea and obviously decided to adopt it themselves, particularly as it is noticeably cheaper to produce.

It is interesting that the same thing has now happened at Daimler Benz, where the C111 three- and four-rotor experimental units, which were originally designed for twin plug ignition, have both appeared with single plugs in their latest form. On the road, however, an owner is unlikely to notice much difference.

In the other perennial development area, tip sealing, NSU engineers under Dr Freude have continued to forge ahead. They have always claimed that the sealing problems of the first production Wankel engine, the single rotor unit fitted to the mid-engined Prinz sports car of the early 1960s, are now very much a thing of the past. Nonetheless we have heard of owners of early-series Ro 80s who have had to have their seals replaced (free, of course) at frequent intervals, and it is presumably to eliminate these costly guarantee replacements that research has gone ahead. At the same time, of course, NSU have been anxious to solve their earlier exhaust emission problems, and it is interesting that early this year both they and Toyo Kogyo succeeded in meeting the current, quite stringent Californian anti-smog requirements.

The third big mechanical improvement has been the elimination of oil changes. Oil consumption on the Ro 80 was a problem at first. By conventional standards the official average of between .13 and .18 litres per 100km (about half a gallon for every 1000 miles) sounds astronomical when one is also faced with a complete change every 3000 miles or so. When this is eliminated, however, the picture changes radically and the Ro 80's oil bill, once one has drained out the running-in lubricant and re-filled with normal stuff, becomes equivalent to that of a conventional car with a six-quart sump which uses none at all between changes.

To aid an owner's memory, there is a warning light which comes on when the oil level needs topping up, but NSU recommend that this is done whenever the level drops below the halfway mark between Max and Min on the dipstick. In practice, at the normal consumption rate, this works out at about every 500 miles.

On the road, the latest car feels very nearly as good as it did when it first appeared. This may sound like a rather backhanded sort of compliment but in fact, as we have pointed out before, advances in the subtler aspects of automotive engineering are made so quickly and yet so unobtrusively these days that a design which seemed sensational at its introduction can often feel totally outdated within a year or two, especially as production tolerances are often so much more lax than those enforced during the pilot runs in which the first demonstration cars are usually built. Only in one respect has the Ro 80 deteriorated, to judge from our latest experience with it, and this is in the important area of wind noise. The first cars were an unqualified sensation in that the faster one drove them the quieter, relatively speaking, they seemed to get. Wind noise at 100mph was almost completely absent and so was engine noise. The engine is still of course extremely quiet, and the absence of all vibration—a factor which

one seldom notices in a conventional engine until it is removed entirely—still gives rise to the sensation that the car is not only going much more slowly than it really is but also that it can never possibly either wear out or suffer any mechanical ill. The door seals, however, to judge by out latest car, are no longer as efficient as they once were and a good deal of roar manages to penetrate at above 80mph or so—intensified, of course, by lack of competition from other sources. This is a great pity and NSU would do well to instigate a blitz on it, as in all other aspects their car is without doubt the quietest in the world.

Is it also the best in the world, as *Motocar* is so often quoted as having said? We don't really think so, although it is hard to beat at the price even after British import duty has been added. Certain features, of course, are outstanding. Among these, apart from its looks, we would list the ride (supple, absorbent, silent, though no better than that of the XJ6 or the BMW 2800), the steering (power assisted r and p, as good as an Aston's—or a Jaguar XJ6's) and the general handling (same applies). Performance is about right for a luxury two-litre car even if you ignore the usual grotesquely boastful speedometer, but it is nothing to get excited about. The freedom from vibration really is something special. All-

of-a-piece handling and superb, fade free braking are features which one has come to expect of all the truly great cars, many of them introduced since the Ro 80 first appeared; it is still true to say, though, that one could not achieve such handling in combination with such roominess *and* such compactness if one had to accommodate a larger, conventional engine.

What is perhaps most impressive about the car, again considered in relation to its price, is the genuine thought given throughout its design to the practical aspects of ownership. From the driver's point of view everything is there: a full set of instruments and carefully thought out controls set without frills in a tastefully designed interior. For the rest of the family there is a huge boot, easy access via wide doors, comfortable seating, comprehensive trim, generous and supremely practical stowage for oddments, everything one could possibly want right down to the vanity mirrors and pencil and note pad holders in the backs of the sun visors. The locking system, the interior lighting, the ventilation, access to such things as the fuse box—every tiny detail is properly carried through, adding immensely to the pleasure of ownership. In these respects, as in its essential balance of dynamic qualities, the Ro 80 was a pace setter when it first appeared. ●

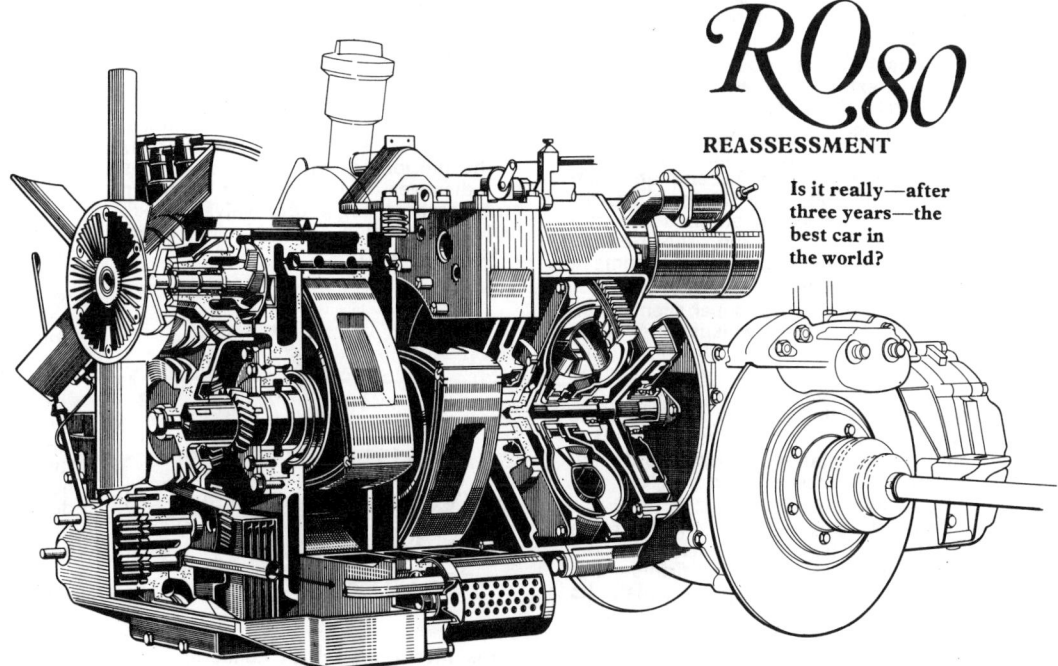

RO80
REASSESSMENT

Is it really—after three years—the best car in the world?

While British makers continue to neglect the Wankel principle, NSU engineers have improved their Ro 80 unit beyond initial hopes

This luxuriously-equipped twin-rotary from Germany is an exciting preview of motoring in the 1970s, MM's Australian testers discover after exacting workout.

NSU Ro80

SELECTING NSU's striking Ro80 as 1968 Car of the Year, was one of the easiest decisions Europe's motoring writers have had to make.

In fact if the model had been released next year, it would almost certainly take the 1970 award.

The Ro80 is more than just a new car. It is a full-scale preview of motoring in the 1970s, and an exciting one at that. Like Citroen's futuristic Parisienne which stunned the car-buying public in 1955, the German product is also destined to become a motoring landmark.

The smooth and super-silent twin-rotor engine that whisps the Ro80 into the sports sedan category is only one part of the story. Add handling which is the equal of any other sedan available in this country, speed-silence which has few rivals, superb brakes and a well-planned, roomy and very comfortable interior, and you are getting closer.

All of this is so much more incredible when you realise that the Ro80 is the German firm's first attempt at a luxury sports sedan. Its normal wares are rather boxy, one-litre affairs that really do not excell in any department.

Although the Wankel rotary engine is only one of the Ro80's outstanding features, the development of this power unit and that of the car, are closely linked.

History tells us that the first rotary-piston machine was a water-pump, conceived in 1588 by an Italian.

However, the story of the rotary engine in its automotive context does not take up until 1951.

It was then that first contacts were made between the NSU Research Department and German engineer, Dr. Felix Wankel — head of the Technical Development Establishment at Landau.

The purpose of the get-together was to discover more about sealing arrangements for rotary valves which had preoccupied Wankel for some years previously.

His inventions which concerned the sealing of oddly shaped chambers formed the basis of the rotary engine.

In 1954, Wankel realised that a four-cycle process could be built into a single rotor engine. An engine was developed and pushed a streamlined 50 cc. motor cycle to a speed of 121.9 miles an hour in 1956.

Nineteen fifty-eight saw the first planetary rotation engine on test at NSU and the firm announced its intention to build Wankel engines late in 1959.

Various versions of rotary piston engines were installed in the pretty NSU Sport Prinz for testing, the most suitable proving to be a 500 cc., 50 brake horsepower single rotor unit.

Late in 1962, production of a Wankel-engined Prinz began on very small volume.

Meanwhile, during 1963, NSU began to look at the prospect of creating a new car around the promising engine, and wind-tunnel tests began on a 1:5 scale plasticine model of what was to become the Ro80.

The decision to make a new and larger Wankel-engined car provided NSU engineers with a great opportunity to create something completely new, unhampered by conventional car design or to a large extent by cost factors, as the model was to be aimed at a higher-priced market.

One of the highest design priorities was that of aerodynamic efficiency, and when the first full-sized Ro80 took to the road in 1965, it had the remarkably low wind-resistance coefficient of 0.355. That is lower than a lot of sports cars; very low for a five-place sedan.

Meanwhile, NSU had begun development of a twin-rotor engine, and this powered a heavily camouflaged prototype Ro (for rotary) 80 (the factory type number) during extensive European tests.

In September, 1967, the model was unveiled at the Frankfurt motor show. Series production started later that year.

But although by European standards scarcely a new model, the car is still a newcomer to Australia.

A heavy European demand and limited production meant that a right-hand-drive version was late coming. The first cars trickled into Australia early this year, and only recently has the car arrived in any volume.

It is estimated that there are now close to 200 in the country, the majority in New South Wales, and there is a healthy waiting list.

Following the absorption of NSU by Audi, a wholly owned subsidiary of Volkswagen in Germany, it was rumored that VW dealers in Australia might get a crack at marketing the car, but this has not eventuated.

Thus the model is handled in Sydney by John Caskey Holdings and in Melbourne by P. J. Regan Motors, from whence our test car came.

The official Australian release only a few months ago, came at a very good time. Mazda simultaneously launched our other rotary-engined car, the R100 Coupe, paving the service path for the Ro80. In fact most of the NSU service personnel have been through the Mazda training course, and conversely if you need NSU ser-

vice, it is only as far away as a Mazda dealer.

Despite a $3600 price difference, there is a lot of similarity between the Ro80 and R100 power-plants.

Each is of twin-rotor design, Mazda

having purchased Wankel manufacturing rights in 1961. The NSUs rotors each sweep 497.5 cc. for a total capacity of 995 cc. and 128.5 bhp; the Mazda has a total capacity of 982 cc. and turns out 110 bhp.

However, two basic differences now exist between the German and Japanes rotaries. One is that the Germans have gone to cast-iron apex seals for the rotors, while the Jap-

anese have stuck to the carbon seals originally used.

The other difference is that the Mazda engine uses side inlet ports while the NSU uses peripheral ports.

NSUs reason for switching over from carbon to cast-iron seals was because of the former's failure under detonation. However, Mazda has countered this quirk by using slightly staggered ignition timing for the two plugs in each rotor chamber, with shielding for the secondary plug.

Mazda's use of side inlet ports stems from the different operating conditions in Japan, where first-class slow-running manners are important, even at the sake of ultimate power.

NSU's Ro80 has been built more with high-speed autobahn cruising in mind, but the standard semi-automatic gearbox with torque converter allows maximum use of power to be made, while overcoming the slow-running problem by keeping revs higher.

Despite the engine design kinship, it is not hard to see where the extra $3600 has been spent on the Ro80.

You get an inkling in the instruction manual under the section "Handling the Vehicle".

"No running-in is required for the Ro80," it says. "Nevertheless . . . for the first 600 miles, do not drive beyond 5500 rpm or 100 mph."

As this bland instruction suggests, the Ro80 is a machine in which high speeds are matter-of-fact.

At the 111 mph we got out of the

49

NSU Ro80

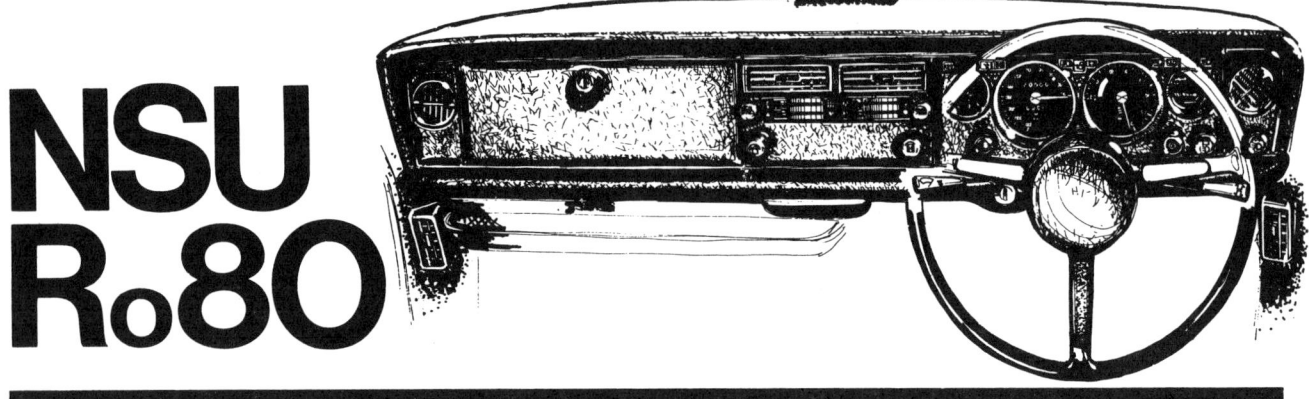

test vehicle, the noise level was ridiculously low. You can listen to the excellent Blaupunkt radio in a traffic jam and still hear it at a true 100 mph without altering the volume.

Very little sound-deadening is used to achieve this superb silence. Obviously the extensive wind-tunnel testing has done its work. From nose to tail, the Ro80 has very clean lines with a minimal frontal area and smooth six-light design. The tail is sharply cut off and the underbody is smooth and bitumen sealed to drown road noise and avoid corrosion.

Not everyone considers the Ro80

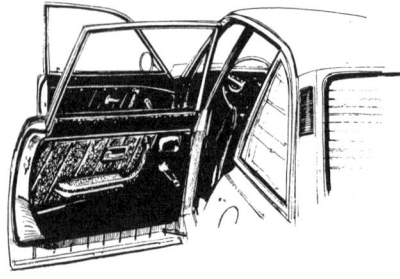

attractive in the accepted sense. But, as the NSU publicity material points out, nothing is less permanent than fashion.

If nothing else, it is distinctive and practical — a refreshing combination in this age of the look-alikes.

It is practical because in its 15ft. 8in., it caters for five passengers, plus a considerable amount of luggage (21 cu. ft. of it) in the fully-carpeted, well-shaped boot.

Being practical is not the end of the matter. Comfort is also high on the list.

The front seats in particular are first rate. Finished in a high-quality breathing vinyl, they are soft, yet sufficiently dished to hold their occupants in place. They are naturally fully reclinable, letting the driver get really comfortable, but their feature we liked best was the good shoulder support.

Back seat passengers do nearly as well. A very wide centre armrest folds down to give room for two sprawling elbows as well as offering lateral support.

Some passengers found the rear backrest a little steeply raked, but there were no complaints about legroom. Rear passengers also get individual ashtrays, grab handles and

string-weave pockets in the rear of the front seats for odds and ends.

The driver is very well looked after, reflecting NSUs experience in motor sport. Immediately in front of him are large rev counter and speedometer dials.

The speedometer is about 10 percent fast, indicating that someone's mathematics were astray when converting from kilometers/hour. The rev counter is red-lined at 6500, but reads to 8000 rpm. NSU approves of short bursts into the "red" when overtaking but not for prolonged periods. In fact the gearing is nearly ideal, with maximum speed coming up at 6200 rpm in top.

Flanking these two dials are a combined temperature and fuel gauge and an electric clock.

Indicative of the thought that has gone into this car is the canting of the speedometer and rev counter dials so that the thickly padded steering wheel boss does not obscure any numerals.

On each side of the steering column are stalks which control windscreen washers, two-speed wipers, headlight dipping, flashing, turning indicators and horn. All within finger-tip reach. Your hands need never leave the wheel.

There is also a very effective heater-demister and flow-through ventilation that really works. Outlets are in the rear screen pillars.

Other examples of design thought

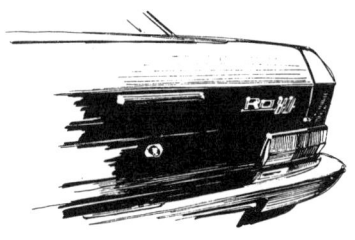

are in the roof-lining (impact absorbing foam) and the sun visors, which are both recessed and have vanity mirrors. The mirror on the driver's side is covered by a flap with Velcro fastening.

Safety standards are high, with crushable knobs, recessed handles and a break-away mirror.

The steering column is extremely

short, placed outside the normal impact zone of the car, and thus less likely to move.

A dual brake circuit is fitted, all-round visibility is first class, and the rear window has the quickest de-icing system we've yet tested.

All-round a very safe package.

There are faults nevertheless. The

window winders for example, operate in reverse and take fully 7½ turns to either raise or lower the big side slabs of glass.

And although the wipers are of the two-speed type, with an anti-lift "wing" on the driver's side, they are not really in keeping with the rest of the car. For a start they are set up for left-hand-drive, and secondly, they only sweep about two-thirds of the huge screen. Also the fast speed is none too rapid. Finally, the rubbers scrape noisily on the laminated screen in less than a downpour.

Driving the Ro80 is a relaxing experience. Some car designers attempt to eliminate driver tension by simply fitting comfortable seats — NSU has eliminated it with an advanced chassis.

The engine, mounted in conventional north-south manner, drives the front wheels. The entire engine/gearbox/differential package is very light and as a result the car is well balanced.

This can be gauged from the tyre pressures, which are only three pounds higher for the front than the rear.

Add independent suspension front and rear of a very sophisticated nature, and the mysteries of the superb handling unfold.

This suspension is in itself interesting. At front it is by McPherson struts, while location is by a trailing arm. There is also an anti-roll bar. A novel feature is the mounting of the

Continued on page 52

DATA SHEET—
NSU Ro80

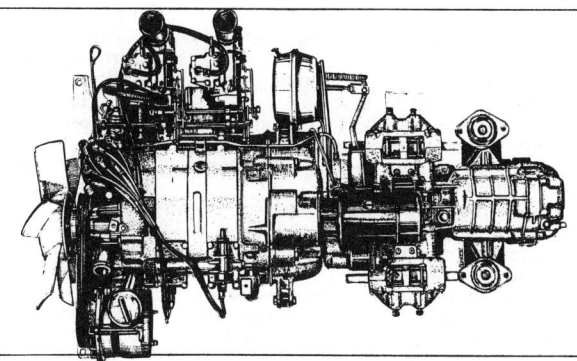

Manufacturer: NSU Motorenwerke Aktiengesellschaft, Neckarsulm, Germany.
Test car supplied by Regan Motors, Elizabeth Street, Melbourne.
Price as tested (includes Blaupunkt radio): $6640.

SPECIFICATIONS

ENGINE:

Water-cooled twin rotor, cast-alloy casing.
Swept volume of each rotor .... 497.5 cc.
Total capacity .... 995 cc.
Compression 9:1
Carburettor ... Twin choke Solex 18 x 32 HHD
Fuel tank .... 18.2 gallons
Fuel recommended .... Super
Max. power (gross) ... 128.5 bhp at 5500 rpm
Max. Torque .... 117.1 ft. lb. at 4,500 rpm
Ignition ...... Duplex ignition, two spark plugs per chamber.

TRANSMISSION:

Three-speed semi-automatic with torque converter.

Gear	Ratio
1st	2.056
2nd	1.208
3rd	0.788
Reverse	2.105
Final drive	4.857:1

CHASSIS:

Wheelbase	9ft. 4½in.
Track, front	4ft. 10½in.
Rear	4ft. 8½in.
Length	15ft. 8in.
Width	5ft. 9in.
Height	4ft. 7½in.
Kerb weight	1 ton 3 cwt. 60 lb.

SUSPENSION:

Front: Independent coil spring suspension with McPherson struts and anti-roll bar at front.

Rear: Independent with inclined trailing arms. Long-stroke spring struts and telescopic shock absorbers.

Brakes: Four-wheel discs with mechanical drum for handbrake on rear. Front discs inboard. Dual-line brake system with vacuum power-assistance.

Steering: ZF power-assisted rack and pinion. 3.7 turns, lock to lock. Ratio, 18.3:1. Turning circle, 38ft. 5in.

Wheels and Tyres: Steel disc wheels with 175 by 14 Michelin XAS tyres.

PERFORMANCE

Top speed	111 mph
Average (both ways)	109.5 mph
Standing quarter mile	19.2 sec.

Speed in gears: (at 6500 rpm) 1st, 47; 2nd, 77.

Acceleration:

Zero to		
30 mph		5.0 sec.
40		6.6
50		9.1
60		12.9
70		16.7
80		21.4
90		31.2
100		44.4

	2nd	top
20-40	6.5	8.2
30-50	6.5	8.5
40-60	6.7	10.1
50-70	7.1	11.7

No braking tests conducted.

Fuel consumption: 18.3 mpg over 359 miles including all tests.

Speedometer error:

Indicated mph	30	40	50	60	70	80	90	100
actual mph	26.5	36	45	54	63.5	73	82	91

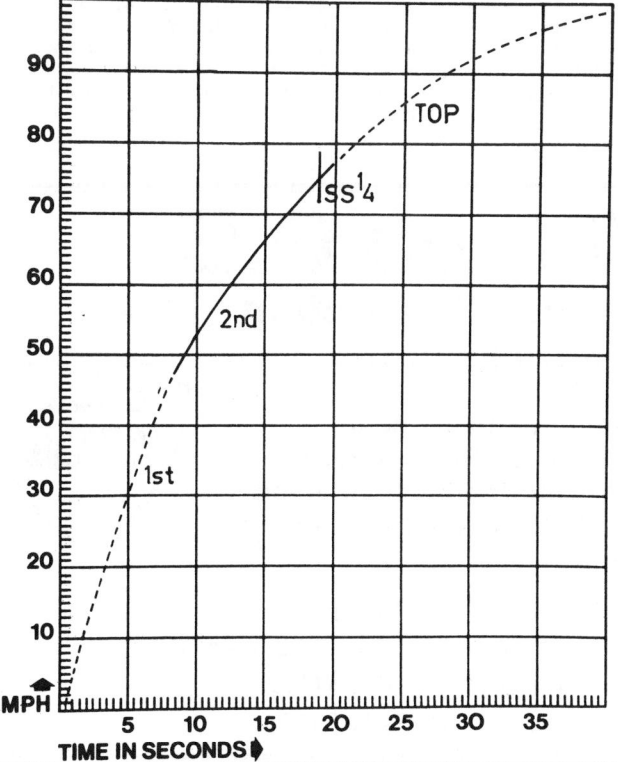

ACCELERATION CHART

(Curve labelled: TOP, SS¼, 2nd, 1st)

MPH axis: 10, 20, 30, 40, 50, 60, 70, 80, 90

TIME IN SECONDS: 5, 10, 15, 20, 25, 30, 35

HOW NSU Ro80 COMPARES

MAXIMUM SPEED (mean) M.P.H.

Scale: 70, 80, 90, 100, 110, 120, 130

NSU Ro80 ($6640)	
Rover 3.5 ($8295)	
Jaguar XJ6 ($8295)	
Mercedes 280SE ($9164)	

0-60 M.P.H. SECONDS

Scale: 25, 20, 15, 10, 5

- NSU Ro80
- Rover 3.5
- Jaguar XJ6
- Mercedes 280SE

M.P.G. Overall

Scale: 10, 20, 30, 40

- NSU Ro80
- Rover 3.5
- Jaguar XJ6
- Mercedes 280SE

STANDING START ¼ MILE (secs)

Scale: 20, 10

- NSU Ro80
- Rover 3.5
- Jaguar XJ6
- Mercedes 280SE

NSU Ro80

(Continued from page 50)

engine casing on telescopic shock absorbers on each side.

Rear suspension is by inclined trailing arms with long spring strut units and double acting telescopic shock absorbers.

What this front-wheel-drive/suspension combination means is all the advantages of front-wheel-drive with none of the drawbacks.

Thrown hard into a tight sweeper, the Ro80 understeers slightly, but nothing more, as the power is kept on. But suddenly backing off does nothing to alter the status quo. The Ro80 does not shift an inch off line, even on slippery, wet roads. Even hard braking in the middle of a corner does not catch this German out of step.

You get tremendous confidence from this predictable behavior when the conditions deteriorate.

The actual roadholding through the 175-14 Michelin XAS radials is of a very high order. Cornered hard, the NSU leans somewhat, but this looks more alarming from the kerb than from inside. Despite the lean, the tyres maintain a flat contact with the ground and grip tenaciously.

Stability, even with gusty side winds, is beyond reproach, a bonus feature of the streamlined body and front-wheel-drive.

All of this behavior is quite extraordinary when you consider the long-travel nature of the suspension, which on paper seems tuned for a boulevard ride.

In fact the ride is smooth, rather than soft, the greatest harshness — speaking relatively — coming from the XAS tyres. The long wheelbase, with wheels close to the corners, eliminates pitch and gives the Ro80 the pothole manners of something a lot bigger.

Rough-going increases the "solid" feel of the car.

All of this would be academic if the NSU did not have good brakes. It has. Four big discs with power assistance

haul the car down from high speeds in a very impressive manner.

The stopping power of this car is as deceptive as its speed, leaving you stationary yards before your estimated full stop.

A look under the spacious bonnet, tells a lot. The big front discs are inboard, next to the differential, and well protected by stone guards. They are very thick, helping to dissipate heat quickly and are well exposed to the airstream. Those at the rear are mounted outboard in conventional fashion, incorporating a mechanical drum handbrake similar to that used by Porsche.

Another superlative can be levelled at the ZF power-assisted rack and pinion steering. This is a similar system used by Aston Martin on the DB6 and DBS models. It has plenty of feel, yet is light enough for the most difficult parking manoeuvres. In fact there is so much feel and self centre — even if ZF has artificially built it in — that most people would not be aware that it was power-assisted.

A valuable feature of the power assistance is that the cornering "tug" of the front-wheel-drive, is not passed on to the driver, allowing him to choose his line with his fingertips rather than his biceps.

What of the rotary engine and its gearbox? This is perhaps the outstanding feature of the car, and like all good things, we've left it until last to discuss.

Except at idle, which is at times as high as 1500 rpm depending on how hot the engine is, the twin rotor unit is dead smooth. At idle it merely rocks oh-so-slightly on its shock absorbers.

With so few moving parts, it is very willing to rev, and observing the red line is not always easy. We experimented with different revs for maximum performance, and found that changing at 7000 rpm produced the best figures. The beauty of the rotary engine is that mechanical clatter is not proportionate to speed, the engine merely working up to a pleasant hum

at high revs.

The three-speed semi-automatic gearchange mated to the engine is a good, although not ideal, choice.

The idea of a semi-automatic change is a good one. Porsche and Volkswagen use it very successfully.

However, with 2700 lb. of motor car to pull around, the NSU would have benefited more from a four-speed unit.

As it is, you must use the gears freely for good performance. As with normal semi-automatic systems, the clutch is built in to the gear lever knob, the touch of a hand declutching the mechanism. This is a sure cure for those drivers who have a habit of nursing the gear lever in traffic.

In theory you can start in any gear and let the torque converter do the work, but acceleration in third from a standing start is rather leisurely. Most people will go through the gears as in a conventional car.

Unlike the Porsche system, the NSU's gearbox does not allow really rapid changes without protest. The synchromesh was regularly beaten during the performance testing, but normally there is no need to change this quickly.

We also found that when changing down at high speed it was sometimes necessary to double-declutch by hand — that is lift the left hand from the lever while revving it in neutral — to get a really silky change.

Still in fairness to the gearbox, it will produce the smoothest changes imaginable when treated normally. After all, this is not a racing car.

As with nearly all German cars, the finish on the NSU is impeccable. The only exception was the lifting of some of the bitumen sealing on the driver's side rocker panel. We also thought bare, exposed light bulbs in the boot and under the bonnet a little skimpy.

At $6400 in this country, the Ro80 is in the middle of a very competitive market, which includes the Rover 3500, Volvo 164, Jaguar XJ6 and BMWs 2500 and 2800, not to mention Mercedes.

Even in this company it can easily hold its own. ●

Although the styling of the NSU Ro80 is now three years old, it still looks modern with its low, road-hugging front and huge windshield.

35,000 MILES IN THE NSU Ro80 WANKEL

Although only about 100 have been sold in the U.S. to date, the advanced Ro80 is a common sight in Europe.

My first contact with the NSU Ro80 was during a press preview in the summer of 1967. The car was up as a candidate for the international "Car of the Year" award which it subsequently won. Like most of my fellow jurymen I thought the car an uncommonly good one, combining handling, roadholding and comfort in a way that set a new standard. I was less impressed with the revolutionary new Wankel engine — the Ro80 was the first large scale passenger car with this new means of propulsion.

It was silent and free from vibrations as a rotary power unit should be, but for a car in this price bracket that had to compete head on with Mercedes six cylinder models it was definitely lacking in power and particularly, in low speed torque. The semiautomatic transmission (that is standard without any options) did not help. What a car, if it just had a real engine, was the general comment.

Having lived now with the Ro80 for two years, I have somewhat changed my opinion. True, it still feels a bit embarrassing to be outdragged by a VW Beetle at the traffic lights, but the Wan-

The European-style headlights look good, but it was found wise to add two halogen road lamps (behind) the grille for more lighting.

In order to avoid obstruction by the wheel, the speedometer only goes to "three o'clock" and the rev counter (right) starts at "nine o'clock."

kel engine has its compensations.

Just after having bought the car second hand in the summer 1968 — it had then done 15,500 miles in the hands of the first owner — I set out for a holiday drive from Sweden to Italy with wife, three children and ample family luggage. Leaving the North German ferry port Trawemunde, we crossed the Swiss border at Basle after six hours driving. The distance is 560 miles giving an *average* speed of 93 mph. The speed in itself is quite remarkable although it could be done in any reasonably fast car. The real remarkable thing was the way the Ro80 did it. My wife is not overly keen on fast driving, normally getting a bit nervous when the speedometer shows over 70. Looking at the Ro80 instrument that most of the time was showing 200 kph (124 mph) she thought

it must be the rev counter or some other technical thing! Nor did the kids, one or the other of them usually getting sick, wanting ice cream or something every half hour, complain.

I have never before experienced this total confidence in a car at high speed that the Ro80 conveys. The Wankel

seems to become quieter and quieter the faster it runs. At the usual cruising speed of just over 110 mph (when the optimistic speedometer shows 124) which is also the top speed, you just can't hear the engine and because of the aerodynamic shape of the body, there is very little wind noise. The only sound is

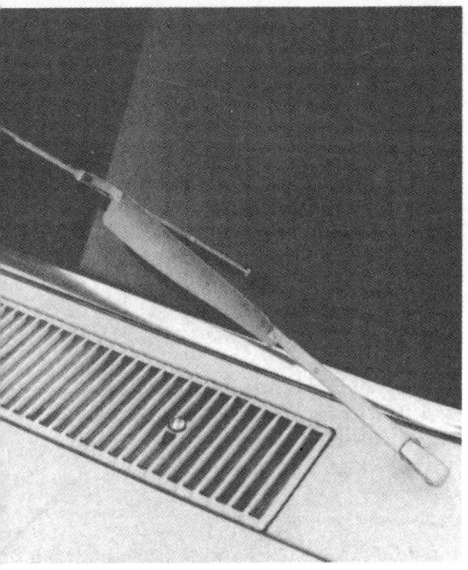

Aerodynamic foils on the wiper arms keep the blades on the glass even at 110-mph speeds. This, actually, was a U.S. invention.

the reassuring hum of the big radial tires. Directional stability is second to none for in a sidewind or not, the car just carries on unaffected. The ride, which is on the harsh side at low speed, levels off beautifully at speed without giving any of those sickening rocking motions that softly sprung cars convey.

The power rack and pinion steering (standard) is a model of how a car should steer. It is light without being overly light as are so many power systems. There is complete road feel and very quick reactions. In fact, the steering

makes the big and heavy Ro80 feel more like a small sports car.

The brakes, discs all round and with a split system that gives braking on the front wheels should any of the circuits fail, have a reassuring bite with just the right pedal pressure — not as light as to promote unintentional wheel locking but light enough to permit a woman to make a full stop from high speed. Needless to say, they stop the car in an absolutely straight line even if you keep your foot right down.

Cornering is every bit as good as the wide track lets you believe. And there is nothing to it. Just turn the wheel and the car corners, seemingly with total disregard for the speed involved. With power on it understeers moderately, with power off it feels just neutral. When it goes, which I have only managed on a closed circuit and at a speed that almost scared the daylights out of me, it slides gently on all four tires. There might be other cars with as high or even higher cornering power but there is none that I know of that can be cornered with this absolute ease.

Next to the Wankel engine the most controversial point on the Ro80 is the semi-automatic transmission. It is similar to the cheapest GM unit you can have in the smaller Chevrolets being a conventional manual three speed gearbox with an electric clutch operated by a switch in the gear lever (when you touch the lever it disengages) and a torque converter. My first impression was that this device combined all the bad things of a manual gearbox with those of an automatic. Today, I think it is wonderful. The torque converter permits you to

The smooth body lines were evolved in a wind tunnel and the resulting aerodynamic efficiency shows in the high top speed for the power output.

start in top gear, should you want to, and the torque multiplication within the gear ratios makes the three speeds completely adequate.

The reason for this setup as standard equipment and without a manual gearbox as an option is the lack of low speed torque with the NSU Wankel engine. (The Mazda Wankel is much better in this respect but loses on top end revability.) Without the torque converter the Ro80 would be a pig to drive at low speeds and even with it, it is far from a sprinter. The acceleration from standstill is definitely poor, not until the engine reaches 4000 rpm is there any marked punch in it.

In second gear you have what in practice is completely automatic driving. Although at the expense of rather slow starting from rest, it spans 0-80 mph with an uncanny smoothness and without going over the 6,500 rpm limit set for constant cruising. For quick bursts of power it can safely be taken to 8,000 rpm — giving 98 mph in second! Even enthusiastic drivers like myself have their spells of laziness, when it is rather pleasant to take advantage of this, particularly in traffic jams when constant gearchanging is a chore, no matter how well you like a manual box on the open road. On the other hand first gear takes you to 47 mph, obeying the limit, and 58 mph at 8,000 rpm, giving spirited

acceleration once the first reluctance of starting is overcome.

The NSU Wankel has become infamous for heavy gas and oil consumption. This is quite contrary to my experience which leads me to believe that most of the inflated consumption experienced by others has something to do with some heavyfootedness. With the torque converter it is obvious that you get a lot of gas consuming slip if you floor the throttle. With proper gear changing and some easy throttle work (which actually gives just as good acceleration) you won't pay for just whipping oil round in the converter.

During the 20,000 miles I have driven my Ro80 the consumption has worked out as an average of 17.8 mpg which is quite normal for any European car of this size and speed potential. During the holiday trip, cruising at top speed as I mentioned in the beginning of this article, the car gave 16 mpg, which is exceptionally good. The few cars that can stand such an average speed get very thirsty cruising at the top end of their ability. This reflects strongly on the

low drag of the body, wind resistance playing the biggest part at high speed.

On the other side I have measured some pretty bad consumption figures during city driving — around 13 mpg — indicating that the torque converter, that is working most of the time at slow speed, is the real villain.

Oil consumption is higher than that of common engines, as it should be. There is a calculated "drip" into the chambers to give the rotor seals lubrication. This oil is, of course, burned up during combustion, leading to a certain inherent consumption. On average, I have had to fill a quart at every other gas fill, giving around 600 miles to a quart. Once used to this, it is not much of a hardship and economically compensated for as the engine does not need regular oil changes. One snag is that it is very difficult to read the oil stick as the oil keeps absolutely clean.

The interior of the Ro80 is in the German matter-of-fact style without any unnecessary decorations, but clever detailing. The driver's seat — a bit too marshmallowy in its soft stuffing for my

This Ro80 has spent most of its 35,000-mile life outside in salty winds and running on salt sprayed roads. Yet, no rust is evident.

taste — has a wide range of adjustment in height, giving plenty of room for my 6 feet plus (of which the legs account for most) and also permits my little wife excellent driving control.

The small diameter steering wheel (with power steering there is no need for extra leverage) is set at a comfortable angle and permits driving with outstretched arms. Instruments (round black dials with white lettering) and minor controls are just right. There is of course a rev counter as standard equipment, as with the unobtrusive Wankel you can very easily overrev it in the lower gears.

Heating and ventilation are first class, something that is very important in this country where temperatures range from minus 40°F to plus 90. There are lots of niceties for driver and passengers like a lighted glove compartment, big shelf

Aerodynamics are followed up in details like rain gutters. Instead of the usual welded ones, they are integral for less wind noise.

under the dashboard, a smaller one (suitable for a pack of cigarettes) in front of the driver, pockets in the backs of the front seats and even a small pocket in the back of the sunvisor for travelling documents and the like. The really capacious trunk is fully carpeted, and like the engine room, lighted. Upholstery is in ventilated vinyl (cloth and leather available) and the soft carpets fitted with foam plastic underlays giving a very cosy interior.

Now to the less pleasant side of being an Ro80 owner. In fact, had the car not been so good in all other respects I would have gotten rid of it in disgust a long time ago. But as it is, it is very easy to forgive its shortcomings. Like most early Ro80 owners, I have had to change the engine. At around 25,000 miles it started feeling rather weak and got into a nasty habit of cutting out at low revs, particularly when steering and braking at the same time when the power taken for these functions seemed to amount to more than the idling Wankel could give.

At 28,000 miles it got to the stage when something had to be done and the NSU agents suggested changing the engine. This has become general practice instead of making repairs. It seems that NSU want all their ailing engines back to find out what went wrong with them. They are probably also as yet not all too convinced about the abilities of their agents' service departments when it comes to such an out of the ordinary engine.

In spite of the guarantee being well out of date, a new (or probably rebuilt) engine was offered free, with only fitting charges to be paid. This was not just because I happen to be an automobile writer; the same treatment has been given every owner with the same problem that I know of.

The second engine lasted precisely three days. Trying to start it one morning, it was locked solid. This was quite obviously due to some manufacturing or fitting error, that should not be typical and I had a third engine installed absolutely free of charge. At 7,000 miles this engine is now just nicely run in and goes better and better. At NSU they say that all previous troubles with the seals have been overcome and that this one should prove reliable, which we shall see. . .

The fitting charges for the new engine amounted not too much more than what one could expect in service costs for any ordinary engine during that mileage and its slow "fade away" did not cause any of the inconveniences a more sudden breakdown always does, so I really didn't mind too much.

What has been worse has been starting troubles during the winter months. The Wankel is somewhat similar to a two-stroke and prone to the same difficulties with spark plugs. The plugs not only sparkle twice as often as they do in a normal four-stroke, they never get the benefit of a cool breeze from an incoming charge of fuel. Consequently they live a very hot life which does not do them any good. Like in a two-stroke, they are also prone to oiling up when the car is used mainly for stop-and-go driving. And that, of course, is the fate of my car as well as most others in the normal weekday life.

The starting difficulties are not bettered by a tendency of the engine to get soaked in petrol after an unsuccessful attempt. Unlike normal engines it can't be dried out just by flooring the throttle and operating the starter. You have to go the whole way, screwing the plugs out and cleaning them, often to find that the starting difficulties persist.

Changing the hyper-expensive special plugs has been a costly pastime during winters. This should, however, be much improved on the current Ro80 engine where only one plug per chamber (mine has two) is used in conjuction with a new transistor-ignition system.

My Ro80 is one of the very first manufactured. As always with early examples, one has to expect teething troubles. Window lifts, door locks, interior lights and other details like that have nothing of that German quality about them, but have been constant sources of irritation. Doors won't lock or open, windows drop down in their frames and all sorts of things seem to come loose. As I have driven Ro80s of later manufacture I know that most of these troubles have been overcome. In my car, I just have to live with them.

Mechanically, I have had little trouble apart from the engine. In contrast to the interior details, the chassis seems to be very rugged. The exhaust system has had to be exchanged, as they rarely last more than two years in any car in this climate. The switch in the automatic clutch has been in need of adjustment once and the lining of the right handbrake (separate drums within the rear disc brakes) got loose and disintegrated for no obvious reason.

The shock absorbers, which after 35,000 miles should be in need for replacement in most cars, are still in good shape and the universal joints, common trouble makers in fwd cars, are still silent. Apart from plugs and one change of breaker points, the electrical system has given no trouble.

Two of the Michelin XAS tires lost chunks of rubber during some high speed driving just after I had bought the car. As these are HR marked they should be well capable of any speed the Ro80 can perform. After a claim, Michelin agreed to manufacturing error and replaced them with an allowance for the mileage they had done. Still they suspected that the previous owner had mistreated them in some way as tread separation with this high class tire is

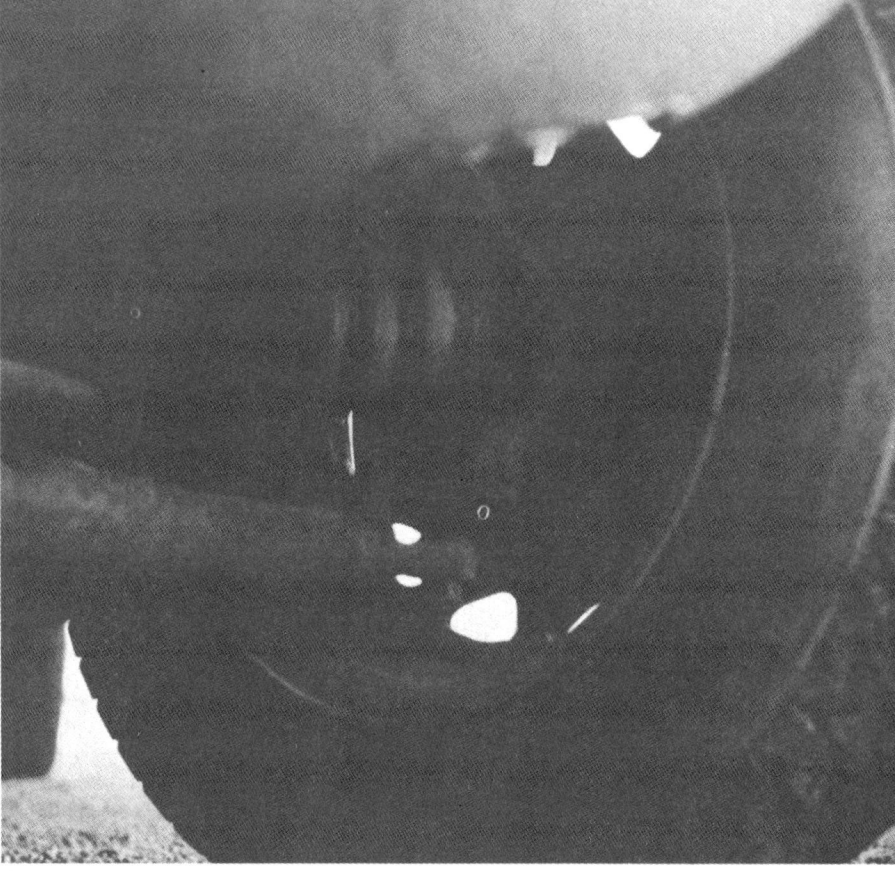

To reduce unsprung weight on the front wheels, the disc brakes are mounted inboard adjacent to the differential. U-joints have survived 35,000 miles.

virtually unknown, both to them and to me. The new ones have given no trouble and have plenty of tread left after nearly 20,000 miles on the front wheels. The rear ones are still the originals, showing hardly any wear at all after 35,000 miles which is quite remarkable as the Ro80 has individual rear suspension that always promotes tire wear, even on a fwd car.

My Ro80 has never seen a garage from inside except during repairs, and as I live by the coast with salty winds blowing over it most of the time and road salt being sprayed on the underside during the winters, the bodywork has led a hard life. Still, apart from the usual blemishes at door edges and around the wheel openings, the car looks almost like new. It has been treated with rust preventing oil inside the body panels (as is necessary in this climate) but has

otherwise had very little in the way of preventive care. The Ullen family considers car washing as something of a luxury that is saved for special occasions, like Christmas and Midsummer!

Although the Wankel engine has given me a fair amount of trouble, I should not like to go back to a normal piston engine again. Its smoothness at normal speeds is fully comparable with the best of your big V8s and at high speed, it is just unique! As you have seen from this appraisal, the Ro80 is not just the engine, but there is no doubt that without the Wankel it would not be the marvelous car it is. The small size of the engine has made the low front and the aerodynamic shape possible, and the low weight and the low position of the engine is responsible for the extraordinary handling. With a normal piston engine giving similar performance, it would have been just another front-heavy lump of understeering automobile. In most car owner surveys there is always the final question, "would you buy another one?" I just can't wait 'til the rumoured three rotor Ro comes out!

—*Jan Ullen*

1. *Thermostatic fan*
2. *Early twin-plug ignition*
3. *Solex 2V 18/32 HHD carburetion*
4. *130 hp twin-rotor Wankel*
5. *Inboard disc brakes*
6. *12-volt, 66 A/H battery*
7. *12-volt, 490 watt generator*
8. *Forward opening hood*

NSU Ro80 4-DOOR SEDAN

PERFORMANCE AND MAINTENANCE

Acceleration: Gears:
    0-30 mph . . . . 5.1 secs.— I
    0-45 mph . . . . 7.3 secs.— I
    0-60 mph . . . . 13.9 secs.—I, II
    0-75 mph . . . . 18.6 secs.—I, II
    0-1/4 mile . . . . 20.1 secs. @ 77.3 mph
Ideal cruise . . . . 100+ mph
Top speed (est.) . . . . 113 mph
Stop from 60 mph . . . . 140 ft.
Average economy (city) . . . . 13 mpg
Average economy (country) . . . . 18 mpg
Fuel required . . . . Regular
Oil change (mos./miles) . . . . None
Lubrication (mos./miles) . . . . None
Warranty (mos./miles) 18/18,000
Type tools required . . . . Metric
U.S. dealers . . . . 78 total

SPECIFICATIONS AS TESTED

Engine . . . . 61.3 cu. in., 2-rotor wankel
Bore & stroke . . . . N/A x N/A ins.
Compression ratio . . . . 9.0 to one
Horsepower . . . . . 130 (SAE gross) @ 5500 rpms.
Torque . . . . 117 lbs.-ft. @ 4500 rpms.
Transmission . . . 3-speed, semi-automatic (Ferodo)
Steering* . . . . 3.75 turns, lock to lock
                               38 ft., curb to curb
Brakes* . . . . Disc front, disc rear
Suspension . . . . Coil front, coil rear
Tires . . . . 175 HR 14, Michelin XAS

Dimensions (ins.):

Wheelbase 112.6	Front track 58.5
Length 188.2	Rear track 56.5
Width 69.3	Ground clearance . 6.0
Height 55.5	Weight . . . . 2820 lbs.

Capacities: Fuel. . . . 22 gals.   Oil. . . . . 6.8 qts.
          Coolant . . . . 8.5 qts.   Trunk. . . 25.0 cu. ft.

*Power assisted as tested

RATING

	Excellent (91-100)	Good (81-90)	Fair (71-80)	Poor (60-70)
Brakes	94			
Comfort	91			
Cornering	93			
Details		88		
Finish		84		
Instruments . .	95			
Luggage	95			
Performance . .			75	
Quietness	95			
Ride	95			
Room		90		
Steering	96			
Visibility	92			
Overall	91			

n/a—not available

BASE PRICE OF CAR

(Excludes state and local taxes, license, dealer preparation and domestic transportation): $5995 at East Coast P.O.E.

Plus desirable options:
$ 425 Air-conditioning
$ 50 Tinted glass
$ 200 Electric sunroof
$ 165 Becker AM/FM radio
$ 260 Magnesium wheels
$ 450 Leather upholstery
$7545 TOTAL
$2.12 per lb. (base price).

ANTICIPATED DEPRECIATION

(Based on current Kelley Blue Book, previous equivalent model): $n/a 1st yr. + $n/a 2nd yr.

N/A—not applicable

TRAIL BLAZER, WHITE ELEPHANT OR BOTH

Which? rated its reliability 'very poor' and claimed it cost over £20 a week to run. Yet of 57 percent of the owners sampled—a very high proportion—said they would buy one again.
Four years after voting it CAR of the Year, we take a harder-than-ever look at one of the most original, most beautiful, most enigmatic family cars of all time: in the NSU Ro80

A PUFF OF SMOKE, AN OILY TRICKLE from the aggressive-looking exhaust outlet, an ominous rattle from under that shapely bonnet. Another NSU Ro80 has fallen by the wayside.

The sight has grown familiar on German autobahns. Owners have become the butt of countless quips. Volkswagen men, current proprietors of the NSU nameplate and inheritors of the Wankel design rights, have learned to shrug their shoulders and murmur 'Not invented here'.

Yet, worldwide, the rotary engine continues to gain ground. The Japanese Toyo Kogyo company now claims that more than 50 percent of its formidable output is Wankel powered. Experimental prototypes are running on at least a dozen proving grounds in other countries. General Motors, by far the biggest spenders on experimental automotive technology, are believed to be close to the production stage with a rotary-powered American saloon. Some observers are even predicting that the entire US industry will have switched to rotaries by 1980.

Meanwhile, what of the Ro80 itself? Like the Citroen DS in its early years, it sails unscathed through a sea of troubles, exciting not only attention but open envy wherever it goes. At a recent gathering of English motoring journalists, summoned to help launch the VW K70 on the British market, the organisers made the mistake of including a couple of Ro80s amongst the fleet of cars assembled for assessment. Eager to refresh their memories, those seasoned scribes fought over the NSU, several of them sparing only a cursory glance for its brand new stablemate . . .

The Ro80 is that kind of car, Many of the early examples still running on British roads are chewing their way through their third and fourth engines. Yet incredibly, some of those cars, with the worst reliability record of any mass-produced modern saloon, *are still in the hands of their original owners!*

The explanation lies partly in the outstanding merit of the vehicle itself (much of it due to design features quite independent of the engine), and partly in the fidelity of the factory, which has kept its original promise to stand by owners with engine trouble to the very last ditch. Only now, after an almost endless succession of problems with cold starting, plug fouling, carburation, lubrication and, above all, premature deterioration of the rotor seals, has a ray of light begun to appear at the end of what must have seemed to NSU's bosses a very gloomy tunnel indeed. 'We have at last got our level of guarantee claims within the bounds that we would regard as normal for a conventional car,' said Ludwig Kraus, Audi/NSU chief engineer, in a recent exclusive interview with CAR. 'But the Ro80 is still uncomfortably close to the top of that bracket.' (You will be able to read the full text of Kraus's remarks as part of our Operation Confrontation series next month.)

To get an accurate picture of this very special car and its place in the British motoring scene, we talked to six owners selected at random (unlike the *Which?* sample) from the importers' sales records. They ranged from an enthusiastic doctor who had bought, and cherished, one of the very first left hand drive examples to a busy company director who turned down a Rolls-Royce to own his second Ro80. But before we set about collecting these men's impressions, we borrowed a current example and put it through our usual test procedure.

Here, Ian Fraser's comments:

Present day motoring in former CARs of the Year almost invariably leads to the conclusion that they are not as good in retrospect as they seemed at first. Old age has not overtaken many of them so much as the spectacular improvements among other vehicles of similar price, size and purpose. Automatically, the newcomers provide wrinkles that are more than skin deep in their older rivals' acceptability.

That's what makes the NSU Ro80 such an oddity. It made a tremendous impression when it took the CAR of the Year honours for 1967/68, yet it is hardly less impressive today.

One of CAR's best-trodden routes away from London is along the East Coast over a variety of roads which take in thick traffic (of course!), fast motorways, standard roads and twisty mud-strewn lanes that are the domain of GT tractors. It is just 100 miles all up, and the fastest we have managed to date was 90 minutes in a Datsun 240Z. I thoroughly appalling condition the V12 E-type—a far less hand car—consumed two hours, b neither of these difficult journe was anything else than ol fashioned hard work; the mo enjoyable part was opening th door at the end of the run.

The 115bhp Ro80, running i the wet all the way, did the sam trip in just a shade over tw hours with no hard work involve It is so much more a harmoniou collection of mechanicals tha just about anything else aroun

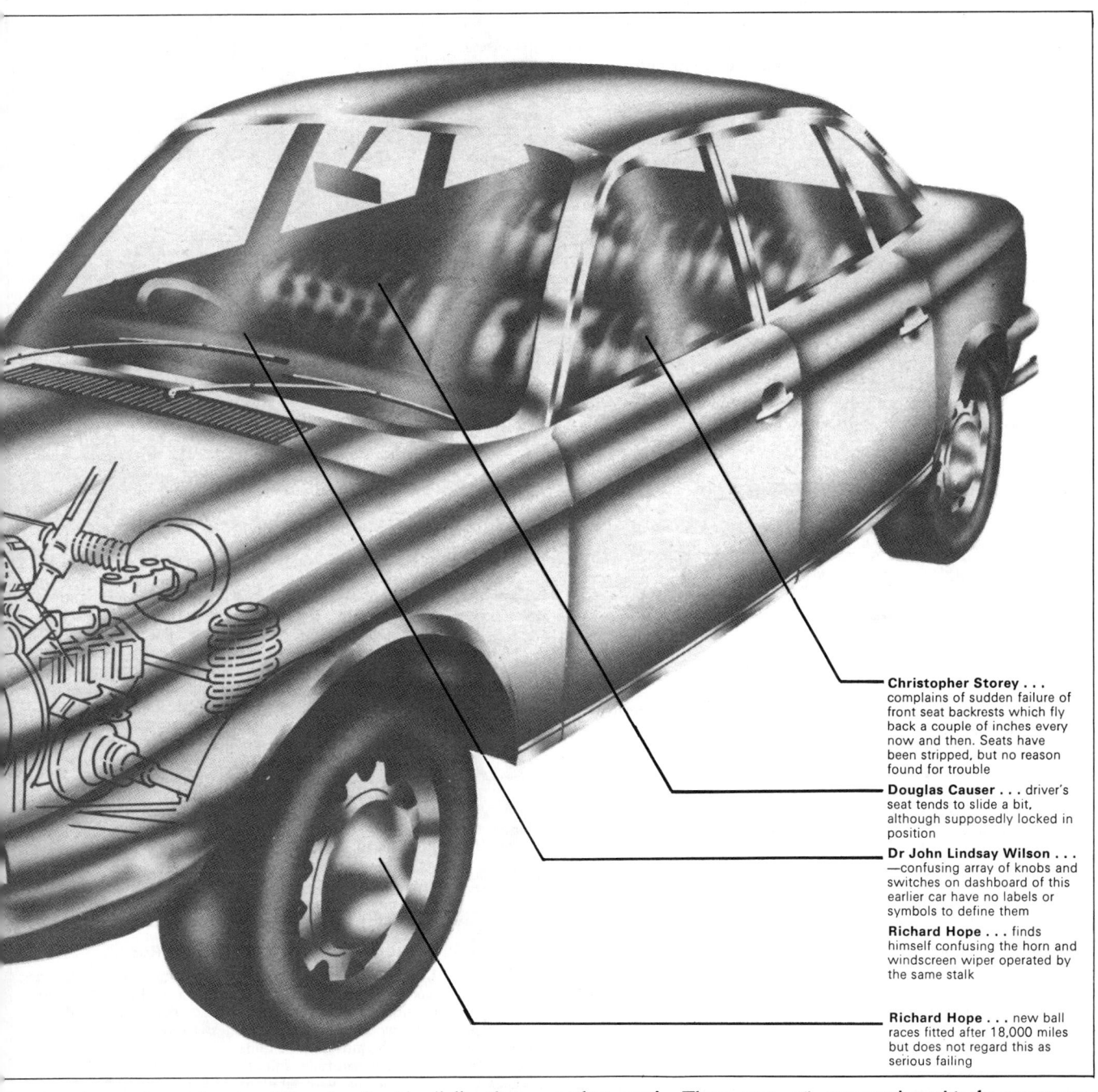

Christopher Storey . . . complains of sudden failure of front seat backrests which fly back a couple of inches every now and then. Seats have been stripped, but no reason found for trouble

Douglas Causer . . . driver's seat tends to slide a bit, although supposedly locked in position

Dr John Lindsay Wilson . . . —confusing array of knobs and switches on dashboard of this earlier car have no labels or symbols to define them

Richard Hope . . . finds himself confusing the horn and windscreen wiper operated by the same stalk

Richard Hope . . . new ball races fitted after 18,000 miles but does not regard this as serious failing

ese days that we have taken to eculating that had the Ro80 en on the CAR of the Year gibility list last time around, ould it have scored a significant mber of votes? The conclusion this address is that even if the SU did not sweep the board (as did originally), it would have ded up in a position of strength.

Despite major engine modifica-ns, including single-plug-per-amber electronic ignition and, ould you believe, an afterburner r the exhaust, it is still largely e same car it was back in 1967.

Although refined in all directions, it is still the same concept built to the same principles. Unlike the Japanese Mazda rotaries when they first appeared, the Ro80 was always intended as a Wankel-powered car with roadability, accommodation and styling to match the ideals behind its propulsion. The time lapse of five years has served to enhance the Ro80 rather than denigrate it, which is the virtue of careful development. Nowhere in the car has anyone said 'well, that was quite wrong, let's do it again

another way'. There was, of course, the plot to produce a cheaper car along the lines of the Ro80, using a reciprocating en-gine (about which NSU also know a great deal), but various financial pitfalls along the way turned that into the not marvel-lously effective VW K70.

Apart from an almost two-stroke idle and a conspicuous lack of low speed torque, the engine has almost endless revability. It is, therefore, excusable to travel at 100mph in places where 65 is the norm, breaking off intellectual

conversation with the passengers only long enough to mouth unseemly utterances at the slug-gards who seem to have chosen this very day to clutter up the road with 35mph four-wheeled jokes. Eventually the penny (whatever that is) drops, often as a dry-mouthed, clammy-handed passenger tries to remark non-chalantly how effortlessly the Ro80 does 105 along the North Circular Road!

That's really the bother with the NSU. Not having great balls of fiery acceleration low down, it tends to sneak up on you at the other end. Can be embarrassing—and expensive if the lawmen decide you are over-playing your hand. The deliberate cruising speed can be anything up to its 112mph top speed, but hard driving does give the Wankel engine thirst enough to make more fuel stops necessary, thus damaging your average. Punting along at a gentlemanly rate, say up to 75mph, you can reasonably expect to get 22mpg, but tread the right pedal consistently harder and you are immediately in the realm of 18mpg, which is bad news, the 18-gallon fuel tank notwithstanding.

Another way to increase the fuel consumption simply enormously is to forget to change into top gear. By reason of the smoothness and lack of recipro-

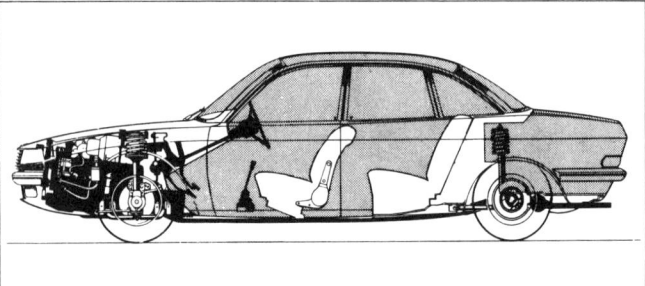

cating fuss it is easy to go for miles in second. But, let it be said, there is little danger of inadvertently entering the rapid-wear zone which is the undoing of rotaries in general. At 7000rpm on the tachometer (500 into the red), a buzzer croaks an undeniable warning that even the most befuddled matronly driver would be hard-pressed to ignore. No one told us of this latest innovation when we picked up the Ro80, so we found out about it the hard way.

We still cannot decide if we really like the NSU's clutchless, partly automatic three-speed gearbox, so reminiscent of Porsche's Sportomatic (and BMC's nightmarish Manumatic of A55 days). Yet, like the rest of the car, the Ro80's transmission works well in its context. The Good Book of Sound Advice for Ro80 owners says that you can forget about first except for climbing out of bogs, and do all the routine plugging in second and top. The torque converter provides the necessary slippage for clean getaways and no doubt eases the fuel consumption. The change follows the normal three-speed pattern and a micro-switch in the gear-

knob disengages the drive to enable changes to be crunchless. Despite the hybrid nature of the transmission it is less offensive in the NSU than in any other car. Certainly it contributes to relaxed and smooth progression.

The ZF power steering is cast in the same mould. You may recall our unbounded enthusiasm for it in the past. Well, nothing has occurred meantime to alter this; it is still one of the best—perhaps even the ultimate—systems around today. It is firm at low speeds so that it is not just a matter of twirling the helm with one finger, yet it is light and positive and works in direct relationship with speed, surface and cornering stress. The brakes, disc all round, are as faultless as the suspension with its long wheel travel and impeccable ride.

Handling is not nearly as front-wheel drive as those of us who were brought up in the Mini syndrome would expect. In fact, it is only in very tight bends with lots of throttle in use that the Ro80 ever reveals through which wheels the rotary is driving. It is extremely quick around any sort of corner, but it does pay to remember that the rear wheels are a long way astern and can be dragged over kerbs or into holes. Lifting off half way through a bend is no more of a hairy experience than it is in a tidy rear-wheel-drive car. We did not meet any corners that fussed the NSU or even gave cause to wonder what was going to happen next; to depart from the bitumen for a journey through the scenery is something a Ro80 driver would really have to work at.

Of course, it is not a cheap car. It never has been, despite a rumoured early intention to sell it—sans power steering, sans semi-automatic—as a sort of Audi-eater. Currently the Ro80 costs £2593. Back in 1968, when it was CAR of the Year, the tag was £2232, so that must make it one of the present-day bargains. ●

DOUGLAS CAUSER, 1970 Model Ro80

'It's the only car I know that is excitingly original, has a reasonable boot, has room for three in the back and yet looks sporty' said **Douglas Causer** when we talked to him about his Ro80. His hobby is cars, and he has had more than the usual experience with the NSU—happy experience, he is quick to stress. His present car has covered 22,000 miles with no problem apart from a faint but aggravating whine from the torque converter.

He finds the roadholding beyond compare, acceleration brisk and cruising speed 'well over the legal limit'. Using 7000rpm he reckons to get 0-60mph in 10sec; in fact he is mystified that road tests show 13sec as the average time taken to reach the same speed, though probably with a lower rev limit. He would appreciate extra power in reserve but wouldn't necessarily use it to the full. A high-mileage driver, he covers about 18 to 20,000 a year, most of it on business in and around Greater London, with the odd monthly trip farther afield. He finds the high fuel

consumption offset by the engine's contentment with two-star petrol.

Enthusiastic and helpful attention is given by the main dealers in London and by the garage in Mitcham where the car was purchased, and Mr Causer has much admiration for them.

The driver's seat tends to slide a bit, although supposedly locked in position. He finds the controls splendid, but the gearlever is just out of easy reach—definitely an individual detail. There are no problems starting from cold with this late-model car, even when it has been left out all night. He would only prefer a three-rotor engine provided its increased mass didn't alter the steering and balance.

Regular passengers have commented on the car's quietness and the ease with which the doors close. Mr Causer feels the optional extra alloy wheels give him even better and safer cornering. He would keep his present car until something went drastically wrong, and would immediately buy any improved version.

DOUGLAS BROWN, 1970 Model Ro80

Douglas Brown has had his Ro80 since June 1970. He considers it to be the best car in the world at any price. The engine is quiet, and he finds the car beautifully smooth and spacious, with fabulous roadholding. He particularly likes the light steering, and thinks that the Ro80 is 'terrifically safe—in fact, the safest car I've ever driven'. He bought it in preference to a Rolls-Royce Silver Shadow after witnessing an accident involving a Ro80 and being mightily impressed by the way the body stood up to frontal impact.

This initial enthusiasm persists despite one change of engine, carried out free of charge. Mr Brown pronounces himself happy with

the importer's explanation that a bad batch of chambers had been machined. The swap took two days.

This demanding owner says he uses all the performance the engine can give him, and makes free use of the gearbox at all times. He thinks the car's 100mph-plus cruising ability at 100+mph is 'fantastic', although he would like more acceleration. He would buy a three-chamber Ro80 if available.

He is also a devotee of the front wheel drive principle, and regards the Ro80 as 'tremendous value for money—a superb example of advanced engineering, with built-in directional stability and immensely impressive total package'.

RICHARD HOPE, 1970 Model Ro80

Richard Hope bought his Ro80 because he admired the engineering concept and the appearance. The Wankel engine fascinated him, and he freely admits that the idea of being a motoring pathfinder appealed to him.

He has had immense satisfaction from the car, and has retained the same model for two years, averaging between 8000 and 10,000 miles a year. He thinks it is a very sound design, but he does criticise some details of the interior. For example, he still finds himself confused by having the horn and windscreen wipers operated by the same stalk. The lack of a parcels shelf is another annoyance. The headlights he finds 'totally inadequate' for the car's performance.

Mr Hope's car is difficult to start when cold, and he complains about the smell from the exhaust when the engine is started. He has grown used to the idea of excessive oil consumption, and comments that if the car doesn't start right away when cold it has to be left for some time before trying again. He has had new ball races fitted to the wheels after 18,000 miles, but doesn't regard this as a serious failing. Nor does a 'bonk' from the front wheels when turning sharply at low speeds alarm him.

He wouldn't buy another one, he says, but neither would he buy a 'less fast' car. He believes all cars will have Wankel engines within 10 years. He mentions a feeling of vulnerability when touring, as service stations that could cope with mechanical trouble in the engine are few and far between.

DR JOHN LINDSAY WILSON, 1968 Model Ro80

Dr John Lindsay Wilson bought his Ro80 after reading complimentary reports and seeing it voted CAR of the Year by CAR magazine. This was one of the early demo models, purchased at a very reasonable price late in 1968. It has left hand drive.

Despite having had a lot of trouble, he considers it easily the best car he has driven over many varied years of motoring experience. He is still extremely enthusiastic about its roadholding ability. He finds the steering superb, likes the gearchange, with reservation, and says the car is ideal for long journeys, being both quiet and comfortable. His dislikes include a disastrous rate of petrol consumption; he spent £50 on a new set of carburettors, thinking they were the root of the problem, but unfortunately has found little improvement. The car is driven mainly in town, and although the engine is quiet at high speeds the lower gears which one is forced to use in town cause rather a high noise level.

Servicing and garage attention have been more than satisfactory, which is just as well as two new engines have been fitted during the car's lifetime. Both exchanges were performed with the minimum of fuss and at no charge. Dr Wilson still finds acceleration poor for a car of this price, but says the cruising speed of 90-100mph is effortless. The confusing array of knobs and switches on the dashboard of this early car have no labels or symbols to define them, but, this apart, he likes the interior layout. There has been much difficulty starting from cold, particularly in winter, as well as a danger of flooding the carburettors. He has now learnt the procedure necessary to avoid this. Dr Wilson questions the comprehensiveness of the stocks of spares carried by main dealers; he has experienced delays in the supply of main engine fittings. He would prefer the car with improved petrol consumption and an even quieter engine.

He has owned BMWs and Rover 2000s, never buying the same car twice. For this reason alone, he doubts whether he would buy another Ro80.

JAMES BRAMWELL, 1971 Model Ro80

Despite warnings of engine problems from a friend in the trade, **James Bramwell** bought a low-mileage second-hand Ro80 because he felt it was a handsome design and the price was right. He had driven the model previously and had fallen in love with its smoothness and excellent steering.

He has since covered 10,000 miles with little trouble, using the car for the rush-hour crawl into London two or three days a week, for long business journeys and weekend family trips, towing a boat. The power steering, he says, is exceptional and road-holding first class: 'There always seems to be plenty in reserve if I take a corner too fast'. He finds the seating comfortable and the car very relaxing for long distances, with noticeable freedom from noise and other adverse effects on the driver and passengers. Petrol consumption in town is poor at 17 to 18mpg, and though the semi-automatic gearbox is quite acceptable he finds the change soggy and sloppy.

His only real let-down with his car was when an oil seal on the torque converter failed. Although it was just out of warranty, an NSU representative agreed that repairs should be made free of charge, which Mr Bramwell felt as generous. NSU even agreed to go half-way on the additional costs that he had incurred because of the failure.

Acceleration up to 40mph doesn't match the car's image, he says. Driving hard, the engine in the lower gears is noisy, but not alarmingly so, whereas at higher speeds the car is smooth and quiet. The interior layout he finds very good, apart from the heating system, which is 'difficult to understand, too complicated and not as efficient as it should be'. There have been no problems when starting from cold. He would certainly buy another Ro80, but would like to see the gearchange improved and performance uprated.

CHRISTOPHER STOREY, 1971 Model Ro80

Christopher Storey, who lives in Haywards Heath, is on his second Ro80, a company car ostensibly provided for his father, who is chairman of the family import/export business. Mr Storey also drives a +2 Lotus Elan. He was disappointed with his first NSU from a mechanical point of view; in fact he says the company would not have bought the second one without the categorical assurance of the importers that it would be far more reliable than the first four-plug version they owned. They had three engines in the first car. Each of the two replacements was fitted free of charge.

Mr Storey says he fully expected trouble with such a radically new car. On the whole he is more than satisfied with the Ro80 in general terms. He found it impossible to drive the first car with the choke out, and starting the old four-plug engine from cold was a tricky operation, the engine backfiring and generating an awful lot of smoke. The new two-plug version is a much easier car to start and to drive, but he points out that the gearbox should be used to keep the revs up; the plugs oil up if the car is driven as a full automatic. He also complains of sudden failure of the front seat backrests. These fly back a couple of inches every now and then—usually at awkward times, such as during high speed cornering or under acceleration. The seats on his car have been stripped, but no reason has been found for the trouble, which remains uncured.

A surprising complaint is that the handling in corners is not as good as expected. According to Mr Storey, a lightness is evident in the steering, indicating to him the onset of understeer at what he would consider to be low cornering speeds. All in all he is very impressed with the car and glad the company bought it in preference to the Silver Shadow which they were contemplating. He would like more power from the engine, if possible. ●

NSU RO80 FINAL REPORT AT 23,000 MILES

By Stuart Bladon

Engine stripped down, inspection and measurement of seal wear. Personal opinions as we say a sad farewell to our Ro80.

It took about an hour to remove radiator, fan, carburettor and other accessories, allowing the engine to be lifted out

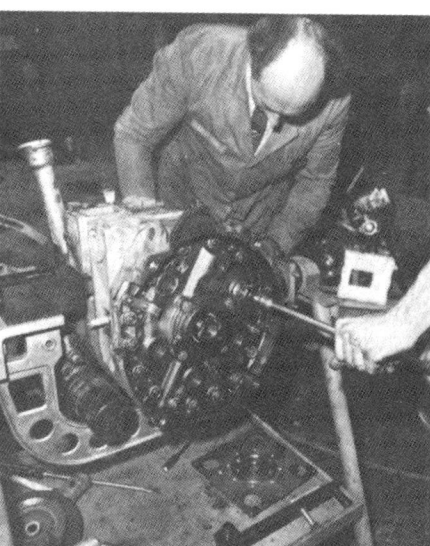

Long bolts securing the two main parts of the engine are held at one end, as they are splined in the centre, and their nuts at the other end are undone

When the front end cover, incorporating the sump, was lifted off, a trace of metal swarf wa. seen lying on the rotor

LAST February a "half-time" report on our NSU Ro80 was published at 14,000 miles. A further 9,000 miles have been covered, taking the total to just over 23,000, and by the end of last month it had completed a year of service and so is now to be replaced. This report is therefore the farewell story, so before going on to deal with the details of its behaviour in the second half, it is appropriate to comment on the Ro80 in general, and to answer the all-important question of whether I would choose to have one again.

It is as a long-journey car that the Ro80 is in its element, cruising fast and tirelessly and carrying its occupants in great comfort. As a driver's car it offers one of the best power steering systems, retaining superb sensitivity and general feel of the car while having the advantage of assistance for hard cornering and manoeuvring. On corners it tends to roll quite a lot, and there is marked understeer, but it is one of those cars in which the driver can feel exactly how it is responding and this, coupled with exceptional adhesion on slippery surfaces, gives an extremely high safety factor. The brakes are also excellent, taking fairly firm pedal loads but giving reassuring fade-free response.

In addition to first class handling and controls, the driving position is good, and when I come back to it after driving various Road Test cars, the Ro80 always seems so controllable that reacquaintance comes as a pleasure. As well as providing the quiet vibration-free running which is such a relaxation when cruising fast, the Wankel engine contributes to the good handling by its relatively low weight. Starting has always been prompt, with seldom need for more than two turns of the starter and, although it takes some while to reach full working temperature, the engine responds at once after a cold start. Obviously it helps here that there are no tight-fitting pistons in cylinders.

In particular, the Ro80 is an outstanding bad weather car — be it torrential rain, snow and ice on the road, or blustery side winds, it treats them all with contempt enabling one to drive with a feeling of great confidence in the car's abilities. The good visibility ensured by vigorous wipers and an unusually quick and effective rear window heating element are a great help, and the intermittent wiper provision is useful in drizzle. For night driving there are excellent halogen lamps with a sharp cut-off to ensure that oncoming drivers are not dazzled, and standard equipment foglamps — also with halogen bulbs — mounted beneath the bumper, take much of the misery out of fog driving.

Semi-automatic transmission is fitted, in which there is a torque converter and three-speed manual gearchange, clutch operation being automatic as soon as the gear lever knob is touched. Many drivers find they take a long while to get used to this arrangement, but in the end most of them join

The rear drive plate unbolts from the torque converter, and transmission, brakes and drive shafts are not disturbed

For dismantling, the engine is held in a clamp which can be revolved giving access to either end. First, the front end cover is removed

This gives access to the oil heat exchanger and pump gear which are also taken off

The engine is then rotated and the end cover is lifted off revealing the rotor. There are no gaskets — all sealing is by O-rings

Rotor tip seals were removed and measured, and wear found to be within very reasonable limits. In this view the seal has been raised, and the spring is revealed behind it

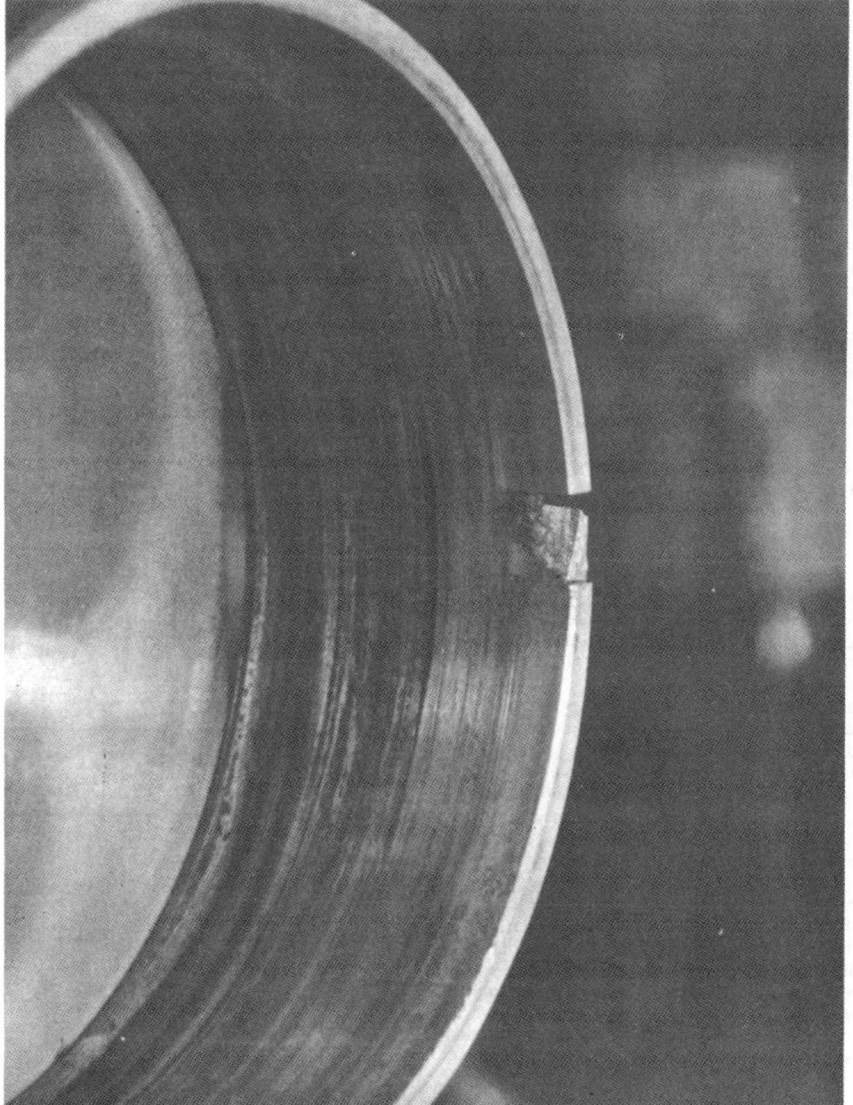

Close-up view of the front bearing, showing deep score marks. The crankshaft was also lightly grooved

NSU RO80

me in liking it. I drive it like an ordinary three-speed manual car, with first gear used for starts from rest, the only difference being that there is no clutch pedal to operate. As the clutch is the main chore of a manual transmission, the arrangement works well. Also, as so many automatic transmissions leave the unfortunate engine struggling in top gear on hills and in acceleration unless you work a selector lever, it makes sense to take on the job of selecting the right gears for the car yourself, while still enjoying the convenience of a torque converter for smoothness and traffic work.

When the car is at rest, and the driver releases the gearknob, the clutch engages at once causing a sharp thump. This can be reduced by adjustment of the screw on the regulator valve under the bonnet, but the jolt is prevented by engaging first gear slightly before coming to rest and releasing the gearknob while the car is still moving; alternatively, the lazy driver stays in second while in town.

Personal enjoyment and convenience of the car have been enhanced by a Philips RN312 AM radio and cassette stereo unit which gives wonderful reproduction from its door-mounted speakers when playing cassettes, but tends to pick up some engine interference when tuned to a fairly low-strength radio signal, as is Radio 3; and by a Carphones radio telephone. Operative in London and within a 30-mile radius of Luton and Birmingham, this covers the areas in which the car has spent much of its time, and it has been a great help on numerous occasions to be able to ring up and keep in touch without having to stop and waste time at a call box — always assuming one could find a call box which the vandals have left in operation. Carphones headquarters are at 65a Station Road, Chingford, Essex.

Snags and weak points of the Ro80 are few, worst being the exhaust smoke during the first mile or two of running after a cold start. Originally this was very bad, to the point of being an embarrassment; it is now much less, yet there is still quite a noticeable puff of blue on accelerating during the first minute or so after starting up. I am also slightly unimpressed by the rather plain facia treatment, and there have been numerous rattles and creaks from the facia which have tended to get worse with time. One grows accustomed to the slow engine response, and when waiting for the opportunity to cross a busy road, for example, it is best to hold the car with the left foot on the brake leaving the right one free to build up revs against the torque converter and thus avoid the momentary delay which otherwise occurs. However, there are many times when it would help to have rather more acceleration in hand for quick, safe overtaking.

Considering how little it has changed over the years, with all development work being concentrated on engine reliability, it is remarkable how well the original design of the Ro80 still stands up to the test of time. It remains a distinguished futuristic-looking car, whose appearance grows in appeal when you live with the car. Coming to the vital question of how I would respond to the prospect of a further 20,000 miles with the Ro80, I can say positively that I would have been delighted to do so and only the fact that we feel there is little more to be learned from further experience of the car enforces the end of the test. This presumes, of course, that reliability of the Wankel engine is at last established, and this we believe to be the case.

In apparent contradiction of this, it was almost immediately after publication of the 14,000-mile report in the 30 March issue, that a slight metallic noise was detected from the engine. It was noticed only on sharp acceleration, and sounded almost like "pinking" experienced with a conventional engine. The noise was so slight that it was difficult to be sure it was there, but it was decided that at least we would "keep an ear on it"

A long period of trouble-free running ensued, in which a routine service was the only entry in the car's record book in 6,000 miles, but by the time the car returned from a trip to the Belgian GP, the mileometer now indicating over 20,000 miles, there was no more doubt about that metallic noise from the engine. It was no longer a slight jingle, but a definite knock. By an ironic chance this was in June, and coincided with a press conference given in London by Audi-NSU at which details were given of all the modifications introduced to obtain extended life from the NSU Wankel engine.

Most of the work had been concentrated on developing new shapes and materials for the tip and side seals of the rotor to reduce the rate of wear. Dr. Walter Froede, head of the Research Department at Neckarsulm, claimed that since introduction of ferrotic seals early in 1970, wear in 60,000 miles had been reduced to only 15 per cent of permissible total limits, and in theory old seals could even be re-used in new engines. After this and other development work, he explained, the rotor bearing became the cause of most of the warranty claims. Modifications to the crankshaft drillings increased oil flow by six times, and eliminated bearing failure even at speeds of up to 9,500 rpm.

When the opportunity came for questions, I established that the new crankshaft had gone into production at about the time when my car was built. Mike Hoppis, technical manager of Audi-NSU in Gt. Britain, then came down to the basement where I had left my car, and confirmed that the noise was that of a failed bearing.

A few days later the Ro80 was due at my local Audi-NSU agent at Boreham Wood in Hertfordshire for routine service, and I handed it in much as might an unsuspecting owner, without mentioning what had been diagnosed. On return there was a certain atmosphere of concern, and I was told with the usual drama that I had "big trouble". They had diagnosed a failed bearing and *possibly* a seal as well — this later turned out to be wrong. I was quoted £260 for a new engine, plus £60-80 for labour. Almost as an afterthought I was told that although the mileage indicated was now over 20,000 it *might* be covered under the warranty

The new crankshaft (installed) is compared with the old one (right), with different drillings. In the new crankshaft, oil is forced round the bearing to find its way back again, and lubrication greatly increased

which extends for the first 18,000 miles. From correspondence with readers and talks with the concessionaires, I am confident that it would have been covered by the warranty, had it happened to a man who had paid good money for one of these cars.

To learn more about the engine problem, I arranged to take the Ro80 — it was still eminently driveable — down to Shoreham to see the engine stripped down. Sharp at 9 a.m., it was run into the repair shop, surrounded by packing cases, as Audi-NSU were getting ready for their move to the new headquarters at Dunstable, and at 10 a.m., after preliminary investigation, work started. The whole strip-down process for the Ro80 engine is shown in picture form on these pages, and there is much to be said for the simplicity of a design which allows the engine to be taken out, stripped to the last nut and O-ring, and put back again ready for full performance, all in the

COST of OWNERSHIP

Running Costs		Life in Miles	Cost per 10,000 Miles
			£ p
One gallon of 2-star fuel, average cost today 34p		18	188.80
One pint of top-up oil, average cost today 21p		600	3.50
Front disc brake pads (set of 4)		20,000	3.92
Rear disc brake pads (set of 4)		25,000	3.12
Michelin XAS tyres (set of 4 changed F to R)		35,000	13.10
Service (main interval and actual cost incurred)		3,000	35.28
Total			**247.72**
Running cost per mile: 2.5p			
Approx. standing charges per year	* Insurance		52.50
	Tax		25.00
Depreciation	Price when new		2,584
	Trade-in cash value (approx.)		1,700
	Typical advertised price (current)		2,000
			884

Total cost per mile (based on cash value) 12.1p

* Insurance cost is based on garaging in Hertfordshire, nett after deduction of 65 per cent no claims bonus; named and approved drivers over 30 only; compulsory £50 excess; Group IV.

A form of scissors clamps are used to hold the rings in place, ready for the rotor to be lowered on to them

Tightening of the main crankshaft securing nut is done by a long-handle torque wrench

day. Even with a hold-up because someone had "borrowed" the chains for the engine hoist, it took only just over an hour to remove the engine from the car, cleared of all its accessories.

A further hour and a quarter saw it stripped down to the centre plate. When the rotor was revealed, the first thing spotted was a small piece of metal swarf which had broken off the failed bearing, but this had not caused any damage to other components. The tip seals were removed and measured, giving a reading of 8.15mm. This compares with the new engine tolerance of between 8.2 and 8.3mm. Minimum acceptable size is 7.7mm, so on the basis of 0.15mm wear for 20,000 miles — this itself assumes that the seals originally fitted were at the upper limit of size tolerance — this gives a theoretical life of 80,000 miles. Of course, it does not necessarily follow that the same rate of wear would continue throughout.

Further dismantling allowed the rotor to be lifted off, and the crankshaft was removed revealing a bearing which had very obviously run and caused shallow scores in the crankshaft. More important, it was confirmed that the crankshaft was of the old type, made before the modification to increase oil flow.

After lunch the job of reassembly started, with new bearings, crankshaft, rotors and seals; work continued steadily for just over three hours, by which time the engine had been rebuilt and installed in the car. It started at once and after tuning carburettors and setting ignition we went straight off for a test run; again, the great advantage of the Wankel, that it needs no running-in, was enjoyed.

Performance figures, taken after the stripdown were not as good as those timed for the 14,000-mile report, but still show a small improvement over the original Road Test figures. The rev counter has started to read high, restricting the maxima in the gears and taking the edge off the top-end performance.

Apart from this engine work, there have been no other faults, and indeed reliability of the car as a whole, excluding its unusual power unit, has been outstanding. At 20,000 miles the original front disc brake pads were replaced although the 6mm thickness of friction material remaining still left ample safe margin. The Michelin XAS tyres give superb grip in all conditions, and the original set still have plenty of tread left. They look like lasting to 35,000 miles, as originally predicted.

If the Wankel engine problems have finally been overcome, the Ro80 is certainly a long-life reliable vehicle; and it really does seem that at last the engine is up to the dependability of the rest of the car.

PERFORMANCE CHECK

Maximum speeds

Gear	mph		kph		rpm	
	R/T	Staff	R/T	Staff	R/T	Staff
Top (mean)	107	110	172	177	5,750	6,500
(best)	108	110	174	177	5,800	6,500
2nd	80	72	129	116	6,600	6,600
1st	47	43	76	69	6,600	6,600

Standing ¼-mile,	R/T:	19.2 sec	72 mph
	Staff:	19.2 sec	72 mph
Standing kilometre	R/T:	36.1 sec	91 mph
	Staff:	35.5 sec	91 mph

Acceleration,	R/T	5.2	7.1	10.1	13.9	18.3	24.8	34.8	48.9
	Staff	4.3	6.3	9.9	13.4	17.6	24.7	34.5	48.7
Time in seconds	0								
True speed mph		30	40	50	60	70	80	90	100
Indicated speed MPH	R/T:	36	46	56	66	77	88	100	110
Indicated speed MPH	Staff:	33	43	54	65	76	87	97	108

Speed range, Gear Ratios and Time in seconds

Mph	Top		2nd		1st	
	R/T	Staff	R/T	Staff	R/T	Staff
10-30	6.2	6.5	4.7	4.7	4.0	3.4
20-40	8.0	8.0	5.9	5.8	4.0	3.8
30-50	8.4	9.3	6.2	6.5	—	—
40-60	10.2	10.9	6.9	6.7	—	—
50-70	12.5	12.9	8.7	7.6	—	—
60-80	16.0	14.5	—	—	—	—
70-90	19.4	16.8	—	—	—	—
80-100	24.1	23.5	—	—	—	—

Fuel Consumption

Overall mpg,	R/T:	18.2 mpg (15.6 litres/100km)
	Staff:	17.8 mpg (15.9 litres/100km)

NOTE: "R/T" denotes performance figures for Ro80 tested in *Autocar* of 1 February 1968.

Yesterday's car of tomorrow

Seven years ago NSU were a small German firm producing only rear engined baby cars. So imagine the incredulity in motoring circles when they became the first company in the world to put a Wankel engined car into production by introducing the futuristic looking Ro80 luxury saloon.

The Ro80's introduction was greeted with a mixture of delight and plain scepticism, and the car has maintained this chequered reputation to the present day. Although NSU had been testing rotary engines for ten years before the Ro80 came out, the early years of the Ro80 were plagued with engine failures due to rapid wear of the rotor seals. As a gesture of faith to their customers NSU generously replaced engines long after Warranties had expired; a gesture which was driving them

to the brink of bankruptcy before they were taken under the wing of Volkswagen in a series of mergers that formed Volkswagen Audi/NSU.

In recent years the engine problems have been completely solved, only for the black shadow of soaring fuel prices to cast more gloom over the car. Wankel engines are renowned for consuming more fuel than their conventional equivalents, a failing which obviously assumes much more significance now than ever.

By virtue of its luxurious nature, NSU have always had their car compared with large and costly to run conventional luxury saloons, such as XJ Jaguars and BMWs, even though its engine size is only equivalent to a two litre conventional unit. In luxury car terms its fuel consumption is quite com-

parable, and to make the car even more tempting NSU recently cut the price by £200 to £3531 and extended the Warranty on the whole car to two years/24,000 miles, demonstrating their faith in the power unit. It is now a highly competitive contender in the luxury car market.

Style and finish

The lines of the Ro80 have been scarcely changed since the car was introduced, yet its clean uncluttered styling still turns heads and its shape can still be fairly called futuristic.

The car was wind tunnel designed for maximum aerodynamic efficiency. The result is a wedge-shaped body that presses the nose down onto the road. Similar use of this

aerodynamically proven "wedge" design can be seen in many Formula One racing cars.

Most noticeable is the complete absence from the exterior of glittery chrome trim and flashy badges. Wrap around bumpers front and rear are of stainless steel as is the window edging. A simple NSU badge graces the front and Ro80 is signed on the rear; nothing else interrupts the smoothness of the lines. The whole car is set off perfectly by the elegant forged aluminium road wheels which are included in the standard specification.

Accommodation

The already large Ro80 is made even roomier by virtue of being front wheel drive, with the resultant absence of gearbox and transmission tunnel from the interior. Legroom and headroom for the tallest passengers front and rear is enormous

The seats are cloth covered, the front seats being large and soft with plenty of padding round the sides for firm lateral support. The rear bench is shaped to seat two, but with the central arm-rest folded away a third person can easily be accommodated. Both front seats can be fully reclined, and although the driver's seat does not have any extra adjustment for height, a good driving position can be found by drivers of differing stature.

The boot of 20.5 cubic feet is large and deep even though the vertical spare wheel fills one corner. Accessibility under the forward hinging bonnet is good — although most owners would not want to do more than routine checks on the thoroughly puzzling engine that sits there.

Equipment

The interior of the Ro80 is finished in a typically plain German manner. Owners of British luxury cars like to see plenty of polished walnut cappings on their doors and dashboards. Germans, it seems, even though they are buying expensive cars, like the simple look.

So the facia of the Ro80 is finished in plain black leathercloth, with just four dials sitting in front of the driver. Two column stalks operate indicators, headlamp flashers, dip and wipers/washers.

A weak point of the car is its ventilation system. It has been criticised in the past and as a result improved by NSU, but it is still not up to scratch. There are fresh air vents in the centre of the facia and under the scuttle, but they rely simply on ram pressure which does not reach satisfactory cooling proportions until the car is travelling fast. A fresh air booster fan would be a great asset.

The list of standard equipment on the Ro80 is very comprehensive. It includes twin foglamps under the bumpers to supplement the already excellent four halogen headlights; reversing lights, rear screen demister, hazard flashers, child-proof rear locks, head rests, door mounted outside mirror, locking fuel cap, and the very efficient Toric inertia reel safety belts. The only extras on our car were a rear fog lamp and an electric sliding sun roof. This latter was very pleasant in warm weather (coming to the rescue of the poor ventilation) but when opened fully wind turbulence could make for some unpleasant buffeting effects inside the car at certain speeds.

Large engine compartment houses the rotary unit under an array of pipework

Comfortable rear seating has good legroom while reclining front seats are well shaped

Low rear sill allows easy access to large carpeted boot containing covered spare

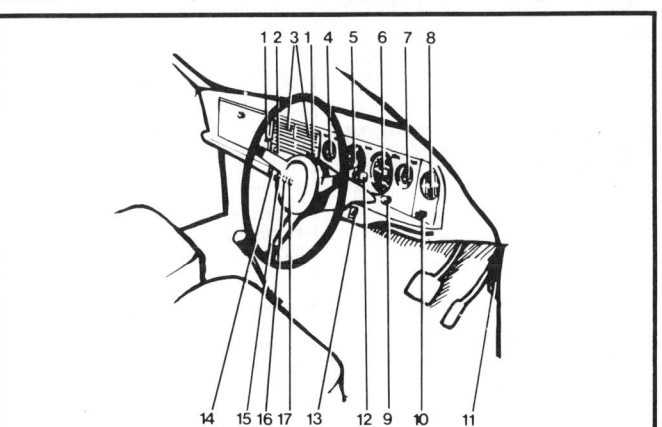
1. Air regulators. 2. Heater controls. 3. Ventilation slats. 4. Fuel and temperature gauges. 5. Tachometer. 6. Speedometer. 7. Clock. 8. Vent. 9. Trip reset/rheostat. 10. Lights master switch. 11. Bonnet release. 12. Wiper/screenwashers/horn. 13. Ignition. 14. Dipswitch/headlamp flashers. 15. Cigar lighter. 16. Heated rear window/foglamps. 17. Hazard warning.

Performance

A brief description of the Wankel rotary engine may interest those who are unfamiliar with the unit. It is still not widely used, only NSU and the Japanese Mazda company using it in production models.

The essential advantage of the Wankel is its smoothness and flexibility of running, stemming from the fact that it has only three moving parts instead of some 160 in conventional piston engines. The Ro80 has a twin rotor engine, each rotor being a curved sided triangle that rotates inside a combustion chamber. The normal four stroke cycle takes place inside each chamber, and the power is applied to each face of the rotor in turn, spinning it round. The engine has a power output of 115 bhp from a total chamber volume of only 997.5 ccs and runs on two star fuel. It also emits very low levels of exhaust pollution.

The engine starts instantaneously if the correct procedure is followed, and runs perfectly from cold. Noticeable immediately is its smoothness as it whirls up toward 6700 rpm where a warning buzzer sounds to stop drivers over-revving (a cause of early engine failures).

NSU have fitted the car with three speed semi-automatic transmission of a type that is used on only a few other cars. The driver still changes gear with a floor mounted lever and this lever also has a solenoid switch in the knob to disengage the clutch on gear-changing, obviating the need for a clutch pedal. However there is also a torque converter as in conventional automatics, so a driver can start in top (or any) gear, letting the torque converter do its job allowing the car to pull slowly away.

Because it is such a rarely used system it takes some getting used to. First attempts at driving often result in horrifying clutch judder because a lazy hand is resting on the gear lever, or gear changes may be made with the left foot banging down on an imaginary clutch which turns out to be the brake pedal! But a day or so's driving and one is at home with the system. Although a semi-automatic lets a driver make full use of the flexible engine by either pressing on through the gears or being lazy and staying in top, NSU might widen the appeal of the car if they gave an alternative manual transmission.

On paper the Ro80 is not an especially quick car; some of its neighbours in the £3500+ bracket being well able to better its 0-60 mph time of 12.8 seconds and top speed of 110 mph. But on the

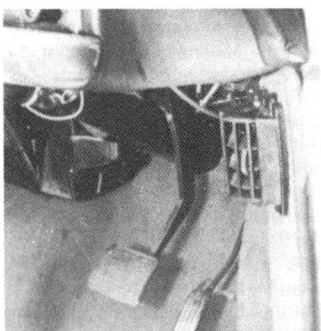

Fresh air vents are not good enough

Rear end design is uncluttered

road the Ro80 is deceptively fast and delightful to drive simply because it is so quiet, probably the quietest car we have driven including such masters of noise abatement as the XJ series Jaguars. Whispering down a highway in virtually complete silence one needs to check the speedometer to believe one is really doing 100 mph. There is no engine noise from the Wankel unit and scarcely any wind noise from the efficient body shape.

Road holding

Sustained silent high-speed cruising is the Ro80's forte, not just because of the silence but also because of the car's superb ride comfort. It rides in a stable fashion, solid as a rock on the road and unaffected by side winds.

For a big car it can also be hustled quite quickly through twisting roads. It is so well set-up that one does not notice that it is front wheel driven. There is no characteristically fierce self centring of the steering wheel and lifting off through bends does not produce the normal "tucking in" of the nose. All the way through corners the car's attitude is strictly neutral. Although there is a fair amount of body roll, the limits of adhesion are very high.

The ZF power steering is faultless, giving good feel at speed when it is needed, and plenty of assistance for low speed manoeuvring. The brakes are discs all round with good stopping power and no snatching. The handbrake operates via two small drums built onto the rear discs.

The costs

There is no way that the Ro80 will be a cheap car to run, but one assumes that buyers with £3531 to spend can afford a car that returns 15.5 mpg overall, and 18.0 when cruising. Insurance at

Group 6 is similar to most of its rivals. The 24-month Warranty is undoubtedly quite a bonus, Rolls-Royce being the only other company to offer it on an entire car, and Mazda offering a similar term on the mechanics of their Wankel cars. With a Warranty this long one might look a little more easily at spares that include spark plugs for £3 plus each, an exhaust system at well over £90, and drive shafts at £70 plus.

The alternatives

Mazda's top Wankel saloon is the RX4 2.6 at £2176, but anyone contemplating alternatives to the elegant Ro80 would certainly be put off by its fussy Japanese styling even if its performance is good.

Price rivals to the Ro80 must be the BMW 520 at £3436, large, comfortable and with similar performance, but not quite the roominess or style of the Ro80; the Jaguar XJ6 was once its obvious competitor, but British Leyland price rises and the Ro80's price cut have widened the gap to £795 in favour of the NSU. The smallest Mercedes, the 230.4 at £3825 is another car worth considering, as might be the much cheaper Opel Commodore GS coupé at £3150.

Verdict

We can only criticise minor features of the Ro80, such as its ventilation and below par performance. It is a fabulous car to drive, one of the most relaxing long distance cars around. It is expensive, both to buy and to run, but we think that it stands up well to comparison with others at the price. However it is hard to see a future at present for the Wankel in anything other than this luxury form where the fuel consumption penalty is not so critical. After all it is equivalent to a two litre car and only returns 18 miles per gallon!

NSU Ro80 £3531

Importer: NSU (GB) Ltd., Volkswagen House, Brighton Road, Purley, Surrey.

Performance
Maximum speed: 110 mph
Maximum in 2nd: 79 mph
Maximum in 1st: 47 mph
Speedometer error:
2 percent fast at 60 mph

Acceleration
0-30 mph: 4.3 secs
0-40 mph: 6.4 secs
0-50 mph: 9.4 secs
0-60 mph: 12.8 secs
0-70 mph: 17.2 secs
0-80 mph: 24.0 secs

Fuel consumption
Full test: 15.5 mpg
Touring: 18.0 mpg
Tank holds: 18 galls
Range: 296 miles
Fuel grade: 2 star
Fuel for 15,000 miles: £450

Specification
Engine: Twin rotor Wankel rotary engine
No. of cylinders: 2
Capacity: 2 x 497.5 cc (equivalent to 1990 cc)
Compression ratio: 9 to 1
Carburation: Solex 32 DT1 TS
Maximum power: 115 bhp DIN at 5500 rpm
Maximum torque: 121 lbs/ft DIN at 4500 rpm
Cooling: Water
Main bearings: 2

Transmission
Clutch: Single dry plate with torque converter

Gearbox: Three speed all-synchromesh
Ratios: 2.056, 1.208, 0.788 to 1
Final drive: 4.88 to 1
Mph per 1000 rpm in top gear: 18.6

Steering: Rack and pinion
Power: Yes
Turns, lock to lock: 3.7
Turning circle: 37 ft

Suspension
Front: Independent, MacPherson struts, lower wishbones, anti-roll bar
Rear: Independent, semi-trailing arms, coil springs

Brakes: Twin circuit servo assisted
Front: 11.2 ins discs
Rear: 10.7 ins discs
Wheels: 14 x 5 ins light alloy
Tyres: 175 x 14 radial ply
Body construction: Steel unitary

Weight: 24 cwt
Distribution (front/rear): 63/37 percent
NCC recommended towing weight: 18 cwt
Payload: 992 lbs

Servicing
Recommended service interval: 5000 miles
Standard charge, labour only: £7.25

Parts costs
Front wing: £31.12
Frong brake pads (4): £12.07
Exhaust system: £97.91
Clutch unit: £51.86
Replacement engine: £432.79
Replacement gearbox: £227.84

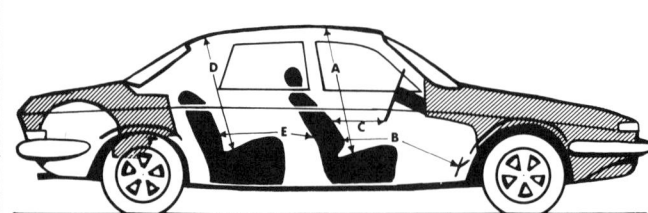

A: 36 ins. B: 33.5 to 42 ins. C: 12.5 to 22 ins. D: 33 ins. E: 22.5 to 31 ins. Length: 190 ins. Wheelbase: 112.7 ins. Track (front): 58.5 ins. Track (rear): 56.5 ins. Width: 69.5 ins. Height: 55.5 ins. Interior width: 56 ins.

HOW IT COMPARES

Price	Car	cc	Speed (mph)	touring (mph)	0-60 secs	30-50 in top	Interior width (ins)	Boot (cu ft)	Length (ins)
£3150	Opel Commodore GS Coupé	2784	120	23	9.3	5.6	59.0	11.8	181.3
£3436	BMW 520	1990	107	23	11.9	10.8	54.3	21.9	182
£3531	**NSU Ro80**	**1990**	**110**	**18**	**12.8**	**9.0**	**56.0**	**20.5**	**190**
£3825	Mercedes Benz 230.4	2307	106	25	12.7	10.3	58.0	20.5	184
£4326	Jaguar XJ6	4235	121	18	9.0	6.5	52.5	17.0	189.5

NSU Ro80

1,990 c.c.

After six years, the Ro80 is as good as ever, despite the high cost and heavy fuel consumption. Good performance and superb ride and handling matched with excellent brakes. The car's long-legged cruising ability is complemented by very low levels of road and wind noise

The exceptionally large windscreen and uncluttered side windows give the occupants really good vision; there are small fog lamps below the bumper, and all the other driving lamps are under a single-piece glass

IN THE 100 or so years' history of the motor car, engineers have been seeking some alternative means of turning the wheels. But in practically every case, they had to admit that there seemed nothing as good as the straightforward reciprocating engine, running on a petrol-air mixture. The rotary engine in various forms had seemed an attractive proposition, but the practical difficulties overwhelmed the drawing-board designs. The man who found the answer was Dr Felix Wankel, and the short period since the little single-rotor NSU Spider was launched and today, practically every large motor manufacturer has given serious thought to this engine. In Japan, Mazda are making their RX range of models, while General Motors in the USA are geared up to produce their Wankel-engined Vega.

It was back in February 1968 that we were able to carry out our first full Road Test of the Ro80 in Italy, and we were impressed. But even in those halcyon days, we criticized the car's poor fuel consumption. Now the price of petrol makes the Ro80, itself a very expensive 2-litre car in Britain, something of a rich man's means of transport.

Although the basic design of the Ro80 has altered little in the past seven years, its body shape and styling is showing that same ageless quality as that of the Citroën DS series. NSU were able to design the car without any preconceived ideas; for them it was physically the largest vehicle they had ever attempted. The bodyshape and its aerodynamic qualities were developed by the Technical University Research Institute at Stuttgart, and the very distinctive appearance has resulted in complete stability at high speeds coupled with an almost total lack of wind noise.

The twin-rotor engine has a swept volume of 997 c.c. per shaft revolution, but for taxation and registration purposes, the capacity is given as a nominal 1,990 c.c., which is more in keeping with its power output. From the very outset, NSU were keen to "sell" the idea of the rotary engine to the United States, and now all production cars are fitted with the full US Federal detox equipment, which includes an air pump, a mass of air bleed pipes and various solenoids. To achieve the anti-pollution standards required was something of a triumph, for the Ro80 has a total-loss lubrication system, which means that oil as well as the exhaust gases have to be dealt with.

Despite all the detox equip-ment, the power output has been increased slightly, from 113·5 bhp (DIN) to 115 bhp, both at 5,500 rpm, while there is also a marginal increase in torque, up from 117 to 121 lb.ft., again with no change in engine speed at 4,500 rpm. The latest engines have only a single sparking plug per rotor; the earlier ones had dual ignition. A single twin-choke Solex 32 DTITS carburettor, with an automatic choke, is now used, in place of the two progressive twin choke Solexes.

Starting from cold never presented any problems, with the automatic choke being set by pressing the accelerator pedal to the floor once. Initial idle is very fast, around 2,500 rpm, but this can be reduced by tapping the accelerator pedal with the toe, which brings the engine speed down to around 1,000 rpm. Once warmed through, the engine normally idles at around 500 rpm in neutral, and at 350 to 400 rpm in gear. Unless the car can be driven fairly briskly from cold, it takes a noticeably long time to warm up.

Transmission is by means of an all-direct three-speed gearbox, with a Fichtel and Sachs torque converter with a stall ratio of 2·3 to 1. Between the torque converter and the gearbox is a servo-operated single dry plate clutch, controlled by a

NSU Ro80

solenoid worked by a micro-switch in the gear lever knob. NSU term the three gears "performance ranges", and in practice, one soon learns to treat them as such, rather than as a conventional gearbox.

To move off, the gear lever is moved into the desired range and the accelerator pressed. With the torque converter cushioning any tendency to snatch, move off is very smooth. To change gear, the lever is simply moved. With the microswitch in the gear lever knob, the driver very soon learns not to drive resting his hand on it! Past experience has taught us that it is essential to get the correct tick-over and clutch vacuum servo settings to achieve smooth changes. If they

Comparisons

MAXIMUM SPEED MPH

Audi 100 Coupé S........(£3,070) 112
NSU Ro80 ....(£3,596) 110
Mercedes-Benz 230/4....(£3,896) 110
Ford Granada GXL (A)....(£2,807) 106
Peugeot 504 inj (A) ....(£2,413) 96

0–60 MPH, SEC

Audi 100 Coupé S ....10·6
Ford Granada GXL (A) ....11·9
NSU Ro80 ....13·1
Mercedes-Benz 230/4 ....13·4
Peugeot 504 inj (A) ....14·8

STANDING ¼-MILE, SEC

Audi 100 Coupé S ....17·7
Ford Granada GXL (A) ....18·1
NSU Ro80.......................19·1
Mercedes-Benz 230/4 ....19·2
Peugeot 504 inj (A) ....20·4

OVERALL MPG

Audi 100 Coupé S ....23·6
Mercedes-Benz 230/4 ....22·7
Peugeot 504 inj (A) ....19·9
Ford Granada GXL (A) ....19·1
NSU Ro80 ....16·0

Performance

ACCELERATION SECONDS

True speed mph	Time in secs	Car speedo mph
30	4·5	33
40	6·5	44
50	9·6	56
60	13·1	66
70	17·4	78
80	24·2	89
90	34·6	99

Standing ¼-mile
19·1sec 84 mph

Standing kilometre
35·0sec 97 mph

Mileage recorder:
3 per cent over-reading

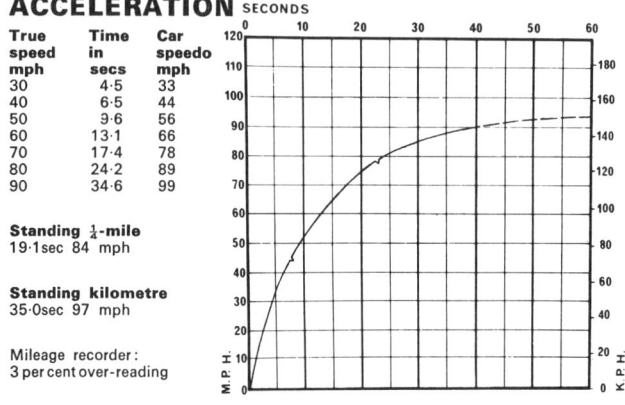

GEAR RATIOS AND TIME IN SEC

mph	Top (3·84–8·83)	3rd (5·88–13·52)
10–30	5·8	4·6
20–40	7·0	5·8
30–50	8·4	6·1
40–60	10·3	6·4
50–70	12·3	7·5
60–80	14·5	—
70–90	18·3	—

GEARING
(with 175×14in. tyres)

Top ....18·6 mph per 1,000 rpm
2nd ....12·1 mph per 1,000 rpm
1st ....7·1 mph per 1,000 rpm

MAXIMUM SPEEDS

Gear	mph	kph	rpm
Top (mean)	110	177	5,910
(best)	112	180	6,022
2nd	79	127	6,500
1st	46	74	6,500

BRAKES

FADE (from 70 mph in neutral)
Pedal load for 0·5g stops in lb

1	35	6	37
2	35	7	37
3	35	8	37
4	35	9	37
5	35	10	37

RESPONSE (from 30 mph in neutral)

Load	g	Distance
20lb	0·30	100ft
40lb	0·52	58ft
60lb	0·80	37·6ft
80lb	0·90	33·4ft
Handbrake	0·28	107ft

Max. Gradient 1 in 3

Consumption

FUEL

(At constant speed—mpg)
30 mph ....30·2
40 mph ....31·3
50 mph ....29·4
60 mph ....25·3
70 mph ....20·6
80 mph ....16·3
90 mph ....11·9

Typical mpg 17 (16·6 litres/100km)
Calculated (DIN) mpg
18·6 (15·2 litres/100km)
Overall mpg 16·0 (17·7 litres/100km)
Grade of fuel: Regular, 2-star (min. 92RM)

OIL

Consumption (SAE 30) 250 mpp

TEST CONDITIONS

Weather: Overcast
Wind: 7–15 mph
Temperature: 1·5 deg C. (35 deg F)
Barometer: 30·00 in. hg
Humidity: 70 per cent
Surface: Dry concrete and asphalt
Test distance: 1,100 miles

Figures taken by our own staff at the Motor Industry Research Association proving ground at Nuneaton.

Dimensions

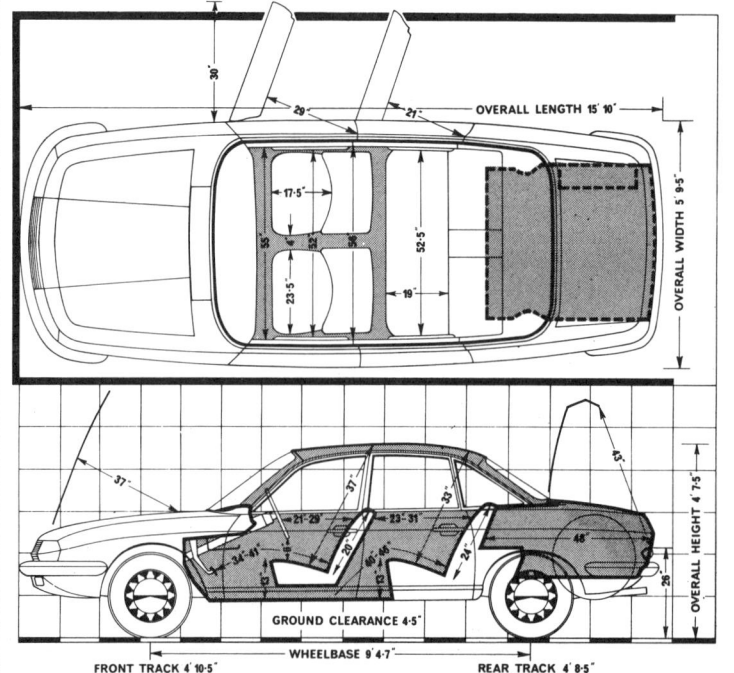

STANDARD GARAGE
16ft ×8ft 6in.

TURNING CIRCLES
Between kerbs
L, 35ft 0in.; R, 37ft 1in.
Between walls
L, 37ft 4in.; R, 39ft 5in.
Steering wheel turns, lock to lock: 3·7.

WEIGHT
Kerb weight 24·0cwt
(2,688lb–1,222kg).
(with oil, water and half full fuel tank).
Distribution, per cent
F 63·1; R, 36·9
Laden as tested:
27·5cwt (3,084lb–1,402kg)

are wrong, gearchanging can become rather jerky.

For maximum performance, all three ratios need to be used, but in town, the Ro80 is quite happy being left in second gear, which gives a maximum speed of 79 mph at the start of the tachometer red line to 6,500 rpm. The starting technique we used when taking the accelera-

tion figures was much the same as for a car with a fully-automatic transmission. The foot brake was held on by the left foot, the engine taken to torque converter stall point, and the brakes released.

The latest car was considerably faster than the original version we tested six years ago, reaching 30 mph in 4·5sec,

against 5·2, 60 mph in 13·1sec, compared with 13·9, and 80 mph nearly a full second quicker, in 17·4sec. The mean maximum speed of 110 mph was 3 mph better than we achieved originally.

On the road, the Ro80 can be deceptively fast, as the engine is so quiet and the power delivery so smooth. The almost total lack

of wind noise also makes it difficult to judge road speed. Unfortunately, the speedometer on the test car was wildly optimistic, being about 10 per cent out throughout its range.

Ride and handling

With front-wheel drive and the wheels very close to the corners, the Ro80's handling is

---

Specification   NSU Ro80

FRONT ENGINE, FRONT-WHEEL DRIVE

ENGINE
Cylinders	Twin-rotor Wankel rotary engine
Main bearings	2
Cooling system	Water; pump, thermostat and viscous-coupled fan
Displacement	2×497·5 c.c. (2×30·4 cu. in.)
Nominal capacity	1,990 c.c. (121·3 cu. in.)
Compression ratio	9-to-1. Min. octane rating: 92RM
Carburettor	Solex 32DT ITS
Fuel pump	Mechanical
Oil filter	Full-flow, cartridge-type
Max. power	115 bhp (DIN) at 5,500 rpm
Max. torque	121 lb. ft. (DIN) at 4,500 rpm

TRANSMISSION
Clutch	Fitchel and Sachs servo-operated single dry-plate, with torque converter
Gearbox	Three-speed, all synchromesh
Gear ratios	Top 0·79–1·82
	Second 1·21–2·78
	First 2·06–4·74
	Reverse 2·11–4·88
Final drive	Hypoid bevel, 4·88 to 1
Mph at 1,000 rpm in top gear	18·6

CHASSIS AND BODY
Construction	Integral, with steel body

SUSPENSION
Front	Independent, MacPherson struts, lower wishbones, telescopic dampers, anti-roll bar
Rear	Independent, semi-trailing arms, coil springs and telescopic dampers

STEERING
Type	ZF power-assisted rack and pinion
Wheel dia.	15·7in.

BRAKES
Make and type	ATE inboard discs front, outboard discs rear, with integral drum parking brake
Servo	Teves vacuum
Dimensions	F, 11·2 in. dia.
	R, 10·7 in. dia.
Swept area	F, 242 sq. in ; R, 216 sq. in.
	Total: 458 sq. in. (331·9 sq. in/ton laden)

WHEELS
Type	Light alloy, 5-stud fixing
	5in. wide rim
Tyres—make	Michelin
—type	XAS radial ply tubed
—size	175×14in.

EQUIPMENT
Battery	12 volt 66 Ah.
Alternator	Bosch 35 amp a.c.
Headlamps	110 watt (total)
Reversing lamp	Standard
Electric fuses	8

Screen wipers	Two-speed and intermittent
Screen washer	Standard, electric
Interior heater	Standard, water valve control
Heated backlight	Standard
Safety belts	Extra, automatic
Interior trim	Cloth seats, pvc headlining
Floor covering	Carpet
Jack	Screw pillar
Jacking points	2, each side
Windscreen	Laminated, tinted
Underbody protection	Sealing compound on all underside and sills

MAINTENANCE
Fuel tank	18 Imp. gallons (82 litres)
Cooling system	15 pints (inc. heater)
Engine sump	12 pints (6·8 litres)
	SAE 30. Change oil after initial 600 miles only
	Change filter every 12,000 miles
Gearbox and final drive	4·5 pints. SAE 90. Change every 12,000 miles
Torque converter	2·5 pints ATF. No change required
Grease	None needed
Contact breaker	0·015–0·016in. gap; 63 deg. dwell
Ignition timing	27 deg. BTDC (stroboscopic at 5,000 rpm)
Spark plug	Type: MAG 340T 2SP. Gap: 0·028in.
Compression pressure	128–156 psi
Tyre pressures	F, 29; R, 25 psi (normal driving)
	F, 32; R, 28 psi (high speed)
Max. payload	992lb (451kg)

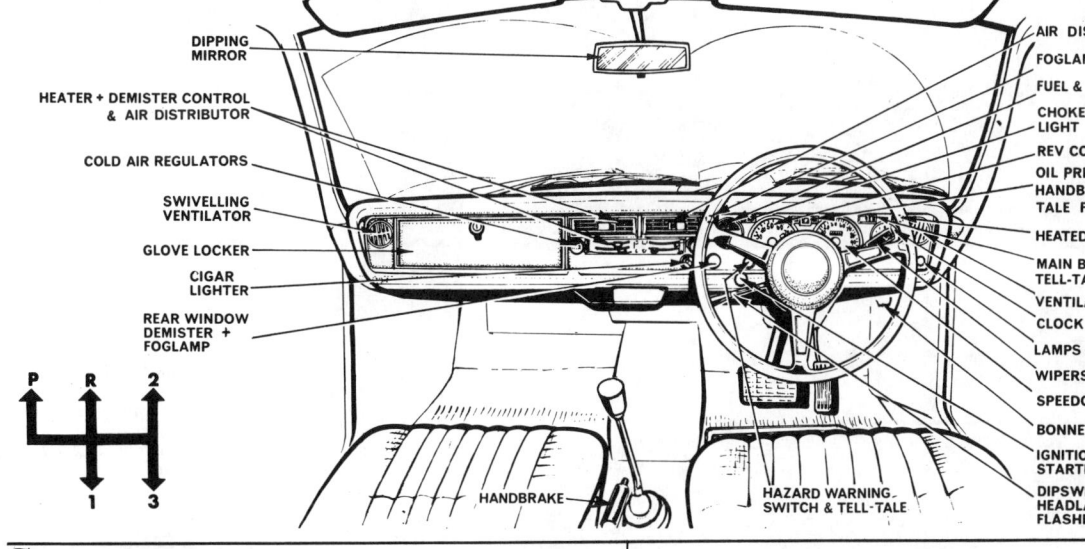

Servicing

	5,000 miles	10,000 miles	20,000 miles	Routine Replacements:	Time hours	Labour	Spares	TOTAL
Time Allowed (hours)	2·25	2·25	2·25	Brake Pads—Front (set)	0·67	£2·21	£12·19	£14·40
Cost at £3.30 per hour	£7·43	£7·43	£7·43	Brake Pads—Rear (set)	0·67	£2·21	£6·29	£8·50
Oil Change	N/A	N/A	N/A	Exhaust System	1·60	£5·28	£240·58	£245·86
Oil Filter	N/A	£3·14	£3·14	Clutch	5·30	£17·49	£48·02	£65·51
Breather Filter	N/A	N/A	N/A.	Dampers—Front (pair)	1·0	£3·30	£11·06	£14·36
Air Filter	N/A	N/A	£5·04	Dampers—Rear (pair)	1·0	£3·30	£32·36	£35·66
Contact Breaker Points	N/A	N/A	£0·76	Replace Drive Shaft	0·7	£2·31	£77·87	£80·18
Sparking Plugs	N/A	£3·42	N/A	Replace Alternator	0·6	£1·98	£51·68	£53·66
Fuel Filter	N/A	N/A	N/A	Replace Starter	0·5	£1·65	£70·22	£71·87
Total Cost:	£7·43	£13·99	£16·37					

NSU Ro80

superb. Independent suspension is used fore and aft, with struts feeding the load to coil springs set high in the wings. The spring rates are quite low and the wheel movements long, which adds to the ride comfort of the car. Rack and pinion steering is used, with power assistance which aids, rather than overwhelms the driver's control. As a result, the steering is delightfully precise without being over-light. The turning circle is rather large, at only just about 40ft between walls.

The car's superb straight line stability might indicate that this is associated with a good deal of understeer, but this is certainly not the case. The Ro80 seems just as happy on twisting roads with barely a hint of trying to plough straight on through corners. It is possible on very tight bends, and in bottom gear, to lift an inside front wheel for a moment.

Lifting off in the middle of a corner produces none of the violent reaction often associated with fwd cars, and the rear wheels always follow the line taken by the front ones. The Michelin XAS tyres give good grip, but they tend to produce a slight roughness in the ride, which is perhaps more noticeable because of the car's quietness. Our test car suffered from a slight whistle from the front passenger door, which seemed rather pronounced.

The ride on rough surfaces is good, with the long, well-damped suspension movement absorbing irregularities with total ease. Despite the softness of the suspension, there is no pitching and roll is well controlled.

Brakes

NSU use disc brakes front and rear, those at the front being inboard and easily accessible from through the bonnet opening. At the rear, small drums are built into the outboard discs for the handbrake. When the car is parked, the transmission can be positively locked in the P position, to the left of the reverse slot.

The response is progressive, and for normal check braking in towns, only 20lb pedal pressure is needed. With 80lb pressure, and a reading of 0·9g, all four wheels locked. A pressure-control valve in the rear braking circuit prevents the rear wheels from locking first. The handbrake recorded a slightly lower-than-average figure of 0·28g, but it held the car firmly on our 1-in-3 test hill, although the car tended to drag the locked rear wheels when facing downwards. Take-off in bottom gear was very easy.

There was virtually no sign of fade, the pressures rising from 35 to 37lb at the end of our 10 stops at 0·5g from 70 mph. Pedal travel remained unaltered, and there was no roughness or squeal from the discs even when very hot.

Fuel consumption

One advantage of the Wankel engine is that it will run on the cheapest, lowest grade fuel. However, allowing for the fact that the Ro80 is a big car, with a very reasonable performance, our overall figure (bearing in mind the 50 mph speed limit) of only 16·0 mpg was not very pleasing. It takes time to learn to drive the car in the most economical manner, but our best brim-to-brim figure was only 18·0 mpg. Because of the total-loss lubrication system, the car used oil at the rate of about 300 miles per pint. A car of equivalent top speed and acceleration, like the Mercedes-Benz 230/4, had an overall consumption figure 14·4 per cent better, at around 23 mpg, although on 4-star petrol. The tank holds 18gal, and fills

Top left: The engine rotor casing and transmission is buried under the mass of auxiliary equipment. Above: Rear seats are well shaped, with wide door openings, and ample legroom. Left: A deep cowl over the facia minimizes reflections; instrument legibility is good. Below: The huge boot is full carpeted

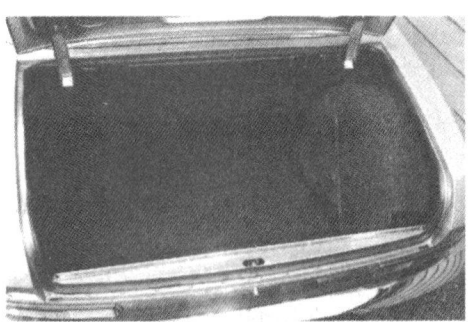

easily without any blowing back. A locking filler cap is standard. A red sector on the lower end of the gauge indicates that about 2gal remain, and a yellow lamp on the facia comes on when the tank is down to its last gallon or so. Because of the comparatively high oil consumption, NSU recommend that the level is checked each time the tank is filled.

Fittings and furniture

It is the mark of a properly-designed car that so few changes have been made to the interior design, although by current standards, the facia layout is perhaps rather cluttered. But at least the layout on the Ro80 was designed by an engineer, rather than being the product of a stylist's drawing-board.

The two, large, centre instruments contain the speedometer and tachometer, with very clear markings. The speedometer trip mileometer is reset by turning the outer ring on the knob, the inner part of which controls instrument lighting intensity.

To the left of the speedometer is the combined unit for fuel tank contents and coolant temperature, while on the right is the quartz-crystal clock. This kept dead accurate time, but was just about the noisiest piece of equipment on the test car, emitting a curious grinding noise! On the far right is the lighting master switch, and to the left of the steering column is the hazard warning switch, and the combined switch for the fog lamps (including the dual high-intensity rear lamps), and the heated rear window, which is standard.

Across the top of the facia, and shielded by the deep, full width cowl, are the various warning lamps. These are operated by a series of relays, and if the idle becomes too slow, and the alternator charge drops, these click in and out, making a noise like a small telephone exchange. Ventilation is comprehensive, but the temperature control is governed by a water valve, which allows little fine adjustment. Four horizontal slides control the air flow to car and screen, the temperature and the supply to the adjustable grids above the controls. On the latest cars, the demister slots below the screen are much larger than previously, giving very rapid clearance. A great deal of thought has been paid to getting stale air out of the car. On the sills there are two circular extractors, which exhaust air from foot level through vents concealed behind the lower part of the rear doors. In addition, there are extractors in each rear pillar. In hot weather, additional fresh air can be fed into the car through directional vents under the facia. Heated air can be boosted by a two-speed fan,

which is fairly noisy even on its lower setting. The test car was fitted with an electrically operated steel sun roof (£198 extra). The weather was not really suitable to use it much during the time we had the car, but it did not appear to cause any low-frequency buffeting when open.

Unlike the original car, the front seats can no longer be adjusted for height as well as reach. They are upholstered in cloth, and at first appear to be rather hard, but even after spending most of the day at the wheel, we found them extremely comfortable, with plenty of support for the spine.

The rear seats, too, are very comfortable, with a drop-down centre armrest. Head restraints are standard on the front seats, and they are small enough not to block rear passengers' forward vision too much. Storage space within the car is very limited. There is just a lockable cubby in the facia and the lower padded rail, the end of which is formed to make a grab handle for the passenger. Maps can be stored in the elasticated pockets on the back of the front seats. Conversely, the boot is huge, and fully trimmed throughout, with the spare wheel, jack and small tool kit under a cover on the right. The fuel tank is well out of harm's way, between the rear wheels. If really long loads – skis for instance – need to be carried, the back seat squab can be removed easily.

Visibility is excellent, although neither the front nor rear extremities of the car can be seen. Slim pillars cut down blind spots, and the front and rear screens wrap round to give a commanding view of the road. The sun-vizors are recessed into the roof lining, with light-coloured trim on their outside, and black on the inside, to cut down glare. Unfortunately, the vanity mirror, protected by a flap, is on the driving side. The car's left-hand drive origins are also made clear by the wiper pattern – and the fact that the deflector is on the passenger-side wiper.

The front interior lamp is neatly blended into the rear-view mirror stem, and there is a separate one, above the rear screen, for the other passengers.

The Ro80's unusual lines are a direct result of the extensive wind-tunnel testing in the development stage

Living with the Ro80

When we first tested the Ro80, the price was £2,249.25. In seven years, this has escalated to £3,822.94, and with the sun roof (the only extra on the car), delivery, excise duty and number plates, the on-the-road price is £4,090.94.

The bonnet of the car is front hinged, and has to be propped open. Initially the sight of the engine bay is rather daunting, with the mass of auxiliary equipment swamping the actual engine rotor block. A good deal of the "plumbing" is concerned with the detox equipment, with the belt-driven air pump mounted on top. The huge air cleaner too takes up a great deal of room. Yet despite all this, routine service points are easily accessible. Battery, screen-washer reservoir and translucent radiator header tank are all on the left-hand wing. The distributor (protected in a plastic bag), coil and the dipstick are to the right of the air pump, and the oil filler to the left. Because of the very high firing rate, the ignition system is very special, using a thyristor pack, mounted on a panel at the rear of the bonnet opening. The spark plugs are easy to reach, but we find that with a lot of slow running, they tended to foul. Normally, this can be cleared by a burst of hard driving, but in one case we had to remove and clean the plugs, which cost £3.42 *each*.

Because the front disc brakes are inboard, the pad material remaining can be easily checked. Another good feature is that the bulbs on the head-lamps can be changed from under the bonnet, after removing the small inspection hatches.

There are eight fuses in a block on the rear wall of the glove locker.

Servicing intervals are at 5,000 miles, and because of the total-loss lubrication system, the car requires only one oil change (at the end of the first 600 miles) in its life, although the filter has to be changed every 10,000 miles.

Whatever the pros and cons of the US exhaust emission regulations might be, the Ro80 has one serious drawback when it comes to replacing the exhaust system. The US regulations require that the engine shall not emit noxious fumes for at least 50,000 miles. This means that an *entire* exhaust system will have to be replaced, and on the Ro80, this will cost £240.58 plus fitting.

In the early days, NSU were faced with many problems with the seals at the rotor tips of the Ro80 engine. These have now been solved, and we see no reason why this engine should not be as long-lasting and as reliable as any normal reciprocating unit.

Indeed, NSU are so sure of their product that they have increased the warranty period on both parts and labour from a mere six months to two years (or 24,000 miles). This is the longest complete warranty offered by any manufacturer. Only Rolls-Royce have a longer one, giving three years or 50,000 miles on the engine and chassis.

Conclusion

NSU had a virtually unparalleled opportunity to produce their ideal car when they set about designing the Ro80. In many ways, the car set new standards of quietness, high-speed cruising ability and logical thought. But because of the very high initial development costs, the car has never been cheap – and now inflation has pushed it up into the luxury price category. Critics have had their doubts about the future of the Wankel engine as a power unit for the motor car. In the days of relatively cheap fuel, one might have argued that a poor fuel consumption was more than made up for by the comfort. Now that argument is carrying less strength. It was a brave attempt – but is there a future for Dr Felix Wankel's revolutionary power unit? □

MANUFACTURER:
Audi-NSU-Auto Union AG, Ingolstadt-Donau, Sommerstrasse 11, West Germany
UK CONCESSIONAIRES:
Audi-NSU (GB) Ltd., Volkswagen House, Brighton Road, Purley, Surrey CR9 2UQ

PRICES		Insurance	Group 7
Basic	£3,017.62		
Special Car Tax	£251.47		
VAT	£326.91		
Total (in GB)	**£3,596.00**		
Seat Belts	£20.00		
Licence	£25.00	**EXTRAS (inc. VAT)**	
Delivery charge (London)	£20.00	*Electric sun roof	£198.00
Number plates	£5.00	*Fitted to test car	
Total on the Road (exc. insurance)	**£3,660.00**	**TOTAL AS TESTED ON THE ROAD**	**£3,864.00**

20,000 MILES ON NSU Ro80

It got itself a bad name in the early days, but what of the Wankel now ? Roger Bell reports on " Motor's " staff car

Garage mechanics tend to be rather more forthcoming than their partners in grime, service managers and receptionists. The man who once serviced our car certainly was, anyway. "Those early four-plug Ro80s were real fliers. Trouble is, they tended to fly apart. Our record was five engines in 9000 miles."

What about the present engines, we asked? Were they reliable? "No trouble at all. Run like clockwork. But they don't seem as quick to me. . . ."

Technical editor Anthony Curtis, introducing a development story on the Ro80 (Motor, w/e July 22, 1972) put it rather more eloquently, though the message was much the same. "Brilliant innovatory designs subsequently dogged by disaster are commonplace in the history of the motor car. In modern times no car exemplifies this better than the NSU Ro80, except that it's a story with a happy ending."

Or so NSU indicated at the time in an attempt to clear the car's bad name. It was to find out for ourselves if it really was a happy ending that we have put as many miles as possible on to the clock of an Ro80 that has already been the subject of a full road test report (Motor, w/e June 22), and featured twice before in our Running Report series.

First impressions

What struck me most about the Ro80 when it arrived last January was how remarkably little the car has changed, either in appearance or feel, since the one Tony Curtis and I drove in Italy for our very first test in 1968. There are a number of obvious detail changes (the seats, for instance, are much better than they were), but essentially our car was all I expected of a model I knew well and much admired. That it didn't feel (and to my eyes didn't look) at all dated underlines what an advanced design it was when introduced seven years ago.

The engine has, of course, undergone an intense durability development programme since then, though with our car it was only the presence of an automatic choke in place of the original manual one that indicated obvious change. I was pleased to find within minutes of first driving the car that the irritating flat spot evident on all previous Ro80s I'd driven had been banished, disappointed a little later on to discover that the engine ran out of breath at 6000 rpm and didn't have the free-revving ability of the earlier four-plug engine—or maybe even the later two-plug one before it got all its emission control plumbing. In retrospect, the reluctance to rev like a turbine may be no bad thing since it was over-revving that destroyed so many of the earlier engines. Of greater importance is that the inherent smoothness and quietness of the Wankel has not been affected by all the changes.

Let's say that my first impressions were as favourable as they were predictable and pass on to other things.

Likes and dislikes

Despite (or maybe because of) rushing around racing tracks at the weekend in harsh and noisy tin boxes, I like to travel in comfort and peace on the road, especially for the daily drudge of commuting between Sussex and Dorset House. Hence my love affair with the Ro80.

As we said in our road test it is not so much what the Ro80 does—the acceleration, for instance, is nothing special for such a costly car—but how it does it. Remember those villains, noise, vibration and harshness that Ford once made a great play of banishing from their cars (and eventually largely succeeded)?

The Ro80 never has suffered from NVH—other maladies, maybe, but not NVH. Being hypercritical, the quietness of the engine is slightly marred by a mild resonant period at about 2500 rpm, and its smoothness by a chatter (from the transmission?) above 6000 rpm. But with a torque converter that allows you to adjust the revs without significantly altering your speed, the resonance is no problem; and the chatter is of no consequence either as I never exceed 6000

Above : 110 mph on the clock on the way to Geneva. The Ro80 really comes into its own on fast, cross-country journeys

Left : Bosch's twin-lamp clusters behind the big glass panels put to shame the headlights of many British cars

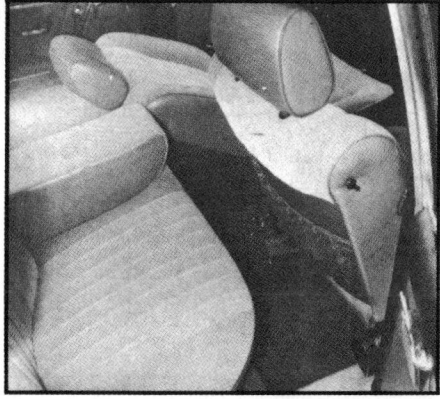

Right : Comfort starts with the seats, and no one who's ever ridden in our Ro80 has complained about them. The head restraints (standard) are adjustable or can be removed altogether

rpm: by then the power is on the wane and the fuel consumption becoming a bit nasty.

Another thing I like about the engine is the way it starts first time, every time (provided you follow the simple cold-start procedure), and then pulls without snatch or hesitation.

Mechanical refinement is not quite so well matched by insulation from wind and road noise, low though it is. I tried Paul Frère's ploy of heaving on the top half of the off-side door frame in the hope that it would bend slightly and press more firmly against the seals to stop a very localised roar that can only be heard from the front passenger's seat. But the Ro80's door seemed too well made to respond to such a crude cure.

There are also those faint whines and zizzes from the transmission, the odd thump from the tyres and, on rough roads, faint

but irritating rattles from within the doors. But despite these minor disturbances, the overall peace and tranquillity of the Ro80 are to me among its most endearing qualities. Passengers who don't know about Wankels invariably remark with genuine awe: "Isn't it smooth and quiet. . . ." Indeed it is.

It is also a very comfortable car. Bell junior naturally welcomes the odd Ferrari or Porsche (and to think that a ride in my grandfather's Austin 10 was an adventure when I was 11), but if there's a long trip ahead, the family want the Ro80. The cloth-covered seats are as comfortable at the end of an eight-hour run as they are at the start, and they do an excellent job of holding you in place when the car keels over, as is its wont, when cornered hard. With no transmission tunnel to get in the way there's enough space up front for the lugubrious labrador as well as the passenger's legs. Such are the strange habits of my offspring that one of the children usually finishes up sleeping on the back floor while the other stretches out on the seat. The boot, too, is what can justifiably be termed family size.

But where, oh where are you supposed to put things inside the car, other than people and dogs? The locker is full of cassettes for the excellent Javelin Europa radio/tape player (an extra and, no, it wasn't a free sample) which leaves nothing but the useful pockets on the backs of the front seats for stowing maps and books. NSU made poor use of the generous available space and, as we've observed before, a Rover-style facia, with panel-top shelf and shin bins beneath, would not only be a lot more useful than the simple flat-faced facia that the Ro80's always had, but would

help give the car an air of greater opulence. Nicely finished, yes, and tastefully furnished, but lacking the ultimate trappings of luxury that you might expect.

Not that I have anything against the modest array of neat, legible instruments and attendant warning lights, or the excellent fingertip switchgear, even though I still sometimes switch on the wipers to indicate a right turn. Most British cars have the indicator stalk on the right, most Continental ones on the left. Standardisation would be no bad thing.

My guess is that NSU were for far too long preoccupied with sorting out the engine—successfully, judging by the reliability of our car to date—to spend much time and effort making improvements elsewhere. No doubt if they had redesigned the facia they would have improved the ventilation system, one of the car's few remaining weaknesses, at the same time. Actually, all it needs is a fan boost: a system that relies on ram pressure alone, and then effectively only when you're travelling quickly, isn't much use in town on a hot, sultry day. In contrast the heater works well, though the levers have always been stiff to operate.

The graze on one of the back corners is testimony to the fact that the Ro80 is not a car you let anyone drive. The blemish was inflicted by some unknown clown who needed to move the car in our crowded park, was clearly baffled by the absence of a clutch pedal, and presumably yanked the lever into reverse while the engine was still revving on the choke: result—a sudden leap backwards into the wire fence. Had he known better, he'd have blipped the throttle after starting to cancel the choke and bring the revs down to normal idling speed of about 1200 rpm, and then plant his foot firmly on the brake before engaging gear. These and other little tricks you learn through experience, which is perhaps why a lot of people don't at first like the semi-automatic transmission.

I have no strong feelings about it either way. It's admirable for my commuter run when I usually start in second (as the handbook suggests) and engage top once on the move. This is probably why I get a much better fuel consumption (of which more later) than some colleagues who seem unable to get over the honeymoon stage of exploiting the engine's effortless ability to spin like a turbine. There are occasions, though, when it would be nice to have four gears (Alpine passes really show up the wide gaps between the ratios), or a fully automatic gearbox. I'm sure the transmission in its present form must put a lot of potential buyers off the car.

Few other things should, however, least of all the handling and roadholding which are excellent, despite the car's tendency to roll too much when cornered hard, and ZF power steering (still among the best) which I'd like even more if it had higher gear-

ing and thus quicker response. You do have to twiddle rather vigorously when taking sharp corners or when parking.

Although an easy car to drive in town—nothing could be simpler, not even a DAF, if you leave the selector permanently in second gear—the car is at its best on fast cross-country journeys and motorways where its impressive stability and effortless cruising really come into their own. Moreover, with a fuel consumption of 22 mpg at a steady 80 mph, the wind-cheating wedge shape of the Ro80 actually helps to make the car less thirsty than some piston-engined rivals, provided it's not driven flat out—which can be done with impunity (top speed equals cruising speed according to the handbook).

Other likes? The splendid all-disc brakes which, because the pedal feels just right and the car always stops all-square without fade, you tend to take for granted; the magnificent Bosch lights which spread a long-range carpet of white light out ahead; those lovely alloy wheels (standard fittings now) which collect very little road muck, though whether by design or through some freak aerodynamic assistance, I wouldn't know; the huge area of glass which not only makes the inside light and airy (I detest the claustrophobic interiors of some over-styled cars), but also gives the driver a panoramic view devoid of any blind spots. Negotiating an awkward Y junction in a car with heavy rear threequarter panels seems a positively dangerous exercise after driving the Ro80. True, you can't see exactly where the front corners are or where the tip of the protruding bumper ends, but I've never found this much of a handicap. Then there's the satisfying way the doors plop shut with a gentle nudge—though the grating noise from the stay-open props isn't so nice.

Other dislikes? Any that I've not mentioned already are either too trivial or will come later in the following sections.

Reliability

The car arrived with **414 miles** on the clock and a couple of small badly touched-in blemishes on its otherwise immaculate brown paintwork. This apart, there was nothing obviously wrong with it, though we got off to a bad start (literally) when, after sitting and gloating in the car for the first time, the engine wouldn't fire. At least, not until I'd churned away for five minutes and obscured the car park in dense blue exhaust smoke. Earlier on I mentioned among my "likes" the way the engine always started first time. And so it does, provided you prime the choke with a couple of dabs on the throttle and don't jiggle the accelerator and flood the chambers. Clearly, someone had done just that before I got to it. It's happened once or twice since, which is why I now always park the car where it doesn't get in anyone's way so I can lock it up. As an Ro80 mechanic at the local agent once

77

observed: "Lovely these big NSUs, but they're one-man cars. Keep it to yourself. . . ." I now do, trusted colleagues excepted.

At **1980 miles,** two screws fell out of the heater lever assembly, making the controls even more difficult to slide; and at **3400 miles** a flying stone chipped the windscreen. As it's a laminated one, though, I don't drive in fear of the thing going bang and crazing over. At **4520 miles** I noted in the log that the outside door catches were sticking in, and that the doors sometimes needed a hefty fist thump to release them. Oiling the locks subsequently cured the trouble.

At **4650 miles** the starter motor failed to engage with the engine, something it's done on very rare occasions since, though I didn't get round to having it investigated until the 20,000-mile service. As a new starter motor costs £120 (according to the receptionist) it's not the sort of problem you leave until the warranty period has expired.

At **4800 miles** the log records that the drive momentarily "flickered," as though there was a faulty contact in the electric clutch mechanism operated by the touch-sensitive gearlever. On previous occasions when the drive had suddenly gone into neutral, it was due to our idle labrador resting her head on the gearlever. This time, though, she was on the back floor and innocent.

At around the same time, I was a little bothered by the flickering brake warning light, indicating that the two brake fluid reservoirs needed topping up. Was the fluid leaking or had the level settled as the pads bedded in? I can only conclude the latter because the level has not dropped since the transparent containers were replenished at the first major service. Simple adjustment to the micro-switch in the gearlever also cured the flickering drive. That first major service, incidentally, came to £18.90 all in.

It wouldn't be quite true to say that the engine has never missed a beat because it does suffer from mild plug fouling. After prolonged running at low speeds with an "old" set of plugs, it will misfire and hesitate for a few seconds at about 4000 rpm before pulling cleanly again. I'd probably not have regarded it as a noteworthy fault had it not happened once in the middle of an overtaking manoeuvre when I needed full power and not a splutter. I say "old" plugs because the very special Bosch ones of the Ro80 need replacing every 5000 miles or so if the fouling is not to become a serious problem. At £3.50 each, I'm glad the engine now has only two plugs and not the four it once had.

Because we wanted to make quite sure the engine was in top tune before we took performance figures for our road test, the NSU concessionaires themselves carried out the 10,000-mile service (all the others have been done at our expense by an NSU agent). The report we asked for said they'd removed the carburetters,

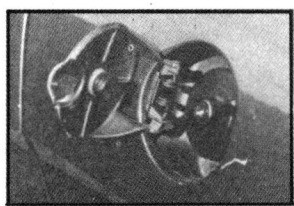

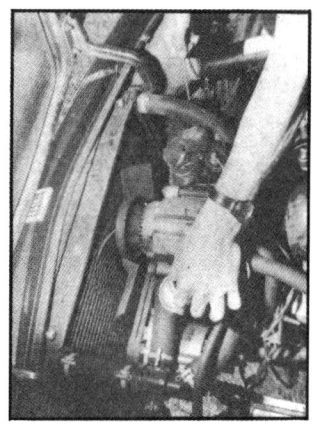

Above left : the splendid alloy wheels need little attention to keep clean. The front Michelins should last for 25,000 miles, the back ones for 43,000. Above : poor detail design — dipstick on one side of the engine, filler cap on the other. Both are used quite often. Left : one of several scratches to have appeared on the dark brown paintwork, this one inflicted by clumsy petrol attendant. Below : neat cassette holder

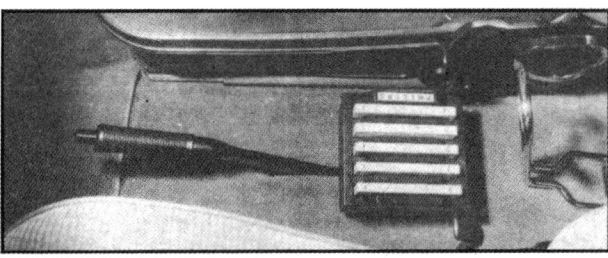

checked the throttle gaps and reset the float level, which was apparently too low. They also adjusted the off-side rear wheel bearing, replaced a circlip missing from the brake servo sensing valve and (inevitably) fitted new sparking plugs. Apart from the plugs, all the other items would have been warranty items, free of charge, anyway.

This service apart, and fuel and oil entries, the log book is blank between 6000 and **12,800 miles** when the idling speed suddenly dropped to 500 rpm from its normal 1200, because one chamber was clearly not firing on the idling jet. This naturally made the engine rather rough and lumpy at tickover but the trouble, whatever it was, did not receive immediate attention because as soon as you touched the throttle the engine ran properly on both chambers and neither the performance nor the fuel consumption suffered.

New plugs (£7) and carburetter adjustments didn't cure the problem at the 15,000-mile service, and I was about to make another appointment when the one-chamber idling suddenly and mysteriously reverted to two. It has remained normal ever since.

The front disc pads (£11.18 per set) were also replaced at this service, as were the points (85p) and air filter (£3.14). With labour, two pints of Castrol to top up the sump, and VAT, this service came to a whopping £57.19—and it would have been even more had they had a filler cap in stock to replace the one that had been lost

—or rather not replaced by a forecourt attendant on the one occasion when I failed to check. As it was, we had to wait many weeks for one to arrive because Audi NSU were re-arranging their spares set-up at the time, according to the storeman. The locking cap cost £5 when finally it did arrive.

In the meantime, I used a piece of polythene-covered rag which proved rather more satisfactory than the cheap rogue cap that a colleague kindly provided. Unfortunately, it fitted too well: apart from being difficult to release, the inrush of air when you did get it off indicated that the tank was being depressurised as the fuel was used up. I have a suspicion that this air-tight cap may have caused a reduction in the capacity of the tank, just as the blocked breather caused the tank of my last car, a Viva 2300 estate, to collapse on itself. Atmospheric pressure is a powerful force on a large tin can with a near vacuum inside.

There's no visual evidence of any partial implosion of the Ro80's tank but after ignoring the low-fuel warning light recently (because I didn't believe it), running out of petrol (inevitably), and then filling to the brim what should be an 18-gallon tank with only 15 gallons, I think the sides must have caved in a bit.

The car has performed flawlessly for the last 6000 miles, completing 20,000 miles at the beginning of September, 10 months after we started the test.

The 20,000-mile service cost £34.65 (including plugs, air filter, points, some oil, labour and VAT), but not the new wiper blades that I requested which were not in stock. I hope they don't take as long to arrive as the fuel cap did. The agents did have in stock (at 50p) a touch-up tube of paint, though. Having got it I must now try and repair that graze on the back.

As this section on reliability has filled a lot more space than I anticipated, let me underline that what faults our Ro80 has had have been relatively trivial, that the car has never been off the road other than for routine servicing and that, overall, I'd rate it as one of the most reliable and troublefree cars we have ever run.

Running costs

The other big question mark that has always dogged the Ro80 is its fuel consumption. As the graph shows, our car does between 16 and 20 mpg, depending on how and where it's driven. I have got as much as 22 mpg on gentle, top gear runs, but this is exceptional. Around the 18-19 mpg is normal, though colleagues tend to get less and I've had letters from other owners who claim much more. The only time the consumption has dropped as low as 16 mpg, incidentally, was on a fast trip to Geneva and back with four up and a full boot. While far from frugal, few piston-engined rivals *of comparable size* that are capable of cruising at 100 mph do any better (and many not as well). Few of them will run on two-star petrol either.

Oil consumption over the past 5000 miles has averaged 320 mpp, which isn't as disastrous as it sounds because with a total-loss lubrication system you don't have any expensive oil changes to pay for when the car is serviced. So oil costs are little if any heavier than normal.

The three services we've paid for, at 5000, 15,000 and 20,000 miles, total £110.74, including labour, materials, replacement parts like pads, plugs, points and filters, and VAT. The fourth one, at 10,000 miles, was done by the concessionaires as we mentioned earlier prior to performance testing. In the summary table we have assumed £35. Clearly, not a cheap car to maintain—though a check with the company's transport office suggests that an all-in cost for maintenance over 20,000 miles of under £150 is not unreasonable for an expensive car. Judging by the price of used Ro80s in the classified section, depreciation is a much greater worry.

The tyres have worn well. As the chart shows, there's still plenty of rubber left on the Michelin XAS radials, despite the frequent hard cornering they're subjected to.

Conclusion

I shall certainly be sorry to part with our car which has proved

very reliable, very comfortable and very satisfying to drive. It's also a car that passengers rate very highly, thanks largely to the comfort of its seats, its spaciousness and quiet running. When you relate the price to what it does with dispassionate objectivity, the Ro80 hardly stands out as a chart buster in terms of value for money. But it's a car with a captivating character, a car of intangible and endearing qualities, as the comments of one of the many Ro80 owners who have written in (most favourably) suggests. The letter concluded: "I find the car quite maddening some of the time, but it has given me enormous pleasure, far more than any other of the 50 cars I have owned. I would not change it for anything."

Second opinion

Anyone who runs a staff car as outstanding in design as the Ro80 is likely to become so dazzled by its virtues as to grow blind to its faults. Certainly the Ro80 would be one of the cars I myself would buy if I had a bit of spare cash—to put away in the proverbial dry barn alongside the Elan, the E-type and the Dino. But Roger has dealt fairly and objectively with his own example, I feel, and has said little with which I disagree. If anything, I consider he has underemphasised the almost miraculous refinement of the Wankel engine: those who think this form of unit is doomed, should try measuring the negligible extra smoothness obtained by substituting a V8 or V12 for a twin-rotor Wankel.

At the same time I believe that Roger has been a little too kind to the car in his assessment of its performance. Although it feels fine when wound up to 90 mph or more and will cruise comfortably at well over 100 mph, it feels positively sluggish to me for a car of its price and class at the lower speeds so vital for mainroad overtaking. It is, moreover, not merely breathless above 5000 rpm but actually rough (by Wankel standards) above 6000 rpm when it elicits a sharp buzz of sympathetic vibration from the gearlever knob.

I share Roger's enthusiasm for the power steering and endorse his criticism of its low gearing which accentuates another minor fault of the car: a trifle too much lurch, roll and understeer in tight bends, though on fast, sweeping curves it is magnificently effortless. I also feel that it is not just the doors that rattle a little but that the whole body creaks slightly, suggesting some lack of rigidity. And yes, the car does become stuffy in traffic when there's no ram pressure to force fresh air into it—but those progressive brakes, those comfortable seats, those stunningly powerful lights! How about giving it to me for the next 20,000 miles?
ANTHONY CURTIS

Make NSU
Model Ro80
Makers Audi NSU, Neckarsulun, West Germany
Concessionaires Audi NSU, Volkswagen House, Brighton Road, Purley, Surrey

Price £3531

WHAT IT COST
(corrected to a 20,000-mile 12-month period)

Petrol[1]	£562
Servicing[2]	£146
Oil	£19
Tyres[3]	£48
Road fund licence	£25
	£800

(Basic cost per mile = 4p)

[1] Two-star petrol at 52p/gallon, assuming 18.5 mpg

[2] Including labour, materials, replacement parts (see text) and VAT, and assuming charge of £35 for 10,000-mile service (see text).
[3] Approximately 60 per cent worn (averaging wear of front and rear tyres). We were quoted prices of between £18.11 and £24.54 for replacement Michelin XAS tyres. Our £48 is based on a price of £20 per cover.
As depreciation and insurance are so difficult to calculate, they have not been included in the lists. Both are likely to be heavy, however.

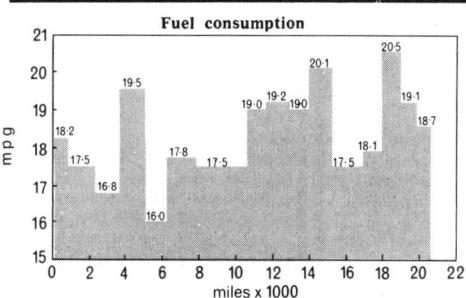

Fuel consumption (on two-star petrol) has varied between 16 and 20 mpg. The 16 mpg "low" was during a high-speed heavily-laden trip to Geneva and back. With gentle driving in top gear, it is possible to do 22 mpg overall

Predictably the front tyres have worn almost twice as rapidly as the back ones. All measurements on the Michelin XAS covers were taken in the centre of the tread, where wear was greatest. Projecting the lines suggests a front tyre life of 25,000 miles, and 43,000 miles for the rear ones

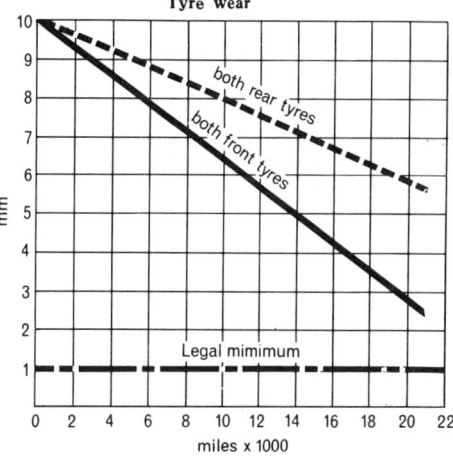

PERFORMANCE

CONDITIONS
Weather	Quite good, wind 0-10 mph
Temperature	59-69° F
Barometer	29.9 in. Hg
Surface	Dry

MAXIMUM SPEEDS
	mph	kph
Banked circuit	106.2	170.9
Best ¼ mile	108.2	174.1
Terminal speeds:		
at ¼ mile	75	120
at kilometre	93	149
Speed in gears (at 6500 rpm):		
1st	47	75
2nd	80	129

ACCELERATION FROM REST
mph	sec	kph	sec
0-30	4.4	0-40	3.3
0-40	6.3	0-60	5.8
0-50	9.2	0-80	9.2
0-60	12.6	0-100	13.4
0-70	16.6	0-120	17.8
0-80	22.0	0-140	28.8
0-90	32.0	0-160	46.1
0-100	47.6		
Stand'g ¼	19.1	Stand'g km	35.1

ACCELERATION IN TOP
mph	sec	kph	sec
20-40	7.2	40-60	4.6
30-50	8.7	60-80	5.7
40-60	10.4	80-100	7.1
50-70	11.8	100-120	7.8
60-80	12.9	120-140	10.1
70-90	16.0		

ACCELERATION IN SECOND
mph	sec	kph	sec
10-30	4.7	20-40	2.8
20-40	5.4	40-60	3.6
30-50	6.0	60-80	3.7
40-60	6.3	80-100	4.2
50-70	7.3	100-120	5.8
60-80	10.2		

FUEL CONSUMPTION
Touring*	23.2 mpg
	12.2 litre/100 km
Overall	18.1 mpg
	15.7 litre/100 km
Fuel grade	92 octane (RM)
	2 star rating
Tank capacity	18 galls
	83 litres

Max range	418 miles
	672 km
Test distance	2020 miles
(see text)	3250 km

*Consumption midway between 30 mph and maximum less 5 per cent for acceleration.

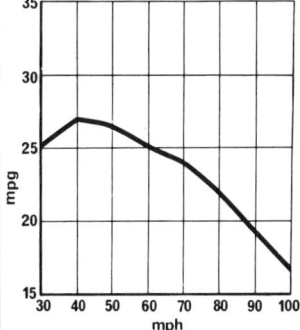

COMPARISONS

	Capacity cc	Price £	Max mph	0-60 sec	30-50* sec	Overall mpg	Touring mpg	Length ft in	Width ft in	Weight cwt	Boot cu ft
NSU Ro80	1990	3531	106.2	12.6	8.7	18.1	23.2	15 8.3	5 9.8	23.5	12.4
Audi 100S Coupe	1871	3014	112.7	10.8	10.5	23.1	30.4	14 5	5 8.75	21.3	12.7
BMW 520	1990	3435	105.8	11.3	11.4	20.1	23.6	15 2	5 7	24.3	13.0
Citroen DS23 EFI	2347	2900	119.5	10.4	12.1	18.6	—	15 11.5	5 11	26.8	11.8§
Ford Granada Ghia‡	2994	3100	110.0†	10.5	3.7	19.4	20.8	15 3	5 10.5	27.2	13.0
Jaguar XJ6 4.2‡	4235	4358	120.0	9.6	3.6	15.0	17.0	15 9.5	5 9.3	33.2	10.5†
Mercedes 230/4	2307	3825	101.6	12.3	10.8	21.8	23.0	15 4.3	5 9.7	26.1	13.5
Rover 3500‡	3528	2941	117.0	9.5	3.9	17.5	21.3	15 0.5	5 7.3	26.1	10.3
Volvo 164E	2978	3387	112.5	8.8	7.5	17.7	—	16 0	5 8.1	26.9	13.5

*in top/kickdown   †estimated   ‡automatic   §boxes not cases

Classic Ro80?

Anthony Curtis puts the case for the adoption of the big NSU

I CAN'T be the only person who sometimes wishes he'd had the sense to buy a 4½-litre Bentley back in the 'fifties when you could get one for about two hundred pounds, or who wonders why he didn't put aside a few dozen of those brass lamps that could be had for pennies at about the same time – or who speculates on the profits he might have made from a couple of roomsful of the Victorian furniture that everyone thought so hideous until John Betjeman began to make the period respectable. The really clever trick, clearly, is to be able to spot the trend just as it begins to develop – and at last I think I've done just that. In fact it's not so much a trend that I think I've spotted but a classic car in embryo, a car which isn't yet regarded as a classic but almost certainly will be: the NSU Ro80.

Few classic car owners, I'd guess, buy their machines as an investment. Instead they value them because they are a joy to drive as well as supreme examples of design or craftsmanship, or both. Still, it's nice if the price of the thing does rise, and you know you possess an asset of value if you are ever unlucky enough to have ruin stare you in the face. So let me start by disposing of the financial attractions of the Ro80 which are based on the current availability of new models from a number of dealers at around £1000 less than the £3531 charged before its regular import ceased. Similarly, good, recent, secondhand examples can be obtained for £1500 and sometimes much less. Anyone wanting one now, though, will have to pay £4500–£5000 for a special order!

My belief is that if Toyo Kogyo (the makers of the Wankel-engined Mazda range) go bust and the Wankel engine dies, the Ro80 will have very considerable novelty and rarity value in 10 or 20 years' time. If the Wankel succeeds, on the other hand, it will still be very valuable as the first production rotary-engined car of any consequence – and it remains a superb machine even if its power unit is ignored completely.

It isn't fears of rapid engine failure which depress the price of the Ro80. Its former power unit problems, caused by premature wear of the all-important rotor tip seals were finally put right (after a number of false starts) for all cars built from the middle of 1970 onwards. Audi-NSU confidence in the cure is demonstrated by the 2-year, 24,000-mile guarantee they offer.

Heavy fuel consumption, however, certainly does influence prospective buyers these days and the Ro80 is reputed to be a really thirsty car. But again, this is no longer true. To appreciate why you must first understand that the Ro80 is a genuinely *big* car, 15ft 8in long, which will seat five in comfort and has a huge boot. It is also fitted out with a semi-automatic transmission system which certainly wastes more fuel than a manual gearbox and probably more than if it were fully automatic, as it tends either to be subjected to excessively high revs in that all-purpose second gear or to

insufficient revs in top and hence an excess of energy-consuming torque converter churning. Despite these disadvantages our sister magazine *Motor* obtained an overall consumption of 18·5mpg in a recent test, which compares quite favourably with the 17·6mpg which the same periodical recorded with the much slower but perhaps slightly more roomy Wolseley Six.

Certainly the fuel consumption was pretty bad (15–16mpg) when the Ro80 was first introduced in 1967, but petrol was quite cheap then, and anyway all the journalists who drove the car wrote a paean of praise about it which finally culminated in the Car of the Year award. Since then the car has not deteriorated over the years as so often happens, and that early praise still seems just.

But apart from its Wankel engine the Ro80 is technically unremarkable. It uses ordinary coil springs, for example, and has a conventional combination of MacPherson strut front suspension and semi-trailing arms at the rear. Instead it is one of those

rare cars, like the recently introduced Alfasud, which owes its excellence to the essential correctness of virtually all its details and to the blending of those details into a near-perfect harmony of design. Perhaps the NSU engineers were able to do so well because they started with a clean sheet of paper, their previous experience being limited to motor-cycles and very small cars.

To offset the necessarily high frontal area, for example, the body was made aerodynamically efficient with the help of extensive wind-tunnel testing, the drag coefficient being as low as 0·365 – a value seldom surpassed in big saloons, even today. The high tailed/low nosed shape not only contributes to this efficiency but also helps to make the car stable in side winds and leads naturally to a large boot. Then there are huge glass areas, a low waistline and exceptionally slender pillars which ensure superb visibility. On top of that the car has beauty – or at least something very close to it.

Although the Ro80's Wankel engine is significantly lighter and more compact than a reciprocating engine of the same power, it is mounted well ahead of the front wheels, partly to improve straight-line stability, partly to leave as much space as possible for passengers and luggage within the wheelbase. But its forward location does mean quite a bit of weight on the front wheels – hence the power steering system which is one of the Ro80's most remarkable features. It is remarkable because it combines the lightness to be expected from power assistance with such excellent feel of the road as to make it almost indistinguishable from a good manual gear. The car's immediate and precise response to this system is coupled with very high cornering powers: the Ro80 always seems to have tremendous reserves of adhesion, even in the wet. Moreover, it will take outrageous liberties such as quite hard braking in the middle of a corner without changing its line at all. It's very much a go-where-you-point-it car. But tyre scrub and understeer do become apparent in a series of tight bends, when quite high roll angles may be attained, though despite the softish springing which these imply, the ride of the Ro80 is no better than fair when compared, say, with an XJ6 or a big Citroen.

But the Ro80's superb handling and roadholding are not its only major virtues: it is also exceptionally quiet and refined. There is nothing special about the extent of the road noise suppression, but even at more than 100mph wind noise is astonishingly low thanks to attention to detail and features like recessed rain gutters in the

screen pillars and roof. As to the engine, I'm always amazed at its almost miraculous smoothness whenever I drive the car, even if I've just transferred from something like a Rover V-8.

For all these reasons the Ro80 received rave notices when it was first introduced, but after a short honeymoon period disaster struck. It was all caused by rapid failures of the rotor tip seals, partly due to a wholly unexpected acceleration of their wear rates during cold start conditions and partly because the very unfussed quietness of the engine tempted so many owners into over-revving it. And worn apex seals didn't just mean poor performance, but often an engine that wouldn't start at all. The load imposed by the power steering didn't help. Cartoons began to appear in German motoring magazines showing Ro80 drivers indicating to each other with the fingers of one, sometimes two, hands, how many new engines had been fitted to their cars. Not all these were due to actual faults, but some to the tendency of the motor trade to take advantage of the generous replacement policy and to their inability to meet exacting service requirements.

The original engine, for example, had two separately timed sparking plugs, so these were replaced in the autumn of 1969 by a single plug working in conjunction with a new and much more efficient transistorised ignition system. At the same time an interim apex seal design was introduced, but the seals which finally solved the problem completely, were not fitted to production cars until the autumn of 1970 – from 9 September, engine no. X7000536 and chassis no. 081100058.

Today, therefore, the Ro80's only significant disadvantage is its alleged heavyish fuel consumption, and even that is only bad in comparison with smaller models. Of course the car is not perfect. Its fresh-air ventilation is not as good as it should be; smooth changes can sometimes be quite difficult to coax out of the semi-automatic transmission, and it still tends to foul its plugs a little in traffic. Nor is it quite true to say, as I did earlier, that it has not deteriorated in any way over the years. It hasn't got heavier as cars often do, but it has certainly got slower, a typical maximum speed now being about 107mph rather than the 113mph or so achieved by early models, though acceleration, both through the gears and in top, is slightly better. But

its design is so outstanding that in the seven years which have elapsed since it was announced no-one has introduced a better car of the same class. It is also a pleasure to look at and to drive. What more can one want of a classic car? ●

At the time that NSU produced the Ro80 they were well known for mopeds and the Prinz range; going to Neckarsulm to try their new big saloon with a Wankel engine before the Ro80 announcement, I didn't know what to expect. Looking at the car for the first time didn't help much either; the grille looked rather amateur and the coke-bottle wedge styling looked overlong and gawky – it wasn't as fashionable then. Driving the car though was something of a revelation; at that stage in mid- 1967 I had only driven the single rotor Wankel Spyder with the Mazda Cosmo 110S yet to come. So the smoothness and quietness of the engine was remarkable with very acceptable performance from the nominal 2-litre. I have always been a left-foot braker with automatics as well as a manual override shifter, so the semi-automatic transmission presented no problems after the first ten miles.

However, I expected to be impressed by the engine, but the more impressive feature of that car was how well the rest of it worked; it was comfortable and held the road with almost rail-like ability; it was quiet with that remote buzz from the engine and very little wind noise thanks to well profiled screen surrounds and a good aero-dynamic shape generally; and it was spacious. That the makers of rather utilitarian small cars should produce a very good sporting saloon first time out was remarkable. At that stage we didn't know much about the probable fuel consumption or the image of unreliability that was going to cloud the car's horizon.

Unfortunately the image is still with us although the car has been developed in detail to a very considerable extent. It is still a quick spacious comfortable car with road behaviour almost as good by comparison with rivals as it was eight years ago when I first tried it; perhaps the roadholding isn't quite as impressive but it is still good. The ability to cruise at 90mph plus with such a low noise level is very rare and such comfort is enhanced by the seats, large but with good support and plenty of leg room for all passengers.

The engine is as ever quite untemperamental, starting easily on its automatic choke and pulling smoothly straight away. Mostly you will start in the left-and-back first gear which is enough for any town speed limit but second takes you through the limits and can be used for gentle starting with a fair amount of torque converter churning. Mostly it seemed easier from rest to go from first to third (top), and very smooth too with the torque converter cushioning the rather in-out action of the electric clutch controlled from the gear lever knob.

Original road test cars used to return fuel consumptions around 15–17mpg with heavy oil consumption but development has proceeded since then and over 700 miles of mixed town, country and motorway driving we returned 21·2mpg of 2-star fuel with economy to spare for those of lighter foot. Oil added during that distance was 2 pints with quite a lot of motoring over 4000rpm.

I leave it to my former colleague, Anthony Curtis, Technical Editor of *Motor,* to put the case for the Ro80's classic rating. **M.H.L.B.**

Ro80 shape has grown more pleasing over the years and is functionally efficient; engine seems little smaller than normal 2-litre but is hidden by ancillaries; interior is well designed and comfortable.

NSU Ro80

Always a classic, ultra-modern body shape, the NSU Ro80 offered excellent all-round visibility and had very low wind resistance. The example below was Autocar's much-loved Long Term test car, seen here on its way to the Scottish Motor Show in 1971

THERE ARE GROUNDS for thinking that NSU's Ro80 is one of the world's most misunderstood cars. Ever since it was launched in the autumn of 1967, the Ro80's twin-rotor Wankel engine took most of the attention and the rest of the car's advanced engineering was virtually ignored. The engine's much-publicised problems and the high cost of rectifying them, submerged almost everything people were thinking about the rest of the car. Yet, for all that, the last NSU Ro80 was not built until March 1977. If the car was such a lemon, surely NSU's owners (Volkswagen) would have ditched it and used the

extensive production facilities years before they actually did?

Technically, of course, the Ro80 is still unique. There have been several other cars with twin-rotor Wankel engines — hundreds of thousands of Mazdas, for example — but none with the front-wheel-drive, the futuristic styling, the great refinement, and the other detail advanced features of the German Ro80. There is therefore almost nothing with which we can compare it, not at least in direct terms. It was nominally a 2-litre four-door saloon car and towards the end of its life it became very expensive, but this is no help. The most effective

comparison we can make, which is to ignore the engine altogether, is with the range of Citroën DS19/DS21/DS23 cars current in the 1960s and 1970s. It comes as no surprise to learn that NSU co-operated closely with Citroën in its general layout, that it used the Citroën "Goddess" as its standard in matters of ride, refinement and road behaviour, and that NSU joined with Citroën in the stillborn Comotor Wankel project.

How many Ro80s?

The car is quite exclusive, but not as rare as all that. This, as far as spare parts provisioning and service exper-

tise is concerned, is reassuring. In just less than 10 years, NSU built a grand total of 37,204 Ro80's, the majority in the relatively "boom" years of 1969 to 1972. Of these, no fewer than 3,614 cars were delivered in Britain in right-hand-drive form, though a few were also imported in 1968 with left-hand drive.

In Britain at least, a growing number of the surviving cars are being treated to extensive transplants, where the troublesome Wankel engine is replaced by modern Ford piston engines — usually 2-litre V4 Capri units, but occasionally even 3-litre V6 units — which can be

The compactness and low mass of the engine illustrated the advantages of the Wankel power unit

The design of the car itself was also ahead of its time, offering excellent accommodation front and rear, and with unusually good ventilation

Approximate selling prices

Price Range	Year
£500—£600	1969
£700—£800	1970 (Mark II)
£800—£900	1970 (Mark III)
£900—£1,000	1971
£1,300—£1,400	1972
£1,500—£1,600	1973
£1,800—£1,900	1974
£2,200—£2,400	1975

Note: The Ro80 has only been available to special order in Britain since 1975, and finally went out of production in the spring / summer of 1977. More than usual, in this case, we must stress that these are top selling prices; the value of a trade-in to a dealer is very much below these levels. A 1975 Ro80, even with a healthy engine, is worth little more than £1,500 to its seller.

Spares prices

Engine assembly — bare (exchange)	£987.72
Short engine (exchange)	£936.67
Semi-automatic gearbox assembly (exchange)	£457.73
Torque converter assembly	£143.21
Differential assembly	£198.05
Brake pads — front (set)	£19.55
Brake pads — rear (set)	£11.55
Suspension struts — front (pair)	£74.02
Suspension struts — rear (pair)	£67.07
Radiator assembly (new)	£139.22
Alternator — exchange	£100.86
Starter motor — exchange	£68.88
Front wing panel	£58.36
Bumper, front	£87.76
Bumper, rear	£76.66
Windscreen — laminated	£67.23
Exhaust system, complete	£253.23

All the above prices include VAT at 8 per cent

mated easily and successfully to the existing semi-automatic Ro80 transmission: Two separate organizations offer this conversion. One is the Ro80 Centre of 59 Albert Embankment, London SE1, and the other is Hurley Motor Engineering of Overbury Road, Coventry, whose London-based associate is Don Marriott of Stock Road, Billericay. Between them, they claim to have completed between 150 and 200 cars so far.

How the Ro80 evolved

When the new model appeared in September 1967, there was absolutely no carryover from existing NSUs. The company had produced a short series of single rotor sporting two-seaters (the Wankel Spider) to gain Wankel experience, but the Ro80 was effectively all new.

The twin-rotor engine displaced 497.5 c.c. per chamber, but as there were twice as many firing impulses for every revolution as would occur in a piston engine the 995 c.c. engine was always rated as a 1,990 c.c. "equivalent", and became a 2-litre car for all performance and insurance comparisons.

Front-wheel drive was a feature, with the water-cooled engine mounted in line and ahead of the transaxle and with the actual gearbox behind the line of the front wheels. The transmission itself was interesting, being the first application of the Fichtel und Sachs "semi-automatic" layout. That is to say that behind the engine was a torque converter, then a conventional friction clutch, and a three-speed synchromesh gearbox of all-indirect layout. However, there was only a two-pedal layout, with the clutch operation being triggered off by a microswitch between the gear lever knob and the lever itself.

The body shell was of conventional unit-construction four-door layout. Independent front suspension was by MacPherson strut and rear suspension by coil springs and trailing arms. Power-assisted rack and pinion steering was a feature and the whole ride/handling equation was trimmed with a view to maximum refinement and precise roadholding.

In the 10 years of Ro80 there were no significant styling or body engineering changes, but it is as well to note that the original cars had vast single headlamps with fog lamps under the bumpers, the "Mk 1" British models of 1968/9 had twinned headlamps and no fog lamps, as did the Mk II single-plug cars of 1969/70. From June 1970 the Mk II models changed to twinned halogen headlamps, incorporating flasher units, all under the same glass covers, and plastic instead of light alloy front grilles were fitted. Towards the end of the car's life (from October 1975) larger wrap-around tail lamp clusters were fitted, along with rubber-faced bumpers. Throughout the life of the car, however, there were no sheet metal changes of any nature — within reason, for instance, doors, bonnets, glass, and other renewable items are common to all types.

All the main changes were confined to the engine. The British Mk I cars (a nomenclature never officially adopted in Germany, incidentally) had "twin-plug" engines — that is to say whose chambers had two sparking plugs per cylinder to give progressive combustion — which were imported only from 1968 to October 1969. Thereafter the chamber design was modified and only a single sparking plug was fitted, along with transistorised ignition. Through the life of the car development changes were made to the engine to maximise on rotor tip seal life and performance, and to minimise chamber surface wear. Towards the end of the car's life, changes were made to satisfy both European and North American anti-emission legislation. A twin-choke Solex carburettor replaced the original dual twin-choke units, while British cars inherited the complete hang-on kit of air pumps and air bleed pipes normally limited to USA-market cars. Performance and fuel consumption capabilities were barely affected, as our *Autotest* figures confirm.

From the autumn of 1975, the Ro80 was only available in Britain to special order, and the last of all was built in March 1977.

What to look for?

We must divide this into two surveys — engine, and other features. The situation regarding engines is discouraging. In spite of all the work put in by NSU (and later VW) even the later engines could not be expected to complete much more than 25,000/30,000 miles before major re-building was necessary. The cost of a new engine was, and is, prohibitive. NSU backed their policy with an extended (two years or 24,000 miles) new-car guarantee, from 1974, and a six-months "Golden Guarantee" on replacement parts in the drive train from mid-1972. It was brave, and generous, but it didn't hide the fact that tip seals continued to wear and chambers continued to be progressively burned downstream of the sparking plug area.

If a secondhand Ro80 is offered with a guaranteed new, or nearly new, Wankel engine, it should be good for at least 25,000 miles, but the use of excessive rpm (more than 6,000 for long periods can be dangerous, not for structural reasons, but because of accelerated wear) will bring this rocketing down. Starting, irregular running, and even poorer petrol consumption, will be the ominous signs. Chamber wear might be followed by cracking, and perhaps even loss of coolant. Re-builds are possible, and some firms (there is an Ro80 centre in London, for instance) tackle this as a matter of course, but the cost is high. Note that a non-multigrade oil like Shell Rotella is recommended for this engine. Fuel consumption even of the cheapest 2-star petrol, is usually poor — anyone boasting of more than 20 mpg is probably stretching a point. With oil consumption no better than 250/300 miles per pint (oil usually has to be added every other time you stop for fuel) this makes the Ro80 quite an expensive car to run.

Early engines sometimes suffered crankshaft (rotor shaft) wear at the bearings, but this problem was soon identified and rectified, and is now not considered to be important.

If you are seriously considering a Ford engine conversion, remember that the V4 transplant (which uses almost all the existing Ro80's auxiliaries) can cost £700 plus VAT, while the more ambitious V6 installation puts the bad news well into the £1,100/£1,400 bracket.

The transmission is reliable,

	Ro80	Ro80 Two-car test	Ro80 Long-Term at 14,000 miles	Ro80
Road Tested in *Autocar* of:	1 Feb 1968	1 May 1969	30 Mar 1972	13 July 1974
Maximum speed (mph)	**107**	**106**	**111**	**110**
Acceleration (sec)				
0-30 mph	5.2	4.9	4.6	4.5
0-40 mph	7.1	6.9	6.6	6.5
0-50 mph	10.1	10.4	9.8	9.6
0-60 mph	13.9	14.0	13.0	13.1
0-70 mph	18.3	18.5	16.9	17.4
0-80 mph	24.8	25.5	24.2	24.2
0-90 mph	34.8	35.8	32.9	34.6
0-100 mph	48.9	—	44.3	—
Standing ¼-mile (sec)	19.2	19.7	18.9	19.1
Top gear acceleration (sec)				
10-30 mph	6.2	6.6	6.1	5.8
20-40 mph	8.0	8.0	6.8	7.0
30-50 mph	8.4	9.9	8.1	8.4
40-60 mph	10.2	11.3	9.4	10.3
50-70 mph	12.5	13.0	11.2	12.3
60-80 mph	16.0	15.2	13.0	14.5
70-90 mph	19.4	—	15.1	18.3
80-100 mph	24.1	—	19.7	—
Overall mpg	18.2	16.4	17.0	16.0
Typical mpg	20.0	18	—	17
Dimensions				
Length		15ft. 10in.		
Width		5ft. 9.5in.		
Height		4ft. 7.5in.		
Unladen weight (cwt)	23.8	—	—	24.0

Milestones and chassis identification

	Series	Chassis Nos.
September 1967: Ro80 announced in Germany. Four-door saloon with twin-rotor Wankel engine (nominal 1,990cc), semi-automatic transmission, front-wheel-drive, power-assisted steering, all-independent suspension. 115 bhp. First chassis numbers:	80	001051
December 1967: Limited imports to the UK in left-hand-drive form, from:	80	001220
October 1968: First imports to UK in right-hand-drive form. Twinned-headlamps and flashers in place of original front fog lamps give identification. Known as Mk I. From:	80	3800103312
October 1969: Engine changes include single-plug/rotor, and transistorised ignition. Now known as Mk II. No recorded chassis number change.	80	—
June 1970: Body changes included headlamps behind single rectangular glass cover. Plastic instead of metal grille. Fog lamps added under bumper. Model known as Mk III.	80	—
October 1971: Audible warning system for over-revving incorporated, from:	0801	082100051
July 1972: Tinted glass, head restraints, metallic paint standardised, from:	0801	0821003258
October 1975: Body changes including wrap around tail light cluster, rubber-faced bumpers, etc. Now available only to special order in UK. From:	081012	0861000269
March 1977: Finally discontinued.	—	—

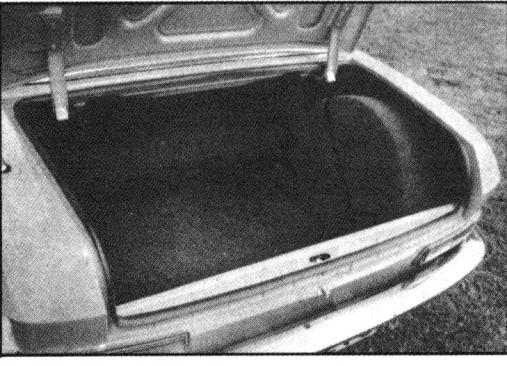

Front drive and the wedge-shaped profile of the body, with high back, allowed a spaciously deep boot, with the spare wheel stowed to one side

though not perhaps up to the same refinement standards as the rest of the car. It was specified to damp down the out-of-balance forces from the rotary engine. The torque converter runs hot, and may overheat with prolonged high-speed motoring; it shares lubricant with the Wankel engine, and problems in one may contaminate the other. A new engine should therefore be treated to a new converter. The gear lever microswitch, incidentally, is adjustable for engagement position, but this is a job best left to NSU experts.

The first signs of transmission trouble usually come in the guise of noisy gearbox bearings. A rebuild is quite costly. Drive shafts are robust — 70,000 miles is quite normal for these items, but do look for split rubber "boots" around universal joints and listen hard for "clicks" when cornering tightly at low speeds. Later cars have neoprene covers, whereas early cars used items of natural rubber.

The body shell, and almost all of its fittings, are of a very high quality. Even Ro80s of the late 1960s are often in very good and rust-proof condition. The exterior brightwork is mainly stainless steel, not chromium plate, and should therefore last well. The front half of the exhaust system is also stainless, and very solid indeed, but the tail pipes are of normal construction, and as fallible as most.

Fittings are of a high standard (check that post-October 1961 cars have an operative rpm-limit warning buzzer!), though the ventilation system has irritatingly cheap plastic parts, the front windows may begin to wind down askew and door locks may tend to stick.

Brake and tyre life should be very high. Premium-type Michelin XAS tyres are normally fitted, and may last for at least 40,000 miles. Front brake pads are relatively huge and although inboard are easily checked for wear (they are extracted upwards into the engine compartment and can clearly be seen at each side of the differential housing). Suspension parts, dampers, and the power-assisted steering are all well made and long lasting, in tune with the rest of the car's structure.

Spares are already quite rare, though VW (GB) have a commitment to support this relatively rare car. But one has to remember that the car was launched here in 1968 for £2,249, last listed in 1977 at £7,765, and that spares prices have been adjusted accordingly.

Our view is that an Ro80 was functionally very enjoyable, technically interesting, and certainly could be considered as a low-mileage-usage latter-day "classic". But in view of what is known about engine life, you have to consider secondhand purchase very carefully — or opt for that Ford engine conversion. Don't forget, too, that if you do this, you will lose performance, for the Ford engine cannot really be used at more than 5,000 rpm. Is a 100 mph maximum still enough? □

Next week we examine Ford V4 and V6 engine transplants for Ro80s

SMOKEY ROTARIES

NSU's advanced Ro80 was a superb car, but it was beset with problems. Stuart Bladon ran two of them

EACH morning it was the same routine: pull out the choke control, turn the key and listen to the smooth throb of the twin-rotor Wankel engine turning over. Then, place the left foot on the brake, move the gearlever into first, without any need to depress the clutch pedal, and accelerate with the right foot, releasing the brakes at the same moment. It was always then that it happened: clouds of blue smoke would erupt from the exhaust of the NSU Ro80 and the smoke trail would continue for the first couple of miles until the engine had warmed up.

On the motoring journal for which I worked, we had been out to Germany to test a left-hand drive Ro80 in 1968, but it was not until three years later that we were invited to get fuller experience of the car and its unique engine by running an Ro80 on a long term test.

I had just started an extended test of a new Audi 100, on loan from Mercedes-Benz, who were handling the Audi concession. Then came the 'coup', when Shoreham-based NSU laid claim to the Audi franchise.

The Audi was recalled, leaving me without a permanent car, so when NSU offered an Ro80 on extended loan, it came my way. I looked forward to it with some misgivings as I already had considerable experience of rotary engines having run one of the original single-rotor Spiders for a couple of years. That had been a good 'fun' car, but the engine was prone to stop for no apparent reason, and refuse to run again for about half an hour, after which it would seem perfectly fit again.

The Ro80 was taken over on March 22, 1971, already with 1,651 miles recorded, and only two days later I set off in it to drive to the NSU and Audi factories in Germany to research a big Audi-NSU supplement for my journal. We had little trouble on this 1,000-mile journey except for a bad wind whistle from the passenger door and a trace of misfiring which developed after leaving Cologne on the return journey. I did not know then that misfiring was to be one of the problems of the Ro80.

On this long Continental trip I came to like the Ro80 very much indeed, appreciating the excellent visibility afforded by its deep windscreen and the impressive stability, ride comfort and good ventilation. There were four of us in the car and it took the load very well.

On the *autobahn* heading north from

Above, an early press shot of the attractive NSU Ro80 emphasising the car's aerodynamics which were the result of exhaustive wind tunnel testing

Frankfurt we ran into torrential rain. It was dark as well and I was most impressed by the feeling of security the car gave with its very accurate power steering, and the good directional stability that was unaffected by crosswinds. The lights were also very effective and I felt we were well equipped to keep out of trouble when the Germans, hurrying home after work, had the inevitable motorway pile-up. In fact my fears were groundless and we cruised on to Cologne without incident.

Legendary smoothness

Suspension of the Ro80 was by MacPherson struts at the front with trailing arms and struts at the rear, and the engine lay in line ahead of the front wheels, which took the drive and had inboard disc brakes. I thought this arrangement of having the front brakes well away from the wheels was very sensible – at least there was never any problem of brake dust on the wheels, and driveshafts able to take the engine torque were well able to cope with braking loads as well.

NSU had been well aware of the inherent roughness of the Wankel engine at low revs, in contrast to its legendary smoothness at high revs, and to counter this the car was available only with the semi-automatic transmission which was popular at the time. It had both clutch and torque converter, and three-speed manual gearbox, but no clutch pedal. A microswitch in the gearlever knob actuated a clutch release servo in response to the lightest touch.

Official recommendation for town driving was to leave the gear in second, but getaway was very slow like that, and I always drove it completely as a manual car except that I would select first gear in advance at traffic halts and hold the car back with the brakes until ready for the 'off'.

What used to fox many drivers was that it seemed odd to change gear without pushing a clutch pedal down, so they used to push the brake pedal instead! Considering how many drivers set off from traffic lights on green and then did a tyre-shrieking crash stop as they trod on the brake pedal when going from first to second, it is amazing that the Ro80 was never clouted in the back. With familiarity, though, this was no problem, and I used to brake with the left foot, as I do with all automatics, yet never used the brake pedal in error. It was just a problem for drivers unfamiliar with the car, and with one particular driver I had to plead with him to put his left foot over on the other side of the car, after he had repeatedly used the brake pedal as a clutch when changing gear.

After running this car for six weeks, it was booked to go into the NSU depot at Shoreham to see if they could do anything about the severe smoking when cold. I also asked for the n/s windscreen wiper to be replaced, as it had a habit of coming adrift, and I wrote in my notebook: 'NEVER SEEN AGAIN.' This referred not to the wiper, but to the whole car!

No explanation was given, but I was simply advised that a new car was being supplied. It came on July 2, 1971 after an interval of nearly two months finished in

SMOKEY ROTARIES

Targa orange. An improvement was that the left door fitted properly, eliminating the bad wind roar which the other had suffered, but it offset this with a number of irritating faults such as a slightly loose driving seat, a bad flat spot which the previous car's engine didn't have and very stiff steering. ZF power-assisted steering was standard, so this was a surprising weak point. On top of it all, the cold start smoking was a bad as with the previous car.

After 1,400 miles, the clutch started to remain engaged. This wasn't as bad as on an ordinary manual transmission car, however, and it was still possible to drive. The only difficulty arose on coming to rest when it was essential to knock the gearlever into neutral in good time. If it was left with third engaged on coming to rest the only way to get our of gear was to stop the engine.

Normand Continental were NSU dealers in London, and the Ro80 went to them for numerous attentions. They rectified the heavy steering and fitted a new clutch at 2,124 miles. The flat spot remained, as did the smoking.

NSU's chief engineer at this time was bearded Mike Hoppis, who amused me greatly by the way in which he was more like a surgeon than an engineer. He would touch something under the bonnet and get a tiny oil mark on a finger, which then had to be wiped off using a white pocket handkerchief. I talked to him about the flat spot, and he said he would have a look at it if I could bring the car down to Shoreham again. He meticulously stripped down the formidable big Solex carburettors, used forceps to extract two tiny springs and measured them. Finding that they were 8mm long, he stretched them slightly, enlarging them to 9mm, and like magic the flat spot was cured!

Alas, the smoking was confirmed as a failing of the engine design. We were using oil at the rate of a pint every 400 miles but it tended to be heavier in local running with many cold starts than it was on a long journey. I came to dread being stuck in dense traffic because this could lead to oiling up one of the sparking plugs; and once this had happened it would never clear of its own accord, in the way that a performance engine comes back on the full song when given a blast to 'blow the smuts out'. For the Ro80 engine, the only solution to an oiled plug was to change it.

Once a plug had oiled, the car became almost undrivable with power cut to about 30% of normal. I always carried spare plugs and an articulated plug spanner in the boot and always changed them as a pair. It took about three minutes. After sandblasting they were usable again, which was as well since new ones cost £3.84 for a pair, at a time when ordinary piston engine plugs were still only about 30p each. There was a lot of discussion as to whether the pink Beru plugs were better than the white Bosch ones, but in the end I preferred the Bosch ones, especially after one of the Beru ones had cracked in ordinary driving conditions.

Once I had discovered what to do I became adept at various DIY jobs on the Ro80, such as adjusting the tickover and resetting the clutch servo by turning the adjusting screw clockwise to make the take-up less abrupt and reduce the jolt on selecting first gear or reverse with the car at rest.

Several other problems to do with the car rather than the engine and its transmission occurred, such as clonks from the steering and blown fuses, but mainly the car was extremely reliable in all other ways and it remained very likeable as one learned to live with the problems. I remember a very fast, trouble-free and enjoyable drive to Scotland to cover the 1971 Glasgow Show when the Ro80 showed its ability to cruise with a wonderfully low level of mechanical noise and near total absence of vibration as a result of the Wankel engine. It also had an impressive body shape giving generous interior space, comfort, low drag and minimal wind noise, although the car always felt and handled as though it was much smaller than it really was. After all, the overall length was 15ft 10in.

As mileage increased, so the problems seemed to diminish — or pehaps it was more that I had learned how to rectify them, such as the ease with which one could unscrew the slow running jets, blow them through and refit them in a couple of minutes getting a better tickover. But in June 1972, with the mileage at 20,000, I began to notice a knock from the engine when it was pulling.

By chance, NSU gave a Press

> *"Stuart, what's your opinion of the Wankel engine?..."*
> *"Sadly, it doesn't seem to live up to expectations."*

Above, NSU rotary predecessor, the Spider. Below, unfamiliar Ro80 engine bay. Right, rotary inventor Felix Wankel with one of his revolutionary engines

Above, the nicely predictable handling of an early Ro80. Right, the author with his first Ro80 on the way to visit the NSU factory in Cologne

conference to explain all the improvements that had been made to the Ro80 engine for improved reliability. They had now overcome all the problems, they assured us, including reducing the cold run smoking. The Wankel engine surgeon, Mike Hoppis, was there, and I asked him to come down to the car park in the basement of the London Hilton and listen to the noise my engine was making. We filled the area with blue smoke, and he diagnosed straight away that it had a bearing failure.

Another 240 miles had been covered by the time I took the car down to Shoreham where it had been arranged that we would take the engine out and go through a complete strip down with photographic coverage. By then the knock had become very bad and I had to take the last few miles very gently.

It took just over an hour to get the engine out of the car, and a further hour and a quarter saw it stripped down to the centre plate. When the rotor was revealed, a piece of metal swarf was spotted which had broken off the failed bearing. It was found that the crankshaft was of early type; a subsequent modification had been made to increase the oil flow to the bearing and avoid the failure which this engine had suffered.

It was all put together again with new rotor seals, although the ones removed were still within production tolerances for a new engine, and I drove it home the same night, enjoying the advantage of the Wankel, that even when new no running-in was needed.

Apart from some details like a new front wheel bearing at 25,000 miles, and the usual problems of blocked carburettor jets and the inescapable smoke after cold starting, the Ro80 served well until November 1972 when, with a mileage of 26,286, it was felt that we had no more to learn about the Wankel engine, and the car was handed back to NSU. In its place I took over an Opel Commodore; it was certainly good to drive without being ashamed of the pollution every time I looked in the rear mirror in the first few miles after a cold start.

The Ro80 itself was certainly a wonderful test bed for the engine, making the best of its advantages of smoothness at speed, compactness and low weight. It was a very safe, comfortable and enjoyable car to drive, but while the good handling and balance owed much to the lightness of the engine, the engine contributed rather low performance in relation to the fuel consumption, which seldom bettered 20mpg.

Long after he had left the staff, our former technical editor, Harry Mundy, said to me: "Well, Stuart, what's your erudite opinion of the Wankel engine?"

I replied: "Sadly, it doesn't seem to live up to expectations."

It was one of the rare occasions when I heard him respond: "I agree." ⬢

In the annals of motor industry misadventure the NSU Ro80 would be worthy of a volume all to itself, a lost cause of heroic proportions. Launched in 1967 – when BMC was still happily churning out crusty relics like the Morris Minor – the impact of the Ro80 ('Ro' stood for rotary, 80 was its design number) reverberated around the motoring world like a small nuclear warhead. Here was a car from another planet, unhindered by compromise, untouched by tradition, unrestrained by any preconceived notion of what a luxury car should be: as a maker of economy cars, NSU had no parts bins to plunder, and carried no prejudicial baggage.

Even without its Wankel engine – a first in a proper production luxury saloon – it would have been a fine car, a clean-sheet design full of superb detail and advanced concepts. The engine was just one part – an important part – of an inspired overall package.

The Ro80's radical wedge body – its low-drag 0.33Cd shape pre-dated the likes of Audi's slippery third-generation 100 by more than a decade – was crafted in a wind tunnel at a time when nobody, Citroën aside, gave more than a passing nod towards aerodynamic theory.

Front-wheel-drive optimised passenger space and the compact, drum-like rotary engine was mounted low for an efficient, air-cleaving prow. The tall glass-house, with that huge front screen, meant excellent visibility, while the high tail – with its deep boot – was portentous of luxury cars to come. Back in '67 it looked like nothing else on the road.

Superb ZF rack and pinion power steering was another star attraction of the Ro80. Exactly right in weight and feel, it was years before it was significantly bettered.

Brakes, too, came top of the class. An all-disc system was mounted inboard at the front to reduce unsprung weight (and make changing the pads easier from inside the engine bay).

Riding a long wheelbase and a wide track, the Ro80 handled and rode brilliantly on its fully independent, long travel suspension – struts at the front, semi-trailing arms with coil springs at the rear.

But, for better or worse, it is for its troubled Wankel engine that the Ro80 is best remembered. From the beginning the car was designed around it and it gave the Ro80 its unique character.

To the Wankel-converted, the twin Rotor unit – nominally rated at two litres and 113bhp – represented the ultimate in free-spinning, high-revving smoothness. Light, compact, powerful and perfectly balanced, it was magically free of the roughness that inevitably beset even the sweetest of four-stroke, four cylinder reciprocating engines. With few moving parts, all going in the same direction, it became smoother the faster it went.

Matched to the clever Fichtel and Sachs clutchless semi-automatic transmission – with three 'performance ranges' – it made the Ro80 lively, and exceptionally refined at high speed.

To the sceptics, though, it was a too much, too soon engine, thirsty for the performance it offered (you'd be lucky to better 18-20mpg in an Ro80) and still relatively unproven: the first rotary engines had run on Dr Felix Wankel's bench a mere 11 years earlier and had only seen

limited production in a short run of NSU Spyders in the early '60s.

The sceptics, sadly, were to be proved right. Rotor tip wear – brought-on by the over-revving and top-gear slogging the Wankel tolerated and encouraged – was soon putting Ro80s out of action. Poor starting, loss of power and increased thirst were early signs of trouble. Wear of the rotor housing itself was a sad knock-on effect and problems with rotor shaft bearings, soon sorted, nevertheless added to the list of Wankel woes.

In its unseemly haste to bring the Ro80 to the market (before Mazda's rotary-powered Cosmo) NSU had pushed through the design of the Wankel too quickly: the tip seals weren't right and the Nikasil plating on the rotor housings, while cheaper than Mazda's chrome plating, was not so hard wearing.

NSU's persistence with simpler peripheral porting on its rotary gave good top-end power but poor low-speed torque compared to Mazda's side ports, hence the need for the semi-automatic gearbox, whose torque converter masked this characteristic to some extent.

Few Ro80s did more than 30,000 miles on one engine and if most of the usage was short-haul, stop-start town work, its life was even shorter: an open choke would put too much petrol into the combustion chambers, washing lubricant from the walls of the chamber, thus hastening rotor housing wear. German Ro80 owners, so the story goes, didn't flash their lights in acknowledgement but waved fingers to indicate the number of new engines they had had under warranty.

In the hands of NSU's testers, who knew how to drive the cars properly, none of these problems showed up and in Germany, where the cars were usually driven flat-out on autobahns, the serious wear was not so widespread.

Generous warranty arrangements (two years or 24,000 miles and a six month 'Golden Guarantee' on replacement drivetrain parts from mid '72) couldn't remove the stain on the engine's reputation and NSU – unlike Mazda – never really got to grips with the Wankel's problems. To be fair, post-1971 single-plug engines, later fitted with a buzzer to prevent over-revving, were undoubtedly better and 60-70,000 miles was a reality with the last of the Ro80s.

But by then it was too late. The whole Ro80 episode crippled NSU, who in 1969 – bankrupted by warranty claims – ran into the open arms of VW. It had been a brave gamble and a vast leap upmarket for the Neckarsulm company which had made nothing more ambitious than humble rear-engined mini-cars before 1967. The Ro80 was never to make it, or its new Wolfsburg paymasters, any profit.

VW, which needed the expertise of Audi/NSU to build its new watercooled cars for the '70s, let the Ro80 continue as the group's executive flagship until 1977. It says much for the rightness of the original concept that so little was changed.

In Germany the car even enjoyed a minor sales resurgence in the mid '70s but in Britain – once the Ro80's biggest export market – it was available only to special order, with a vastly inflated £7000 price tag.

During its final run-out year the Ro80 came

TONY BAKER

Brave new world

NSU's advanced Ro80 of 1967 would have been a world-beater – if it had worked. It's taken a long time to catch up on reliability, says Martin Buckley, but the running survivors can still cut it in the '90s

down the Neckarsulm production lines along-side the new Audi 100, its spiritual successor and, in five-cylinder form, the new group flagship. As late as 1982 one VW boss still preferred an Ro80 as his personal transport, fitted with the latest prototype '3-litre' Wankel engine.

The taint of unreliability, and the fuel crisis, put an end to any thoughts of reviving the NSU wankel in the new big Audi, though a prototype was built and can still be seen in the Neckarsulm museum.

I love the radical shape – still so futuristic – the mechanical smoothness, the purity of the concept and the high quality of the engineering of these cars. In the idealised Buckley motor house there will always be room for an Ro80.

NSU Ro 80. Success through engineering.

Though it appears much smaller, the Ro80 is about the size of a Rover P5, but with more interior space. A low waist and deep glazing adds to the feeling of airy spaciousness.

You climb in over wide, high sills – part of the ventilation system – and settle into hard but well-shaped cloth-covered seats, about the only part of the functionally luxurious five-seater interior that changed in a decade's production. Early cars had less shapely chairs, often austerely trimmed in vinyl. Doors extend into the sills and shut with a dull thunk of quality that permeates the feel of the car.

Floorspace is flat and open-plan, with no chunky centre console, the dash similarly flat and rational. Bereft of unnecessary ornament or artifice it looks the work of an engineer, not a stylist.

There is no choke on this later single-plug special-order car and like any healthy Ro80 it starts on the first or second spin of the starter motor – hot or cold – and soon settles into a 1000rpm idle.

With your foot on the brake you can engage first – left and back – and hear the vacuum servo mounted on the inner wing hiss. Take your hand off the mushroom-shaped knob and, with your foot still hard on the brakes to smother the clunk, you are in gear.

The car moves smoothly away, the refined buzz of the Wankel at these low speeds made more two-stroke like by the non-standard all-stainless exhaust on this car, which rasps like a muted Lambretta under load.

First takes you to 40mph, second to 80 if you obey the 6500rpm limit, though the rotary is just as smooth at 8000 - good for your ego, if not your apex tip seals. Most town work is done in second and the car will pull smoothly, if not vigorously, away in that gear from rest.

Red-hot 0-60mph times were never the Ro80's forte - 13 secs is about the best independently recorded - a corollary of weak

ROTORHEAD

Simon Kremer of RoTechniks (01344 860510) on Mazda conversions and buying a Ro80

In 1981 when Simon Kremer first contracted the Ro80 bug, Ford V4 conversion was still the only practical way to go.

"The cost of a new factory rotary engine, as a proportion of the value of the car, was so high that a V4 conversion at a third of the price looked attractive to many people." says Kremer who rates the worst conversion – out of a bizarre rag-tag of engines fitted in desperation to poorly NSUs since the late '70s – as a Golf turbodiesel: "From the world's smoothest engine to the roughest."

Fourteen years on, Simon's first rotary rebuild is still on the road, and Ro80 enthusiasts are converting back to Wankel power, be it NSU or Mazda RX7: "The Ford V4 was so rough after the rotary that some owners couldn't face converting and just put the cars away when the engines went down," says Kremer who now works on both the ill-starred NSU and the much more successful Mazda RX7 range.

Offering an extensive range of spares and fixed menu servicing and repairs Simon can fit the latest high-spec' NSU rotary engine to your Ro80 or do a professional Mazda 12A 2.3 litre conversion, bringing more power and the promise of longer life: "We wanted our conversion to look as if NSU had done the job in 1977." says Kremer, "with no overheating problems, extra mickey mouse fans and switches or an ugly underhanging sump. It needed some careful engineering."

The RoTechniks Mazda 12A conversion, with adaptor plates, new recon' radiator specially designed for the job and Mazda oil cooler, carb and alternator is guaranteed for two years or 24,000 miles and costs £2995 plus VAT (see case history on p141 for our verdict on the RoTechniks development car).

Simon can also supply a sports handling pack which lowers the car by an inch with uprated springs and shocks to tame some of the body roll on tight corners.

Now is a good time to go Ro80 hunting as the market is quiet: "One of the best ways of buying an Ro80 at the moment," reckons Kremer, "is either to find one with a clean body and a popped rotary engine or a V4 fitted: either way the cars should be cheap – a few hundred pounds – and you can then have an NSU unit put back in or a have a proper Mazda conversion, and know the car is then good."

Kremer bemoans the passing of this milestone classic and feels it was German pigheadedness, as much as anything, that killed it: "They should have picked up the phone in 1977 and ordered a few thousand 12A engines from Mazda, just to keep it going."

BUYING AN Ro80: SEVEN-POINT CHECK LIST

1 Check the engine from cold if possible. It should start first or second time and not smoke excessively or show signs of overheating. It shouldn't stall in gear. A compression test is desirable: look for seven bar across all six 'spikes' of compression.

2 Mazda conversions should look neat and tidy with no low-hanging sumps, oil leaks from torque converter, or bonnet bulges. On poor conversions gears can 'snatch'.

3 Sunroof models rot more than non-sunroof cars. Check sills, tops and bottoms of doors, front wings around bumper attachment, front valance. Inner sills can be checked with a torch through vents inside the car. Wings and doors are getting

rare, but second-hand bonnets and bootlids should not be a problem. Most glass is still available from NSU breakers.

4 Brightwork around doors and windows is anodised: it goes cloudy if not maintained and can't be polished. Lights and bumpers are freely available from breakers.

5 Interiors wear well; if not, there are plenty of good, clean interiors about. Dashes crack along top, back shelves rot due to water ingress. Look for water in footwells, too.

6 Brakes will need overhauling if car has been standing, but all parts are available.

7 Gearboxes tend to be trouble-free, but look for leaks from torque converter seals, noisy bearings.

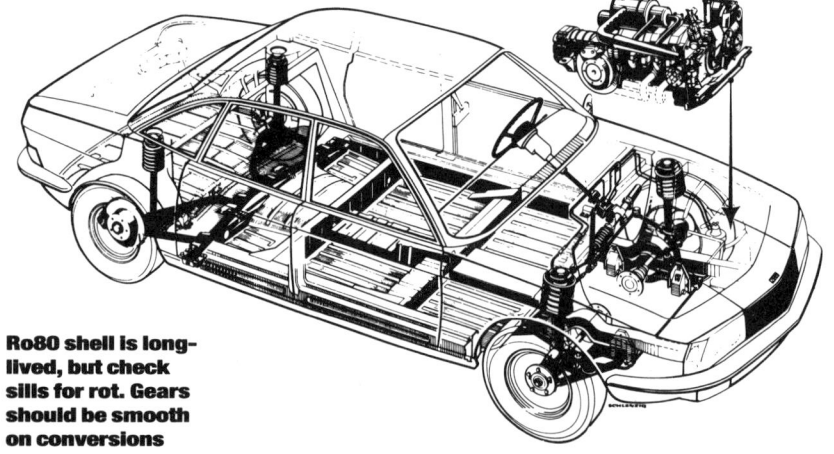

Ro80 shell is long-lived, but check sills for rot. Gears should be smooth on conversions

Ro80 is magnificently composed, and makes the most of its modest 175 section rubber. ZF power steering outstanding in '67

Engine looks lost under ancillaries. Above: cutaway of twin-rotor unit shows how few moving parts there are

Left: interior is plain, functional. No clutch pedal – it's actuated by microswitch in gear lever knob

Ro80 MILESTONES

September 1967 Ro80 launched in Germany.
December 1967 limited UK imports. LHD only.
October 1968 first RHD imports with twin lights in place of original front fog lamps.
October 1969 single plug and rotor, transistorised ignition. Known as MkII.
June 1970 new one-piece headlamp glasses, plastic grille, fog lamps under bumper. Known as MkIII.
October 1971 audible warning system for over-revving incorporated.
July 1972 tinted glass, metallic paint standard.
October 1975 body changes include wrap-around tail light clusters, rubber faced bumpers. Special order only in UK.
March 1977 production ends. Total number built 37,204. 3614 sold in UK with RHD.

BIRTH OF THE Ro80

It was a dream assignment for NSU designers Ewald Praxl and Claus Luthe: design the car of the future for the engine of the future, the rotary Wankel. The initial 1961 parameters were for a Cortina-class car with front-wheel drive and 80bhp watercooled twin rotor engine. It was a brave brief for NSU, an erstwhile motorcycle builder only just gaining acceptance for its air-cooled, rear-driven mini-cars.

Total belief in the future of the NSU rotary patents, and the expected royalties, soon dictated a more upmarket strategy driven not least by Felix Wankel's desire for revenge on his former employer, Daimler-Benz.

Luthe sketched a six light greenhouse with a bulbous venturi creating a ground effects floorpan (in 1963!) a low bonnet line and a raised tail. With a heavy nose, it was reasoned, the car should track arrow-straight at 180kph. By March 1964 the first clay model was presented to the board and was approved virtually as seen: the only changes were that the window line was raised and the car was widened by 5cm.

In September 1965 the clay model spent two days in the wind tunnel at Stuttgart university. It was not found lacking in any area.

Engine development continued. Various seal and housing materials were formulated and discarded as NSU sought to overcome fragility and abrasion: over 400 friction-reducing combinations were rejected before Nikasil coated the alloy housings and hard carbon tipped the cast-iron rotors.

Air suspension was considered, but discarded in favour of long-travel struts, while a Simca-sourced hydrostatic transmission was also considered and rejected, because it was too noisy. An all-synchro four-speed transmission used in some of the 16 prototypes highlighted engine snatch and clutch judder, overcome by a Porsche-inspired manumatic box. It also provided a multiplication effect, eliminating the need for a fourth ratio. The transmission was a unique selling point in a market filled with manuals.

The launch was planned for the 1967 Frankfurt show. Praxl pleaded for more time to eliminate the sealing nightmare but NSU had none, having spent its all on the Ro80 and found few takers for the engine patents. Launched with a known engine malady, the Ro80 drove the company into the red as surely as it tracked down the autobahns.

Did Praxl and Luthe really conceive the car of the future? Consider first that, in 1991, Mazda vanquished Jaguar, Porsche and Mercedes at Le Mans. Then strip the 1963 design of its age-related chrome bumpers, mirrors and spindly wipers. Next, park the RO80 next to the 32 years younger Audi A8 and decide. Most telling is that, in its 10-year life, NSU did not lift a pencil to Luthe's shape. But then engine changes did tend to concentrate its minds.   **Dieter Renkin**

High tail predates current fashion by 20 years. Try parking it next to an Audi A8...

low-speed torque and a large, heavy body. It was never meant to be a dragster, but the Ro80's performance is never found wanting on the road. Those smoothly ascending revs and the engine's high-speed refinement effectively hide the car's true pace.

As speed builds, the engine's buzz becomes smoother, a distant hum, until at 100mph (about 5500rpm) you're much more aware of road rumble from the puny 175 section Michelin tyres and annoying wind whistle – from a poorly seated driver's side door rubber – than you are of mechanical commotion.

I don't recall a '60s car that feels more directionally stable at these sort of speeds. Nothing – be it gusting side winds or the wake of a speeding HGV – seems to knock it off course, adding to the feeling of '90s modernity on the motorway. Like so much about the Ro80, the ride gets better the faster you go.

Once mastered, the semi-auto is good fun. As long as you remember not to rest your hand on the gear knob (thus disengaging the clutch and sending the revs soaring) or grab the lever before you have released the throttle you can treat it like a good manual shift. The gate is close and well defined, if a little notchy.

The smooth-acting throttle is ideally placed for heel and toeing, and I tended not to left-foot brake - as I would in a conventional automatic - as it confuses the issue: looking for a non-existent clutch pedal, I've hit the brakes by mistake more than once on previous Ro80 jaunts. Smoothly progressive and very powerful when called on, the brakes are truly excellent.

Left foot tucked safely away, you learn to enjoy the gearbox and make full and frequent use of it across country to get the most out of the engine. In search of extra punch out of a

tight, slow corner you can resort to first which, assisted by a timely throttle-blip, slips in easily.

Anybody used to the latest executive saloons might be initially perturbed by the amount of roll and understeer this softly sprung German can generate on tighter corners: the body heels over and as you wind on lock the front wheels begin to scrub and run wide.

None of this is untidy, mind: you always feel in complete control, torso firmly embraced by the excellent seats, hands made fully aware of what the front wheels are up to by fluid and informative power steering. Sure, at 3³/₄ turns between locks it makes you work hard sometimes, yet the lack of kickback and ideal feel and weight - so good that you aren't really aware the steering is assisted - make it easy to see why this ZF system was such a '70s standard-setter.

Open, faster corners are the Ro80's true domain of course. Foot down, your line set, the sense of command heightened by the fine view out along the descending bonnet line, the Ro80 sweeps through turns with an incorruptible stability. The rear wheels always follow the line of the front, no matter what you do with the steering, brakes or throttle. There's no question of unseemly tuck-in or unruly oversteer. Grip seems abundant despite the puny dimensions of the Michelin rubber, and nothing can knock the car off your chosen course.

It doesn't take much imagination to see why, by the standards of 1967 - when herds of Hillman Minx still roamed British roads - the bold, brave Ro80 was such a sensation. We will never see its like again.

NSU Ro80 Club GB: Eric Dalton, 9 Manor Close, Congleton, Cheshire CW12 3LB.